# CHARACTER BUILDING
# ACTIVITIES FOR KIDS

## Ready-to-Use Character Education Lessons & Activities for the Elementary Grades

# DARLENE MANNIX

THE CENTER FOR APPLIED
RESEARCH IN EDUCATION
Paramus, New Jersey 07652

**Library of Congress Cataloging-in-Publication Data**

Mannix, Darlene.
     Character-building activities for kids: ready-to-use character education lessons and activities for the elementary grades/Darlene mannix.
          p. cm.
     ISBN 0-13-042585-0
     1. Moral education—Handbooks, manuals, etc. 2. Character—Study and teaching (Elementary)—Handbooks, manuals, etc. 3. Activity programs in education—Handbooks, manuals, etc. I. Title.

     LC268.M199 2002
     372'.01'14—dc21

                                                                                    2001042536

*10 9 8 7 6 5 4 3 2 1*

ISBN 0-13-042585-0

---

**ATTENTION: CORPORATIONS AND SCHOOLS**

The Center for Applied Research in Education books are available at quantity discounts with bulk purchase for educational, business, or sales promotional use. For information, please write to: Prentice Hall Special Sales, 240 Frisch Court, Paramus, NJ 07652. Please supply: title of book, ISBN, quantity, how the book will be used, date needed.

---

**THE CENTER FOR APPLIED
RESEARCH IN EDUCATION**

Paramus, NJ 07652

www.phdirect.com/education

# for Mom

# About the Author

Darlene Mannix is presently a remedial reading teacher in LaPorte, Indiana. She has previously been a teacher for students of all ages who are at-risk; language disordered; and emotionally, mentally, and learning disabled. She has also taught alternative education classes for middle school students.

Ms. Mannix holds a Bachelor of Science degree from Taylor University and a Master's in Learning Disabilities from Indiana University. She is an active member of the Council for Exceptional Children.

She is the author of several resources published by The Center for Applied Research in Education, including *Oral Language Activities for Special Children* (1987), *Be a Better Student: Lessons and Worksheets for Teaching Behavior Management in Grades 4–9* (1989), *Life Skills Activities for Special Students* (1991), *Social Skills Activities for Special Children* (1993), *Life Skills Activities for Secondary Students with Special Needs* (1995), and *Social Skills Activities for Secondary Students with Special Needs* (1998).

# About This Book

Character Education is a relatively new buzzword for schools, home, and society in general, although any teacher will argue that character education is taught daily through values, examples, and academics that are already a part of the daily classroom. What exactly is meant by this term as it applies to children? Let's think through the process and the content of character education and what it means in a practical sense to teachers, parents, and other adults who are responsible for the well-being and emotional growth of children. What should we teach and how should we teach it? Finally, we must consider the philosophy behind teaching character education in a school setting.

## The Content

Let's begin with the question of **content**. What should be included in character education? Most people can readily identify a few characteristics that are indicative of a person of character: honesty, responsibility, loyalty, and so on. But rather than present children with a "grocery list" of many, unrelated characteristics, streamline the skills into basic, general categories. Keep it simple! The content of this book divides the many, varied character traits that are often selected as representative of good character into three basic categories:

1. characteristics that show respect for yourself (honesty, integrity, humility, responsibility, effort, and pride)

2. characteristics that show respect for others (peace-seeking, generosity, compassion, forgiving, understanding, and loyalty)

3. characteristics that convey a positive outlook on life (sense of humor, fairness, open-mindedness, initiative, optimism, risk-taking)

## The Process

The term "education" implies that character can be taught. Our task, then, is to determine how best to provide instruction that will encourage children to understand and apply character traits to their lives. We as teachers know something about education—we have been teaching math and reading for a long time and probably feel as though we have a good handle on writing objectives, providing interesting and thoughtful activities for achieving those objectives, and then evaluating the students' performance. Once we have identified characteristics that seem appropriate, how do we actually teach character education? What objectives, activities, and evaluation will guide the teaching/learning **process** to result in students who are skilled in this new realm?

The process of teaching character education in this book basically follows this format:

1. *Define the character trait.* Children need to understand what we are talking about when we say we want them to be *honest* or to be *generous* or to play *fair*. They need to be able to define, in words appropriate to their age and education, what it means to be honest. The first part of each lesson provides opportunities for children to define the character trait that is being considered.

2. *Recognize the character trait.* Reciting a definition is simply not enough. A child may be able to define a *cat* as a small domestic mammal with four legs and pointy ears, but unless he or she has had experience with a cat, we might be unconvinced that the child really understands what a cat is, the essence of "catness." Similarly, children need to be able to clearly recognize *honesty* in action, point out examples of *generosity*, and be able to identify best *effort* vs. sloppy work when evaluating their schoolwork.

Each lesson contains many examples of situations in which the targeted characteristic is portrayed, as well as the opposite of each characteristic. A child needs to know that *dishonesty*, for example, is as undesirable as honesty is desirable!

3. *Apply the characteristics to daily life.* An honest person does certain things that reveal he or she has applied this characteristic in a habitual manner to his or life. For *honesty*, for example, we would expect an honest person to say and do things that are consistent with what we have defined and recognized as honesty. This is the crucial matter; this is the heart of character education. All of the definitions and examples of desired characteristics mean little if the child has not internalized the importance of being a person of character. Each lesson provides opportunities for children to apply these character traits to his or her own life.

## General Philosophy

We expect students to be *honest*, but what about those "gray" areas that are seemingly not so clear? Should a child answer the telephone and insist that his parents are in the next room when they are really not back from work yet? If your friend asks if you like her new haircut, and your opinion is that it is horrible, should you be honest and inform her that you hate it? If a robber asks if you have money in your purse, should you deny it? Are you always supposed to be totally honest?

The following principles are the basis of the philosophy of the content of this book:

1. *Use common sense.* Most issues can be readily resolved if the person thinks clearly. Throwing complex, impossible situations at young children is not only confusing to them, but it also promotes the idea that right and wrong are relative. Throughout the book, examples and situations are primarily clear-cut and governed by common sense. Tact and safety are important life skills as well!

2. Realize that when determining a course of action, in general *do what is best for the other person,* even if it seems that you are losing something. When you return a wallet full of money, you are losing the opportunity to get some easy money, but you did the right thing. When you give up your seat on a bus for someone else, you are losing a good seat, but again, you made life better for someone else. This quality of self-sacrifice is what makes us human. The "right" answers to many situations in this book are the answers that involve doing something for someone else's benefit, *not* your own.

3. *Don't expect a reward.* When we tell children that doing the right thing will result in some kind of reward—praise from others, a good feeling, recognition—we are setting them up for disappointment. The motivation to be a person of character should not come from seeking gain. Most good deeds will go unnoticed. Some will even be punished. How can you convince a low-income child to work hard to get an honest job when he sees the local drug dealer driving off in a brand new car? The philosophy of the lessons in this book will reflect the position that you behave in a certain way because it's the right thing to do, not because you will feel good about yourself or see your name in the paper. Do the right thing because it *is* the right thing.

*Darlene Mannix*

# How to Use This Book

Before beginning actual instruction with children in these lessons, you should make sure the children understand the philosophy presented in this book of character education. If these principles are in line with what you feel are important, then it is strongly suggested that you spend at least one session explaining and reviewing these principles of building character.

Briefly, they are:

1. *Use common sense.* As stated in "About This Book," most of the situations that students will encounter in their daily life will be straightforward. We must give them credit for being able to make good judgments by using common sense. Doing something questionable because "you didn't say I couldn't do it" is out of line. We don't buy that. No way. Another example is that of reminding students that in many social situations, it is important to use tact rather than cruelty in the name of brutal honesty. It's not acceptable to plead, "Well, you asked for my opinion! I was just telling you the truth!" We as human beings have brains, the ability to think and reason, and can learn to make social judgment calls.

2. *Do what is best for somebody else.* Part of developing good character is the ability to sacrifice. If we view relationships with others as part of a continuum, we could place dinosaurs devouring each other at one end of the line—each out for themselves—and a person dying for another person at the other end, the ultimate sacrifice. We fall somewhere in between. We may want to place our own needs and desires first, but think of how people give up things and sacrifice for each other: a mother spending time reading with her child rather than going out with friends; an adult son taking care of an aged parent at home rather than in a nursing home; everyday instances of ordinary people giving up a seat on a bus, holding a door for someone else, letting someone else take that taxi, giving their own blood or donating a kidney to a relative; and so on. This concept—that it is better to give up than to demand their own rights—is difficult for children to understand. Think, however, how the world would be if everyone adhered to this philosophy. If everyone were trying to do what would benefit someone else, eventually someone would do something that would affect you!

3. *Don't expect a reward for doing the right thing.* If the previous concept is difficult, this one is off the charts! What incentive is there to be good and to do the right thing if there is no apparent reward? Why return a wallet with money in it if the person doesn't give you a reward? It's always a nice surprise to be acknowledged for doing something right, but in the event that it doesn't happen, we need to be prepared to do the right thing anyway. Again, as humans we must adhere to a higher code than always looking for the payoff—the money, the praise, the attention, the good feeling. If something is broken, fix it. If you can do something good, do it. In a way, it is hard to understand, but if we are "only human," let's teach children to be the best humans they can be.

Here is an introductory worksheet to help you get started. Its objective is to teach students three basic principles of character building.

1. Pass the worksheet to students.

2. Read or paraphrase the three principles listed previously that explain the philosophy of building character. Tell students that all of the lessons and activities they will do in this book will use these principles to help teach them to build character, or to be a stronger, better person.

3. Have students take turns reading the examples on the worksheet.

4. Discuss why these principles are important. (We should be kind to each other and not try to hurt feelings; it's nice to share, etc.)

Name _____  Date _____

# Introductory Worksheet

Read and discuss the examples of the important ideas below.

© 2002 by The Center for Applied Research in Education

## 1. Use common sense.

Do you like my dog?

NO

Well, since you asked... No, I think your dog is ugly and ill-mannered. I think you resemble each other in the face too. I'm just being honest!

YES

I guess I'm kind of afraid of big dogs, but he sure seems to like you!

## 2. Do what is best for somebody else.

If I hurry, I can be the first one to get to the cake. Then I can have the biggest piece!

Why don't you go ahead of me? I know you like the frosting and there's a big rose on the corner piece.

NO

YES

## 3. Don't expect a reward for doing the right thing.

Hey! Hey look! Did you see me help that little old lady cross the street?

Someone just threw trash all over the floor. I'll pick it up so the custodian doesn't have to.

NO

YES

# Contents

## Section I: Having Respect for Yourself .......................................... 1

## Section II: Having Respect for Others .......................................... 129

# Section I
# Having Respect for Yourself

What do we mean by the term "respect?" This is one of those words that we hear a lot ("*respect your elders,*" "*respect the umpire's decision,*" "*respect your neighbor's property*"), but may use without defining it for students. When we ask students to have respect, we are asking them to take the time to carefully consider the matter or person at hand, and then to place importance upon it. This is the first vocabulary word that students need to learn and understand: respect—being careful with something because it is important.

Section I of this book deals with developing characteristics that are important for being a person of character. We would expect a person with good character to be honest, keep his or her promises, and put forth good effort, among other things. If a person has respect for him – or herself, that person will develop characteristics that are positive and show strength as a person. The main characteristics for self-respect that will be taught in this book are the following:

- **honesty**—saying or doing what is true
- **integrity**—keeping your promises
- **humility**—not bragging about yourself
- **responsibility**—seeing what needs to be done and doing it.
- **effort**—doing the best job you can
- **pride** (in yourself)—doing things that promote health, not harm, to your body and mind

# Lesson I-1: Defining Honesty

**The contents of Lesson I-1 include:**

- Journal Ideas
- Pre-/Posttest on selecting responses to situations in which honesty is involved
- Worksheet I-1A, What Is Honesty?
- Worksheet I-1B, What Honesty Is and Isn't
- Worksheet I-1C, Listen and Respond

## Journal Ideas

The journal questions can be used on a daily or occasional basis for students to reflect, write, and share their ideas and opinions regarding honesty.

## Pre-/Posttest

Pass out the pre-/posttest to students, depending on how you want to record and evaluate student learning. This can be given to students before the characteristic of honesty is discussed in class to give you an idea of how students feel they would respond to typical situations. This can be used for purposes of discussion, although it will be interesting to administer it as a posttest to see if responses have changed.

### Answers

There is room for difference of opinion on some of the answers, but these are solid honest responses: 1. c; 2. d; 3. c; 4. a; 5. a

### Discuss

Discuss each response and why it does or does not reflect honesty.

## Worksheet I-1A, What Is Honesty?

1. Write the definition of *honesty* on the board or display on a poster where it is easily viewed by students. *"Honesty means saying or doing what is true."*

2. Pass out the worksheet and have students complete the worksheet by first completing the definition of honesty at the top. They then circle yes or no to indicate whether or not the characters are showing honesty according to the definition given.

### Answers

1. no (not doing or saying what is true); 2. yes (doing and saying what is true); 3. yes (working together is acceptable here); 4. no (not doing what is honest)

### Discuss

1. How can you show honesty by what you do? (Can you lie with your actions?)
2. How can you show honesty by what you say?

## Worksheet I-1B, What Honesty Is and Isn't

1. Review the definition for honesty with students. Note that the opposite of honesty (dishonesty) is now a part of the review.

2. Pass out the worksheet and have students complete the worksheet by filling out the review section at the top.

3. Read the directions for the bottom part of the worksheet. Students are to write IS or ISN'T to indicate if this situation shows honesty or dishonesty.

**Answers**

1. ISN'T (outright lie); 2. IS; 3. ISN'T (they were not honest in meeting the teacher's expectations); 4. ISN'T (she made an assumption that may or may not be true; she did not put others first); 5. ISN'T (did not behave in an honest way; he did not use common sense); 6. ISN'T (was not truthful about motives; did not really have a stomachache, wanted to stay inside)

**Discuss**

In examples 3 and 5, the students never said a word about the situation and never told an outright lie. Why are they still considered dishonest in their behavior if they didn't say anything or actually hurt anyone? (**Idea:** *We should behave in an honest way with or without words to back us up. The teacher had expectations for them that they understood. They were dishonest with that expectation by not obeying her instructions.*)

## Worksheet I-1C, Listen and Respond

1. Review the definition of honesty with students.
2. This worksheet is used to clarify what is meant by honesty by contrasting several choices of behavior when given a situation. Read the story on the first part of the worksheet; pass out only the cartoon sheet to students. They should follow along as you read each ending (cartoons are labeled A–G to correspond to the various endings).
3. This should be conducted as a discussion activity, so students are not required to write yes/no on the worksheet.
4. After each ending, allow time for students to discuss their thoughts on the situation. Refer students to the definition for honesty as they make their decisions.

**Answers**

A. yes (she did and said everything honestly); B. no (she told her mother about the candy bar, but she did not follow her mother's expectations—knew her mother wanted the money back); C. no (complete lie, blaming someone else); D. no (she was good-hearted, but did not follow her mother's expectations, and then she lied when she got home) [**Note:** In some families, the expectation might be that it is acceptable to give to poor strangers; this will vary from family to family. Since we don't know Jenny's family situation, we have to go with the expectation that all of the change would be returned.]; E. no (her words were accurate, but not truthful—didn't use common sense); F. no (her words were accurate, but not truthful—didn't use common sense); G. no (she is trying to make it sound as though her mother has to name every single item she can't buy, making it her mother's fault for neglecting to do that; didn't use common sense)

**Discuss**

1. Do you think Jenny's mother might have agreed to let her buy a candy bar if she knew they were on sale?
2. Was Jenny's mother being mean by not wanting her to give money to a poor person? *(You may not know what the poor person is going to do with the money; a legitimate donation to the Scouts or a church might be a safer place for spare money to go.)*
3. Was Jenny's mother placing her own needs ahead of the poor person's needs? *(Use common sense—Jenny's mom obviously was counting on what little change there would be for the son's field trip; money is part of survival for this family. Generosity will be discussed later, but it should not come at the expense of basic needs.)*

# Journal Ideas: Honesty

1. *Rate yourself:* Do you think you are an honest person? Why did you rate yourself the way you did?

    0—honest

    1—sometimes honest

    2

    3—usually honest

    4

    5—always honest

2. Think of a time when you had a chance to show that you were honest. What happened because of your honesty?

3. List examples of honesty you have seen on TV or in the movies. What was the situation?

4. In the fairy tale, Pinocchio's nose grew every time he told a lie. What do you think would be a funny way to find out if people were lying?

5. Find a newspaper or magazine article in which someone's honesty is written about. Summarize the story and write what you think about it.

6. In an election year, there are a lot of claims made by politicians and stories told about each other. What are some examples of honesty and dishonesty that you have found about politics?

7. For what jobs or careers would honesty be extremely important? What if someone in that job was not honest? What could happen?

8. Think of a person who has an honest reputation. Why did you think of this person?

9. Why shouldn't you give your honest opinion sometimes if someone asks you what you think? Should you always be brutally honest?

10. What are some situations for which it is really hard for you to be honest? Why?

# Honesty: Pretest/Posttest

Read each situation and all of the choices. Then circle the answer that shows the most honest response/what you would do.

1. You go to the cafeteria and buy potato chips. You give the cashier some money, but she is distracted and gives you back too much change. You would:

   a. Keep the change; it's her mistake.

   b. Tell the principal that the cashier is careless and should be fired.

   c. Return the money.

   d. Tell the cashier that she made a stupid mistake and then return the money.

2. You are taking a test at your desk and notice that the answer key is in plain sight behind the teacher's desk. You would:

   a. Peek at the answers just to make sure you have them right.

   b. Use the answers to write down your answers since it's the teacher's mistake.

   c. Tell a friend to check the answers.

   d. Try not to look at it.

3. You are babysitting for the neighbors and the kids are awful. Upon her return home, the mother asks how the kids were. You would:

   a. Honestly tell her they were horrible.

   b. Say they were angels so she wouldn't feel bad.

   c. Say they could have been better and then wait to see if she wants more information.

   d. Say they were OK.

4. Your father asks if you have finished mowing the back yard and you realize that your friends are waiting for you to leave with them. You are only about halfway done, but you know you can easily finish in a few minutes. You would:

   a. Say: "Just about finished, Dad, just a few more minutes."

   b. Say: "Yep, all done."

   c. Say: "No, but is it OK if I finish later?"

   d. Say: "No, but I'm too busy to do it right now."

5. You borrow your friend's expensive video game and accidentally drop it. You realize it isn't working right. You would:

   a. Apologize for dropping it and offer to pay for it.

   b. Say you don't know why it doesn't work.

   c. Tell your friend that there was something wrong with the game when you got it.

   d. Say that someone else knocked into you so it wasn't your fault.

Name _____  Date _____

# I-1A. What Is Honesty?

Honesty means s_____ or d_____ what is

t_____.

Look at the situations below. Which are showing honesty? Circle yes or no to show your answer.

1. Is this showing honesty?   YES   NO

2. Is this showing honesty?   YES   NO

3. Is this showing honesty?   YES   NO

4. Is this showing honesty?   YES   NO

Name _____ Date _____

# I-1B. What Honesty Is and Isn't

**Review**

Honesty means s_____ or d_____ what is

t_____. The opposite of honesty is d_____.

**Directions:** Read each situation below. Write IS if it shows honesty. Write ISN'T if it shows dishonesty.

1. Jamie was supposed to lock the door when she left for school but she forgot. When her father asked if she locked the door, she said: "Yes, Dad, I did."                    _____

2. Aimee paid $5 for a movie ticket and the clerk at the theater gave her too much change. Aimee handed the correct change back to the clerk.                    _____

3. The teacher left the room and told the students to stay in their seats. Three students ran to the window to look at a dog outside. Then they ran back to their seats before the teacher returned.                    _____

4. Mrs. Peters, the lunch lady, told the students that they could each come up to the counter and take one ice cream bar. Amanda took two of them since it looked like there would be some extra ones.                    _____

5. Tony very quietly opened book during a quiz to check on an answer he wasn't sure about because the teacher didn't say they couldn't use their books.                    _____

6. Donny wanted to go to the nurse's office instead of going outside in the cold for recess. He told his teacher that he had a stomachache, because earlier that week he really did have a stomachache.                    _____

# For the Teacher
## (Script for Worksheet I-1C, Listen and Respond)

I am going to read a short story about honesty. After I read the first part, I will finish the story for you in several different ways. You can look at pictures that show each ending on your sheet. I want you to think about honesty and whether or not the girl in the story showed honesty. Be careful—some of these are not easy answers. Be prepared to tell me what you think about these endings and whether or not the ending shows honesty.

---

**Remember: Honesty means saying or doing what is true.**

Think:    1. Did the girl say what was true?

2. Did the girl do what was true?

3. Did the girl do the right thing?

---

Mrs. Alexander gave her daughter Jenny a $10 bill and some instructions: "Go to the store and get me some bread and spaghetti sauce. Be sure to bring back all of the change because I will need it to pay for your brother's field trip at school tomorrow."

## Ending A

Jenny bought the bread and spaghetti sauce and went home. Mom said, "Did you get what I asked you to?" Jenny said, "Yes, Mom," and she gave her the change. *Does this ending show honesty?*

## Ending B

Jenny got the bread and spaghetti sauce, but she picked up a candy bar at the checkout counter. She returned home. Her mother said, "There's not enough change here. What happened to the rest of the money?" Jenny said, "Oh, there seemed like a lot of money left over, so I bought myself a candy bar. I figured you would think it was all right." *Does this ending show honesty?*

## Ending C

Jenny picked up a candy bar after shopping. When she returned home, her mother said, "Jenny, there's not enough change. What happened?" Jenny said, "Oh, no! I wonder what happened! Maybe the clerk counted wrong." *Does this ending show honesty?*

## Ending D

Jenny got the items for Mother and as she was walking out, she noticed a very poor man standing by the door with his hand out. "Hello," he called to her. "I don't have any money. Could you spare some?" Jenny felt sorry for him, so she gave him some of the change. When she got home, her mother asked, "Is this all of the change?" "Yes," said Jenny. "That's it." *Does this ending show honesty?*

## Ending E

As Jenny was walking out of the grocery store, she noticed a poor man with his hand out. "Can you spare some change?" he asked her. Jenny gripped the money tightly and said, "I don't have any money," and walked quickly by him. *Does this ending show honesty?*

© 2002 by The Center for Applied Research in Education

## Ending F

Jenny bought the items and a candy bar for herself. When she got home, her mother asked why there wasn't more change. Jenny held out her hand and said, "This is all the change that the clerk gave me. This is everything." *Does this ending show honesty?*

## Ending G

Jenny came home with the bread, spaghetti sauce, and a dozen brownies. Her mother asked her why she bought the brownies. Jenny said, "You didn't say I couldn't get anything else, so I thought it would be OK. And here is the change, like you told me." *Does this ending show honesty?*

Name _____ Date _____

# I-1C. Listen and Respond

a.

b.

c.

d.

e.

f.

g.

# Lesson I-2: Recognizing Honesty

**The contents of Lesson I-2 include:**

- Worksheet I-2A, Honesty with Common Sense
- Worksheet I-2B, An Honest Reputation
- Worksheet I-2C, Being More Honest

## Worksheet I-2A, Honesty with Common Sense

1. Pass out the worksheet to students. Have them complete the review section at the top. (Notice that the first-letter prompts are now missing.)
2. The directions for the remainder of the worksheet involve selecting the response that best shows honesty, but still uses common sense in how students respond.

### Answers

1. first child (side steps actually answering, but the second child is mean); 2. second child (there is a safety issue involved here); 3. second child (if the mother wants more information about her children's behavior, she will probably ask); 4. first child (this is a good answer); 5. second child

### Discuss

1. What's the difference between being honest and being tactful?
2. Why shouldn't the girl who was babysitting for the badly behaved children tell on them? *(the mother probably doesn't need or want to know about every behavior; unless it was a major safety concern, it won't change anything)*

## Worksheet I-2B, An Honest Reputation

1. Pass out the worksheet to students and have them complete the review section.
2. Discuss what is meant by "reputation." *(what other people say about you, based on what you have done)*
3. Have students take turns reading the cartoon character's comments and circle Honest or Dishonest on their sheet.

### Answers

1. honest; 2. dishonest

### Discuss

1. Do you think it takes a long time for someone to decide on another person's reputation or can you "size someone up" based on one incident?
2. Why is it sad that the girl already has a reputation for dishonesty?
3. What could she do to start changing that reputation?

## Worksheet I-2C, Being More Honest

1. Pass out the worksheet to students and have them complete the review section.
2. Have students take turns reading the items and allow time for them to write their responses as to how the person in each situation could show a more honest response than he or she is apparently showing.

**Answers**

1. Mention it to the clerk and make it right; 2. Say that he forgot to do the assignment; 3. Better to say she doesn't know for sure (use tact); 4. Give the boy his money; 5. Make plans with Mother to finish it either right now if it's important or at a later time if he truly needs to rest; 6. Quietly mention it to the teacher

**Discuss**

1. In situation 2, Felix might get in trouble for forgetting to do the work, but he might get by with giving a dishonest excuse *(didn't understand)*. What do you think most teachers would rather deal with?

2. Is it OK if you are silent about a matter (not mentioning a mistake in money or reporting dishonest behavior), especially if you are not directly involved? Does it really hurt anyone if the girl in situation 6 took the answer key and no one told on her?

Name _____ Date _____

# I-2A. Honesty with Common Sense

**Review**

Honesty means _____ or _____ what is

_____. The opposite of honesty is _____.

**Directions:** Read each situation. The children are trying to be honest, but some are not using common sense. Circle the best response to each situation.

1.

Do you like my new dress?

You'll get a lot of attention with that!

You look like a clown! Ha ha ha!!

2.

Hello, young man. Are your parents home?

No, I'm all alone in the house.

I'm sorry, they can't come here right now.

3.

I'll bet you had fun babysitting my little angels. Were they good?

I have a list here of everything they broke.

It was a very busy evening.

4.

Tell me! Are my friends having a surprise party for me?

I can't tell! Then it wouldn't be a surprise, would it?

No, there is no party. Don't ask me again.

5.

Tell me when the teacher isn't looking and I'll get the answer key. Is she gone?

I don't think you should do that, but she's gone.

No, that's not right. I will not help you.

Name _____ Date _____

# I-2B. An Honest Reputation

**Review**

Honesty means _____ or _____ what is

_____. The opposite of honesty is _____.

**Directions:** You might know some kids like these. Read what others say about them and decide if they have a reputation for being HONEST or DISHONEST. Circle your answer.

**Mark**

Mark's brother says:

> Mark always does whatever Mom and Dad ask him to do. Sometimes he's a little slow to get started and they have to remind him, but he will do what they ask him to do.

Mark's teacher says:

> I never worry about leaving my purse out in the classroom when Mark is there. I know he would never take anything out of it.

HONEST    DISHONEST

**Kaaren**

Kaaren's aunt says:

> Kaaren is a nice girl, but she doesn't always tell the truth when she thinks she might get in trouble.

Kaaren's neighbor says:

> I left some really expensive toys in my back yard one day and they were missing. Kaaren said she thought I didn't want them anymore, so she took them. But they were inside my back porch!

HONEST    DISHONEST

Name _____ Date _____

# I-2C. Being More Honest

**Review**

Honesty means _____ or _____ what is

_____. The opposite of honesty is _____.

**Directions:** Read each situation below. Decide how the person involved could be more honest in his or her response. Write your answer on the line.

1. Debbie bought three things at the store, but the clerk only charged her for two. Debbie didn't mention it to the clerk.

   _____

2. Felix was supposed to answer all of the questions in his reading book, but he forgot. When the teacher asked about it, he said he didn't understand the assignment.

   _____

3. Jenny asked her friend Liz if Jason liked her as a girlfriend. Liz knew that Jason couldn't stand her, but she didn't want to hurt her feelings so she said yes.

   _____

4. There was some loose change on a table in the gym and no one was around, so Anthony took the money. Later, a boy came back from class looking for his money. Anthony pretended he didn't know anything about it.

   _____

5. Rudy was supposed to work for two hours cleaning out the garage on Saturday. He was tired after an hour, so he stopped. When his mother asked if he was finished cleaning, he said yes.

   _____

6. Mr. Arthur, the teacher, couldn't find his answer key to the math test. He asked the class if anyone knew where it was. Kaila had seen another student take the test, but she didn't say anything.

   _____

   _____

# Lesson I-3: Applying Honesty

**The contents of Lesson I-3 include:**

- Worksheet I-3A, Honesty Around You
- Worksheet I-3B, What About You?
- Quiz on Part 1: Honesty
- Game: Climb the Ladder

This lesson is directed toward students applying honesty to their own lives. The worksheets are open-ended to allow for specific needs. By this time, students should be able to write the entire definition for honesty with few prompts.

## Worksheet I-3A, Honesty Around You

1. Ask students how they feel about their knowledge of honesty right now. Discuss whether or not they feel they have a good understanding of what honesty is and are able to recognize honesty in situations around them.

2. Mention that now they are taking a big step by applying honesty to their own lives. In this lesson, they will be thinking about their own honesty and ways to be more honest.

3. Pass out the worksheet and have students complete the review section.

4. Briefly discuss some areas of the students' lives that are important to them (this may vary). Ask for volunteers to offer ideas to get them started about writing examples of specific ways they can show honesty in these various places.

**Discuss**

1. Are certain places more difficult than others to be honest?

2. Is it harder for you to be honest if people/peers around you are not? Is it hard to be different if you know being honest is the right thing to do but no one else is?

3. How can you be an example of honesty in these places?

## Worksheet I-3B, What About You?

1. Pass out the worksheet to students and have them complete the review section.

2. Explain that each of them already has a reputation. People who know them have already formed at least a partial opinion about their honesty based on what they have seen them do or listened to them say.

3. Have students complete the worksheet, writing "balloons" to show what they think people would say about them.

**Discuss**

1. How have your reputations been formed by these people?

2. How could you convince someone by your actions and conversations that you truly are an honest person?

## Quiz on Part 1: Honesty

This can be used as a follow-up to Part 1 lessons.

**Answers**

1. *(definition)* Honesty is saying or doing what is true.

2. *(examples)* a. dishonest; b. dishonest

3. *(applying)* Answers will vary.

## Game for Part 1: Climb the Ladder

Directions and sample game pieces are given at the end of this lesson.

Name _____ Date _____

# I-3A. Honesty Around You

**Review**

Honesty means _____.

The opposite of honesty is _____.

**Directions:** How can you show honesty around you? What are some ways you could prove that you are honest at home? at school? and at other places? Write your examples in each space.

| HOME  | SCHOOL  |
|---|---|
| SPORTS  | ON THE BUS  |
| IN MY NEIGHBORHOOD  | (other) |

# I-3B. What About You?

**Review**

Honesty means _____.

The opposite of honesty is _____.

**Directions:** How honest do other people think you are? What do you think other people would say about you if asked if you were honest? Complete the balloons to write what you think these people would say.

 Your mother or father

An aunt/uncle or other relative

 A neighbor

A friend

 Your teacher

Your bus driver/ coach/other adult leader

 Your brother or sister

Your principal

Name _____     Date _____

# Quiz on Part 1: Honesty

1. What is meant by honesty?

_____

_____

2. Are these students showing honesty or dishonesty?

a.

*If you are finished with your work, you may get a library book and read.*

*I would rather read, so I'll tell the teacher that I can finish the work faster at home and I'll bring it in tomorrow.*

_____

b.

*I really want to get that new book on horses!*

*I know that Marcia wants that book too—so I'll tell her that it's already checked out so my friend can get it.*

_____

3. What is a way you could show honesty in your house? Choose one of the following situations to write about. Circle your choice.

   a. doing a chore   b. telling about getting in trouble at school   c. keeping a secret

_____

_____

_____

_____

# Game for Honesty: Climb the Ladder

**Materials:**

You need a ladder gameboard for each player, a token for each player, and Honesty Cards. You might want to laminate the gameboard for repeated use.

**Objective:**

To be the first player to reach the top of the ladder

**Directions:**

1. Each student has a ladder gameboard. (If students want to play as teams or individuals, this is a possible variation.)

2. Each player chooses a token to represent himself or herself moving up the ladder.

3. The Honesty Cards (examples are included) are shuffled and placed in the center of the playing area where they are accessible to all players.

4. Players take turns drawing from the top of the card pile. Each player reads his or her situation out loud (a situation in which the character displays either honesty to gain points or dishonesty to lose points), and then moves the token the appropriate number of spaces up or down.

5. The winner is the first person to make it to the top of the ladder. (The player does not have to have the exact number to win.) All players should compliment the winner on his or her honesty! (to make it fun)

6. If a player draws a card that requires him or her to move back farther than the lowest rung, the player just stays at the bottom until his or her next turn.

You're a winner!

Start

| | |
|---|---|
| You return a lost wallet.<br>**Go ahead 2 rungs.** | You return a lost wallet<br>with money in it.<br>**Go ahead 3 rungs.** |
| You cheat on a spelling test.<br>**Go back 1 rung.** | You look at your<br>neighbor's paper on a test.<br>**Go back 2 rungs.** |
| You promised your mom you<br>would wash the dishes, but<br>you took a nap instead.<br>**Go back 2 rungs.** | You accidentally took a<br>can of soda from the gas station.<br>You go back and pay for it.<br>**Go ahead 3 rungs.** |
| You said you would babysit on<br>Friday for your neighbor, and you<br>show up like you said.<br>**Go ahead 3 rungs.** | You tell your grandmother that<br>you did not get an A on the test for<br>which she helped you study.<br>**Go ahead 1 rung.** |
| You promised a neighbor you would walk<br>her dog while she was on vacation, but it<br>was more work than you thought so you<br>told her you were too busy.<br>**Go back 4 rungs.** | You return an overdue<br>library book and pay the fine.<br>**Go ahead 1 rung.** |
| A friend asks if you will help him<br>study for a test, but you don't want to,<br>so you say you have a cold.<br>**Go back 2 rungs.** | You are embarrassed about taking<br>medication at lunch, so you tell people<br>that it is for somebody else.<br>**Go back 1 rung.** |
| You won the race at the track meet,<br>so you tell everyone that you are<br>going to the Olympics.<br>**Go back 3 rungs.** | You were second at the<br>track meet, but you tell everyone<br>that you won.<br>**Go back 2 rungs.** |
| You were picking partners for a project<br>and didn't like who you were paired with,<br>so you tell the teacher that your mother<br>said you have to work with someone else.<br>**Go back 2 rungs.** | Your father asks if you<br>finished all of your homework.<br>You did!<br>**Go ahead 3 rungs.** |

| | |
|---|---|
| You are late for school, so you tell the teacher that the bus driver drove too slowly.<br>**Go back 2 rungs.** | You are late for school, so you tell the principal that you are sorry that you overslept.<br>**Go ahead 2 rungs.** |
| Your friend asks if you like the new poster she just bought. You don't, but you tell her that it's not really your taste, but you're glad she likes it.<br>**Go ahead 3 rungs.** | Your friend is sad because her mother is sick. You tell her that you will be there with her after school and you make sure you are.<br>**Go ahead 2 rungs.** |
| The teacher asks if the students were quiet while she was out of the room. They were and you say that everyone was fine.<br>**Go ahead 2 rungs.** | You forgot to bring your gym shoes to school, so you tell the P.E. teacher that you thought it was on a different day.<br>**Go back 1 rung.** |
| You tell a friend that she's supposed to call her mother from the office, but it's just a joke.<br>**Go back 3 rungs.** | You tell your little brother that you will play basketball with him after school, and you do.<br>**Go ahead 3 rungs.** |
| The librarian asks how much the book you want to buy at the sale costs because she doesn't have the list in front of her. You tell her it is $5.00, which it is.<br>**Go ahead 1 rung.** | You are correcting your friend's spelling test and notice that she put down an "o" instead of an "a" in the word <u>animal</u>. You take your pencil and make the letter into an "a" so she'll get it right.<br>**Go back 3 rungs.** |
| You tell your bus driver that your mother said he is a lousy driver.<br>**Go back 2 rungs.** | You tell your bus driver that you have a note that says you can get off at a friend's stop instead of your regular stop. She asks to see it so you give it to her.<br>**Go ahead 3 rungs.** |
| Your father asks why you stopped mowing the lawn. You tell him that the lawn mower is making a funny sound and you think you should stop, but really you are hot and tired. **Go back 3 rungs.** | You told your mother you would walk the dog on Saturday morning if he could sleep in your bed. You get up, walk Rusty, and tell your mother that it's taken care of.<br>**Go ahead 3 rungs.** |

# Lesson I-4: Defining Promise-Keeping

**The contents of Lesson l-4 include:**

- Journal Ideas
- Pre-/Posttest on situations involving promise-keeping
- Worksheet I-4A, What Is Promise-keeping?
- Worksheet I-4B, What Promise-keeping Is and Isn't
- Worksheet I-4C, The Three Promises

## Journal Ideas

The journal questions can be used on a daily or occasional basis for students to reflect, write, and share their ideas and opinions regarding promise-keeping.

## Pre-/Posttest

Pass out the pre-/posttest to students and explain that they are to read the situations on the sheet and select the answer that best shows promise-keeping. If used as a pretest, you may want to discuss students' ideas after they have taken the test.

**Answers**

1. b; 2. c; 3. a; 4. c; 5. d

## Worksheet I-4A, What Is Promise-Keeping?

1. Write the definition of promise-keeping on the board or display it on a poster where it is easily viewed by students. *"Promise-keeping means making promises that you can keep, and then keeping them."*

2. Pass out the worksheet and have students complete it by circling yes or no to indicate whether or not the person in each situation is keeping his or her promise.

**Answers**

1. no; 2. no; 3. yes; 4. yes

**Discuss**

1. Why weren't the promises kept in situations 1 and 2?
2. If you forget something, are you still responsible for not keeping your promise?

## Worksheet I-4B, What Promise-Keeping Is and Isn't

1. Review the definition of promise-keeping.

2. Pass out the worksheet and have students complete it by writing IS or ISN'T to indicate whether or not each example shows promise-keeping.

**Answers**

1. IS; 2. ISN'T; 3. ISN'T; 4. ISN'T; 5. ISN'T; 6. IS

**Discuss**

1. What are some ways that the forgetful people could keep their promises?
2. In situation 4, Rob did let his brother borrow a camera, but he knew that the camera did not work. Did Rob keep his promise or not? (Is this a good promise or one that he does not intend to carry out as he knows he is expected to?)

## Worksheet I-4C, The Three Promises

1. Review the definition of promise-keeping.

2. Pass out the cartoon portion of the worksheet to students.

3. Explain that you are going to read a story about keeping promises and students should follow along (following the numbers of the cartoons) as you read.

4. Follow the instructions on the teacher portion of the worksheet.

5. Allow time for discussion at each of the three stopping points.

### Answers

- (after picture 5) The three promises: pick up his clothes from the floor, take Joey with him, have Joey back at 3 o'clock

- (after picture 6) Brad kept his first promise.

- (after picture 8) Brad kept his second promise.

- (after picture 9) Brad didn't keep his promise because he didn't have a watch to let him know what time it was.

### Discuss

1. Is it OK to negotiate on promises (*Brad didn't want to clean up his entire room, just pick up his clothes*) or should Brad have cleaned up the whole room?

2. Would it have been all right for Brad to leave his cousin with the girl if he knew that she was reliable and that Joey would be safe and maybe even have more fun?

3. How could Brad have made sure he was ready at 3 o'clock? Even if he forgot a watch, how could he have kept his promise?

# Journal Ideas: Promise-Keeping

1. *Rate yourself:* How good are you at keeping your promises to other people?

   0—I break promises all the time

   1—I sometimes keep promises

   2

   3—I usually keep promises

   4

   5—I always keep my promises

2. What is the last promise you made to someone? Did you keep it or have you not had the opportunity to keep it yet?

3. How do you feel when someone makes a promise to you and then he or she breaks it? Is it easier to handle a broken promise when you understand the reasons why it was broken? How does it make you feel if you think the person who made the promise didn't really care that much?

4. What promises do you hear parents or adults make to small children? Why do you think they do that?

5. Make a list for one day of the promises you make to others. Then go back at a later time (a day? a week?) and check yourself. How did you do? If you broke some promises, why did that happen?

6. Adults often use contracts to make sure their promises to each other are kept. With what types of contracts are you familiar? Why do you think people need to have contracts to buy things, such as a car or a house?

7. Why is it hard to use words like **always** and **never** when you make a promise to someone else?

8. What are some silly promises you have made to others (or others have made to you), knowing that they won't be kept?

9. Have you ever made a promise to someone else and realized immediately afterwards that you couldn't keep it? What was the promise? How did you feel? What did you do?

10. Is it ever OK to break a promise to someone else? Under what circumstances?

Name _____  Date _____

# Promise-Keeping: Pretest/Posttest

Read each situation and all of the choices. Then circle the answer that shows the response that best demonstrates promise-keeping.

1. Philip was babysitting for his little brother, Tommy, who did not want to go to bed. Philip had promised his mother that he would make sure Tommy got to bed on time. How could Philip best keep his promise?

    a. He could tell Tommy that he would call the police.

    b. He could tell Tommy that he would read him a story if he went to bed on time, and he got a book.

    c. He could tell Tommy that he would call Mom on the phone and tell on him, and he went for the phone.

    d. He could tell Tommy that they would both lie to Mom about bedtime.

2. Angela went shopping with her friends, but she promised her mother that she would be waiting outside the mall at 5 o'clock, so her mother could pick her up right after work. Which ending shows the best way for Angela to keep her promise?

    a. Angela stopped to go to one more store and got there at 5:30.

    b. Angela couldn't find her watch, so she got there at 5:15.

    c. Angela hurried through the last store so she would be on time.

    d. Angela called her mother at work to ask if she could stay longer.

3. Carlos and Tina were going to take care of the neighbor's fish while the neighbors went on vacation for a week. They promised the neighbor that one of them would be there each day. Which ending best shows promise-keeping?

    a. The two friends took turns going to feed the fish.

    b. Carlos decided he did not have time to do this, so he asked Tina to do the whole week, but Tina didn't want to.

    c. Tina forgot that she had cheerleading, so she fed the fish twice on one day and skipped the next.

    d. Carlos had a friend who wanted the job, so Carlos said the friend could do it instead but the friend decided after one day that he really didn't want to do it.

4. Sandy was having a birthday party and asked her friend if she would bring the balloons and other decorations. Her friend said she had some leftover stuff from another party and would bring them for Sandy's party. How could the friend show promise-keeping?

    a. She could ask another friend to bring the balloons.

    b. She could tell Sandy to come and pick up the stuff at her house.

    c. She could bring the balloons and decorations over to Sandy's the night before the party.

    d. She could tell Sandy that she changed her mind and didn't want to give her the decorations.

5. Paul was reading a really popular book that everyone wanted to borrow. He promised his friend Joe that he could have the book next. Joe got sick and was going to miss a week of school. A lot of kids wanted to borrow the book since Joe was going to be gone anyway. Which ending best shows promise-keeping?

    a. Paul let someone else take the book first.

    b. Paul told the kids that he left the book at home so no one would ask for it.

    c. Paul called Joe and said that the book was missing.

    d. Paul asked Joe if he would mind if someone else got the book first.

Name _____ Date _____

# I-4A. What Is Promise-Keeping?

Promise-keeping means m_____ p_____ you can
k_____, and then k_____ them.

Read each situation below and decide whether or not the person is keeping his or her promise.
Circle yes or no.

|  **Now...** | **Later...** |
| --- | --- |

1.

"I'll be here at 5 to pick you up. Don't be late!"

"OK, I'll be here."

"Oh, let's look at these cool jeans. Mom won't mind waiting an extra minute or two."

YES    NO

2.

"I will water your plants for you while you're gone."

"It's cold outside! I'll go tomorrow."

YES    NO

3.

"I can help you with your science homework. I know how to do all that stuff."

"Here I am. I brought an extra dictionary and some science notes I had."

YES    NO

4.

"I promise I'll vote for you for class president."

Nancy ‖‖‖ ‖‖‖‖
Alex ‖‖‖‖

YES    NO

Name _____  Date _____

# I-4B. What Promise-Keeping Is and Isn't

**Review**

Promise-keeping means m_____

p_____ you can keep, and then

k_____ them.

The opposite of a promise-keeper is a promise-

_____.

**Directions:** Read each situation below. Write IS if it shows promise-keeping. Write ISN'T if it shows promise-breaking.

1. Johnny went to the dentist and found out that he had several cavities. He told the dentist he would brush his teeth every day. He made a chart and marked it off every day after he brushed his teeth. So far he hasn't missed a day.  _____

2. Latoya's mother asked her if she would lock the door before she left for school each morning. Latoya knew it was important, and she agreed to do that. The school bus came early one morning and Latoya rushed out the door without locking it.  _____

3. Sandi told her best friend Aimee that she would let Aimee borrow her bike for the weekend. When the weekend came, Sandi told Aimee that she had changed her mind.  _____

4. Rob's mother made him promise that he would let his little brother borrow a camera to take pictures of his baseball team. Rob didn't want to let him borrow his camera, but he found another camera that didn't always work right and gave that one to his little brother.  _____

5. Alison's teacher, Mrs. Frye, asked Alison if she would spend her recess time going around to other classrooms delivering the school newspaper. Alison told Mrs. Frye that she would do it, but at recess time she forgot and went outside instead.  _____

6. Jamie and Kyle were going to meet at the movie theater. Jamie told Kyle that he would probably get there first, so he would save Kyle a seat. Sure enough, Jamie got there early, got his ticket, went into the theater, and saved Kyle a seat so that when the movie started, Kyle got right in and sat down.  _____

# For the Teacher
## (Script for Worksheet I-4C, The Three Promises)

I am going to read you a short story about keeping promises. You can follow along with the pictures as I read. I am going to stop the story at several points to ask you if the boy is promise-keeping or not. Remember to use the definition of promise-keeping when you answer.

> **Promise-Keeping means making promises you can keep, and keeping them.**
>
> Think:   1. Is this a promise that someone can keep?
>
>            2. Did the person keep the promise?

**(Picture 1)** Brad loves to sleep late on Saturday mornings. He also loves to keep a messy room. One morning, his mother bravely pops her head into his room to give him some news. "Guess what, Brad?" she says. Brad says, "MMMMMMMMM." His mother says, "We're having company today—your aunt and uncle and cousin Joey are coming today for a visit."

**(Picture 2)** Brad is less than thrilled to hear this news. Joey is a five-year-old terror who loves to break things, drop things, and mess up Brad's piles of mess. "No!" he cries, "not that little brat!" "Oh yes," says his mother. "I need you to play with Joey while we adults go out to do some errands." Brad sits up suddenly. "Mom, you can't do this to me! I wanted to play baseball with my friends today! I can't babysit Joey!"

**(Picture 3)** "It will be *fun*," his mother insists. "But I need you to promise me some things. I want you to clean up your room, entertain Joey, and have him back here at 3 o'clock so your aunt and uncle can leave right away. Can you do that for me?" Brad thinks for a minute. "I don't want to clean my room; I like it just like this." His mother makes a face. "You have to clean it. We can't even see the floor. This is disgusting." "I will pick up the clothes off the floor so you can walk through. How's that?" Brad asks.

**(Picture 4)** "Now let's talk about playing with Joey," Mom continues. "Can't he play baseball with you and your friends? He loves to play with the big boys." Brad throws the covers over his head. "No, Mom, he can't! He will just get in the way. Can't he stay home? Or with a paid professional babysitter?" Mom shakes her head. "Will you take him with you wherever you go today?" she asks. Brad groans. "If I have to. Yes, I'll drag him with me."

**(Picture 5)** "Now, about this afternoon," Mom continues. "You have to make sure he is here at 3 o'clock because your aunt and uncle are in a big hurry to get home. Put your watch on and make sure you are back at the house on time, OK?" Brad puts his feet on the floor and realizes he has to get up. He nods his head and moans.

**STOP.** What promises did Brad make? *(pick clothes off the floor, take Joey with him, have him back at 3 o'clock)*

**(Picture 6)** After his mom leaves, Brad throws all the clothes on the floor into a laundry hamper and makes sure there is a little path around his room. He leaves the rest of his mess just where it is.

**STOP.** How is Brad doing on his first promise? *(he kept it)*

**(Picture 7)** Soon after, the happy family arrives and little Joey scampers into Brad's room. He makes paper airplanes out of Brad's math homework and builds a tower out of soda cans that he found under Brad's bed. Brad realizes he has to get this little monster out of his room, so he takes him with him to the playground.

**(Picture 8)** At the playground, Brad finds his friends all ready to play. "What did you bring him for?" asks his friends. Brad explains the situation. One boy says his older sister is home and would probably watch Joey for them. Brad thinks about it, but decides he has to keep Joey with him at all times so he says no. The boys think for a minute and decide to let Joey hold the second base. Joey begins tearing up the base, so they try letting him BE second base. This seems to work well.

**STOP.** How is Brad doing on his second promise? *(he is keeping Joey with him)*

**(Picture 9)** It gets later and later in the afternoon. Brad realizes he has no idea what time it is because he forgot to wear his watch. When he sees his mother drive up honking the horn on the car, he realizes he has missed the 3 o'clock meeting time. "I'm sorry, Mom," Brad said. "I really meant to have him back at 3, but I didn't know what time it was."

**STOP.** What do you think about this promise? *(he didn't keep it because he didn't have a watch to let him know the time)*

**(Picture 10)** "You promised you would have him back at 3," his mother says. "Now your aunt and uncle are going to be late." Brad says he is sorry, but they were having such a good time he just forgot. Then his aunt and uncle come up. "It's OK," they say. "We are so happy to see little Joey having a good time with his big cousin. We will just stay overnight and let you two have more fun together. Wouldn't that be fun, Joey?" Joey is delighted. Brad makes another promise—this one to himself. He promises he will start wearing a watch all the time!

# I-4C. The Three Promises

1.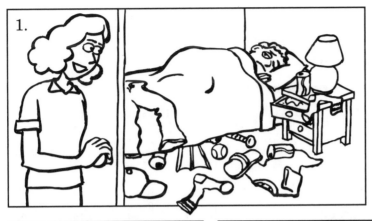

2.

3.

4.

5.

6.

7.

8.

9.

10.

# Lesson I-5: Recognizing Promise-Keeping

**The contents of Lesson I-5 include:**

- Worksheet I-5A, Promises You Can Keep
- Worksheet I-5B, Promise-keeping with Common Sense
- Worksheet I-5C, What's a Good Promise?

## Worksheet I-5A, Promises You Can Keep

1. Pass out the worksheet to students. Have them complete the review section at the top.
2. Have the students write yes or no to indicate whether or not the promises made could likely be kept.

**Answers**

1. yes; 2. yes; 3. no (very long range); 4. yes; 5. no (unlikely—that's a lot of reading for a typical student); 6. no; 7. no (probably involves a lot of people!); 8. no (unlikely); 9. yes; 10. no (probably requires permission from a parent)

**Discuss**

1. Why were some of the promises on this list unlikely to be kept?
2. Why is it important to really know the person before you decide whether or not he or she is making a possible promise? *(maybe someone is a terrific reader and can read 100 books—you would need to know this before you could evaluate the reality of the promise)*

## Worksheet I-5B, Promise-Keeping with Common Sense

1. Pass out the worksheet to students. Have them complete the review sentence.
2. Directions for the remainder of the worksheet require students to read each item and use common sense to decide whether or not the character really intends to keep the promise. This is a discussion page, so no writing is required.

**Answers**

1. no (she intends to cheat); 2. no (had his fingers crossed); 3. no (overdoing the project— most likely will not be able to do that much work); 4. no (unlikely that he will win the lottery and he's too young to get his own ticket); 5. no (unlikely that he will do that much homework for that long); 6. no (will the other girl really love a haircut given by this girl who has only cut dolls' hair?)

**Discuss**

1. Why were all of these promises likely to be broken? *(the characters either never intended to keep them or made such outlandish "deals" that they most likely could not be kept)*
2. What do you think about the excuse "my fingers were crossed" for not keeping a promise?

## Worksheet I-5C, What's a Good Promise?

1. Pass out the worksheet to students and have them complete the review section.

2. Have students read each item and choose the best promise that the person in each situation could make. They are to circle A or B.

### Answers

1. B (probably easier to do it before bed than getting up early and rushing for the bus); 2. A (better to promise to do it more often and succeed than set too high of a standard— "never"?); 3. A (helping someone is better than doing the project for him); 4. B (more reasonable); 5. A (depending on how upset the person is about his friend stealing)

### Discuss

1. Is it better to make a wonderful promise that you probably won't be able to keep or to make a promise that is more realistic but not so dramatic?

2. In situation 1, do you think some people work better at night and others work better in the morning? Could possibly either answer work depending on the person? Does it matter when the work is done as long as it gets done?

3. In situation 4, Alison wants her friend to be as angry at Isabelle as she is, although Kara may not be angry at Isabelle at all. To what extent should you be angry for a friend? How does this affect making promises on his or her behalf?

Name _____ Date _____

# I-5A. Promises You Can Keep

**Review**

Promise-Keeping means _____ _____ you can

_____, and then _____ _____.

**Directions:** Are these promises that someone could keep? Write YES or NO in the blank after each item. If not, what is wrong with these promises?

1. I promise I will clean up my room this weekend. _____

2. Yes, Dad, I will take out the garbage before I go to bed. _____

3. I promise I will get all A's on my report card for the next three years. _____

4. I promise that I will read a book for an hour after school all week. _____

5. I will read 100 books in the next month and do book reports on all of them. _____

6. I am going to be the first man on Mars. _____

7. I will invite the whole school to my birthday party next week. _____

8. I know your parents are getting a divorce, but I will get them back together. _____

9. I will get you a picture of a puppy to hang on your wall. _____

10. My dog, a St. Bernard, just had puppies so I will give you one or two of them. _____

Name _____ Date _____

# I-5B. Promise-Keeping with Common Sense

**Review**

Promise-Keeping means _____ _____ you

_____ _____, and then _____

_____.

**Directions:** Read each situation below and think about whether or not this person intends to keep the promise he or she made.

1. Jill

I know I flunked every spelling test this whole year so far, but, Dad, I promise I will have a perfect test score on the next one.

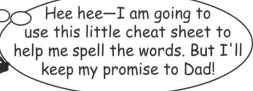

Hee hee—I am going to use this little cheat sheet to help me spell the words. But I'll keep my promise to Dad!

2. Carlos

No, I won't fight with my little brother anymore.

I had my fingers crossed when I said that. As soon as Mom leaves the room—POW!

3. Angel

Oh, Mrs. Tyler! I love to color maps! Give me all of the maps for the United States! I will color all of them for you! And then give me Europe! I will color all of the European countries, too, and then the world! I will color every country in the whole world for you!

4. Bob

Please let me borrow $100 from you. I am going to buy a lottery ticket from my uncle and I just know that I will win and then I can pay you back.

5. Stevie

Fred, if you take out the garbage for me, I promise I will do your homework for you every night for a month.

6. Sylvia

I know how to cut and dye hair! I did it on my dolls all the time when I was little. Let me cut and dye your hair and I promise you will love it! Hand me the scissors!

Name _____ Date _____

# I-5C. What's a Good Promise?

**Review**

Promise-_____ means making _____ you can

_____, and then _____ them.

**Directions:** Read each situation and choose the best promise that the person in each story could make. Circle A or B.

1. Mother tells Lisa that she has to go to bed in a half hour, but Lisa doesn't have her homework finished yet. She has a big test and a book report due. What could Lisa promise?

   A. "I promise I'll get up early tomorrow morning and get it done in the half hour before the bus comes."

   B. "I promise I will work on my homework for 45 minutes, and then I will go to bed."

2. The dentist is very unhappy with John's teeth because there are lots of cavities. What could John promise?

   A. "I promise I will brush my teeth a lot more often than I have been."

   B. "I promise that I will never get another cavity."

3. Pete's friend asks him to help him draw an art poster, but Pete is very busy this weekend with some things he has to do at home. What could Pete promise?

   A. "I will come over on Saturday and help you for a little while."

   B. "I will do the poster for you next week and give it to you to turn in."

4. Alison is really mad at Isabelle and does not want anyone, especially Kara, to talk to her or have anything to do with her. If Kara talks to Isabelle, Alison will be extremely upset with her. What could Kara promise?

   A. "I will never talk to Isabelle again. I will stay away from her so that you and I will remain friends."

   B. "I might have to work with Isabelle at school, so I will have to talk to her, but I will not say anything about you to her."

5. Jeff takes some money out of the teacher's desk when she is out of the room. He asks his friend Keith to promise not to tell on him. What could Keith promise?

   A. "I won't say anything if you return the money."

   B. "I won't tell on you, but I think what you did is wrong."

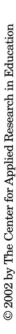

# Lesson I-6: Applying Promise-Keeping

**The contents of Lesson I-6 include:**

- Worksheet I-6A, Making a Promise to Someone
- Worksheet I-6B, A Day of Promises
- Quiz on Part 2: Promise-Keeping
- Game: Promise Circles

## Worksheet I-6A, Making a Promise to Someone

1. Pass out the worksheet to students. Have them complete the review section at the top.
2. Explain that now they should be thinking about how they can apply what they have learned about making and keeping promises to their own lives.
3. Have students complete the worksheet by thinking of people to whom they have made promises (or likely will in the near future). Explain that they should select a specific person and a specific situation, and write an example of a specific promise.

**Discuss**

1. Is it harder or easier to make a promise to someone you know well or care about?
2. Have you made a promise that you felt uncomfortable making and you knew immediately that you wouldn't be able to keep it? What could you have done?
3. How does being a promise-keeper affect someone's reputation?

## Worksheet I-6B, A Day of Promises

1. Pass out the worksheet to students and have them complete the review section at the top.
2. Explain that now they are going to take a close look at how they are doing on their promises by recording and examining promises made in a day.
3. Discuss guidelines for recording their promises; for example, they may use the worksheet to write promises throughout the day, or record them at the end of the day, etc.
4. After some time has passed (the next day?), have students review their promises and evaluate how they did by adding some comments. The comment section might include problems they encountered in keeping their promises.

**Discuss**

1. Was it difficult to remember the promises you had made?
2. Did it help you to specifically say, "I promise…" when you made a promise to someone?
3. What problems did you run into with promises you did not keep?

## Quiz on Part 2: Promise-Keeping

This quiz can be used as a follow-up to Part 2 lessons.

**Answers**

1. (*definition*) Promise-Keeping means making promises you can keep, and then keeping them.

2. (*example*) a. no (not realistic); b. no (the sister went out the door); c. yes (the person promised to try, and she kept her promise even though it didn't go the way she wanted it to)

3. (*applying*) Answers will vary.

## Game for Part 2: Promise Circles

Directions and sample game pieces follow at the end of this lesson.

Name _____ Date _____

# Worksheet I-6A. Making a Promise to Someone

**Review**

Promise-Keeping means _____

_____.

The opposite of Promise-Keeping is _____.

**Directions:** What is a good promise you could make to these people? Fill in a specific name, think of a specific situation, and then write your promise.

To your teacher…

_____

_____

_____

To a brother or sister…

_____

_____

_____

To a good friend…

_____

_____

_____

To an adult you like…

_____

_____

_____

To someone younger than you…

_____

_____

_____

To a parent…

_____

_____

_____

To a school person…

_____

_____

_____

To a kid you don't know well…

_____

_____

_____

To an adult you don't like…

_____

_____

_____

To someone a lot older than you…

_____

_____

_____

Name _____ Date _____

# I-6B. A Day of Promises

**Review**

Promise-Keeping means _____
_____.

The opposite of Promise-Keeping is _____.

**Directions:** Go through an entire day listing the promises you make to other people. Keep track of how you are doing at keeping your promises.

| Time | Person | Promise | Kept? | Comments |
|------|--------|---------|-------|----------|
|      |        |         |       |          |

Name _____ Date _____

# Quiz on Part 2: Promise-Keeping

1. What is meant by Promise-Keeping? _____

_____

_____

2. Are these children Promise-Keepers? Circle yes or no.

a.

*We're going on vacation. Will you pick up our mail while we're gone?*

*Not only will I pick it up every day, I will open it, read it, and pay your bills for you.*

**YES   NO**

b.

*I have to go to the store. Will you keep on eye on your little sister?*

*Yes.*

Later...

**YES   NO**

c.

*Save me a seat at the lunch table, OK?*

*Sometimes it gets crowded, but I will try.*

Later...

*You can't save seats. It's too crowded in here.*

**YES   NO**

3. What could you do if a friend wanted you to promise something that you were not comfortable with? Choose one of the following and write about it on the back of this sheet.

   a. changing religions

   b. not talking to someone

   c. not telling about a dangerous secret (physical harm, dishonesty)

# Game for Promise-Keeping: Promise Circles

**Materials:**

You need promises (written on circle cards) and a gameboard for each player. You might want to laminate the gameboard for repeated use.

**Objective:**

To be the first player to fill up his or her board with four different types of promise cards plus a "free" promise card

**Directions:**

1. Pass out a gameboard to each player.
2. Shuffle the promise cards.
3. Explain that there are four types of promises in the deck:
    a. promises that are fun, but silly
    b. bad promises (involving doing something wrong)
    c. promises over which you have no control (weather, winning)
    d. good promises (can be kept)
4. Students take a promise card off the top of the shuffled deck, read it, and place it on the corresponding promise circle.
5. If students pick a "free" circle, they can play on the "free space."
6. If students already have a promise circle covered, they put back the card.
7. All five circles must be covered to be a winner.
8. Examples of promises to copy onto circle cards. Be sure to include "FREE" cards, too.

**Silly Promises**

I promise I will give you $1,000,000.

I promise I will take you to the moon.

I promise I will fly you to Walt Disney World after school.

I promise your Teddy Bear will magically appear at school.

I promise you will get a pony, a puppy, and a dinosaur for Christmas.

I promise I will give you my dad's wide-screen TV set.

I promise you will wake up tomorrow and be 6 inches taller.

**Bad Promises**

I promise I will lie for you.

I promise I won't tell that you were smoking.

I promise I will steal that book you want from the library.

I promise I will make noises when the teacher comes in the room.

I promise I will trip Bobby when he walks past.

I promise I will hit you if you tell on me.

I promise I will help you cheat on the test.

## No-Control Promises

I promise it will be sunny and nice out tomorrow.

I promise your team will win the game.

I promise that everyone in the class will come to your birthday party.

I promise our team will win the baseball game.

I promise that your sick dog will not die.

I promise that the boy/girl you like will call you every night this week.

I promise that it will rain tomorrow.

## Good Promises

I promise I will take the dog out after school.

I promise I will wash the dishes.

I promise I will help my brother with his homework.

I promise I will sit down and be quiet.

I promise I will lock the door behind him.

I promise I will pay you back the dollar I borrowed from you.

I promise I will return the library book tomorrow.

A Silly Promise

A Good Promise

Free!

A Bad Promise

No-Control Promise

# Lesson I-7: Defining Humility

**The contents of Lesson I-7 include:**

- Journal Ideas
- Pre-/Posttest on situations involving humility
- Worksheet I-7A, Bragging or Telling?
- Worksheet I-7B, What Is Humility?
- Worksheet I-7C, Accepting a Compliment

## Journal Ideas

The journal ideas can be used for daily or occasional writing activities. Responses should be shared with others occasionally.

## Pre-/Posttest

Pass out the pre-/posttest to students and explain that they are to select the response that best shows humility.

### Answers

1. c (acknowledges the response but does not take credit); 2. b; 3. a; 4. d; 5. a (c would also be appropriate)

## Worksheet I-7A, Bragging or Telling?

1. Write the definition of *humility* on the board or other visible place. *"Humility means not bragging about yourself."*

2. Pass out the worksheet and have students complete the review section at the top. Then direct students to the remainder of the worksheet where they should put a T (telling) or B (bragging) in front of each statement.

### Answers

1. B, T; 2. T, B; 3. B, T; 4. B, T; 5. T, B; 6. B, T

### Discuss

1. Is it OK for someone else to brag about your accomplishments?

2. Is it important to consider who your audience is when you are talking about your accomplishments? *(e.g., talking about expensive clothes in front of people who don't have much money)*

## Worksheet I-7B, What Is Humility?

1. Review the definition of humility.

2. Pass out the worksheet and have students complete it by circling the person who is not bragging.

### Answers

1. no (just telling); 2. yes ("best"); 3. yes (expensive); 4. no (just happy); 5. yes (has to tell how many kids he beat); 6. no (just telling)

**Discuss**

1. The students in situations 1 and 6 are telling about their accomplishments, but they are not bragging about them as far as we can tell. How would the tone of voice that they use affect whether or not they were bragging? *(a different tone probably would indicate that they were bragging)*

2. In situation 4, the boy is very happy but he is not saying anything that would make someone else feel bad. What might he say if he were bragging?

## Worksheet I-7C, Accepting a Compliment

1. Review the definition of humility.
2. Pass out the cartoon section of the worksheet to students.
3. Explain that you are going to read a story about how to accept a compliment when someone else is bragging about you. As you read, stop periodically to ask questions and give students time to discuss their thoughts.

**Answers**

- (after picture 1) Yes, bragging about how rich her parents are.
- (after picture 3) Yes, bragging about the expensive professional pictures. Mindy complimented her on her skating, pictures, and trophies.
- (after picture 4) The mother complimented her on her looks; she responded in a snotty way.
- (after picture 5) She was complimented about her skating backwards; the boy did not want to be instructed by her.
- (after picture 6) Della thanked her guests for the special day. She continued to brag about the skating contest. Not many people will probably show up.

# Journal Ideas: Humility

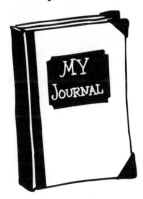

1. *Rate yourself:* How humble are you?

   0—I brag all the time.

   1—I brag often.

   2

   3—I brag sometimes when I do something important.

   4

   5—I never brag about myself.

2. What are some things you would like to brag about? What would you like people to know about you that you think is important?

3. When was a time you really bragged about yourself? What did you say? To whom did you brag? How did it make you feel?

4. Think about someone (don't name names) who brags a lot. It may be a sports figure or a celebrity. What does this person say about himself or herself? Does it make you think more highly of this person? Do you think it's funny?

5. What are some compliments you have been given? How did it make you feel to be complimented? What did you say?

6. What was the last *sincere* compliment you gave to someone? Why did you say it to the person? How did he or she react?

7. What was the last *insincere* compliment you gave to someone? Why did you do this? How did the person react?

8. If someone were to give you a trophy for doing something great, what would be engraved on it?

9. When you play on a team, sometimes bragging or boasting is a good way of getting your team "up" for the game. How is this different from bragging about yourself? Do you think this is right?

10. How does it make you feel when someone brags and adds: "I'm just telling the truth"? What would you rather hear this person say?

Name _____ Date _____

# Humility: Pretest/Posttest

Read the situations below and choose the response that best shows humility.

1. Denise won the hurdles race for her track team. After she crossed the finish line, a reporter for the school newspaper said to her: "You were fabulous!" How could Denise respond to show humility?

   a. She could smile and say nothing.

   b. She could say, "I am really good."

   c. She could say, "Today was my day!"

   d. She could say, "It was easy to beat those losers."

2. Everyone knows that Elliot is the smartest kid in the class. When it was time to pick kids to be on the school quiz team, someone said, "Be sure to pick Elliot. He's really smart." What could Elliot say or do to show humility?

   a. He could stand up and take a bow.

   b. He could say, "I would love to be on the quiz team."

   c. He could say, "I'm smarter than those other kids."

   d. He could say, "I got all A's last semester. This will be no problem."

3. The Red Rockets is the name of the girls' soccer team that meets on weekends to play other teams. They are in first place for their division. What could they say to each other to get psyched up to play before the game?

   a. "We will play hard and play fair and follow the rules!"

   b. "We will kill our opponents! Watch out!"

   c. "We are mean and rough and tough and we eat other soccer players for breakfast!"

   d. "We will do anything short of cheating to win this game!"

4. Elaine is really beautiful. Whenever there are a group of girls and their mothers, the adults always hang around Elaine and tell her how pretty she is and how she should be a model. What could Elaine say or do to show humility?

   a. She could say, "Thank you, I know."

   b. She could flash and smile and pose like a model.

   c. She could say, "I got these good looks from my mom and dad."

   d. She could say, "Thank you, that is so nice of you."

5. Daniel loves to draw and his painting won a blue ribbon at the county art show. His painting is displayed in the front of the school where everyone can see it when they come into the building. Rick also loves to draw, but no one noticed his charcoal drawing that he spent weeks working on. When they were in art class together, the teacher said to Daniel, "Your art project was tremendous. You showed a lot of creativity and hard work in that project." What could Daniel say or do to show humility?

   a. "I like to draw. So does my friend Rick."

   b. "It's fun to be the best drawer in the school."

   c. "That ribbon will go in my scrapbook."

   d. "I worked hard on that project. I deserved to win."

# I-7A. Bragging or Telling?

Humility means not br_____ about y_____.

The way you say something can make a difference in what people hear. If you are bragging, it means you are telling more than the person really wants to hear or making yourself sound better than other people. Read each pair of statements below. Put a **B** in front of the one that shows bragging. Put a **T** in front of the one that shows telling.

1. _____ My dad is the best basketball player on the team.

   _____ My dad is a good basketball player.

2. _____ I got a lot of nice toys for my birthday.

   _____ I have more toys than anybody else in the class.

3. _____ These jeans cost over $50.

   _____ These are nice jeans, but they cost a lot.

4. _____ We live in the nicest house in the neighborhood.

   _____ We have a nice house that we really like.

5. _____ I love to swim and I swim whenever I get the chance.

   _____ I have lots of medals for being the best swimmer on the team.

6. _____ Everyone says I could be an actress because I am in plays all the time.

   _____ It's really fun for me to be in plays.

Name _____ Date _____

# I-7B. What Is Humility?

**Review**

Humility means not br_____ about yourself.

**Directions:** Read each situation below and decide whether or not the person is bragging about himself or herself. Circle yes or no.

# For the Teacher
## (Script for Worksheet I-7C, Accepting a Compliment)

When someone gives you a compliment, it is an opening to start bragging about yourself. I want you to follow along with the pictures as I read a short story about Della, a girl who did not know how to accept a compliment. Instead, she used compliments as an opportunity to brag about herself. Follow along and see what happens.

**(Picture 1)** Della is having a birthday party. Her parents say that she may invite as many friends as she wants since it is going to be a skating party. She goes to school on Monday and announces, "It's my birthday on Friday. I want everyone in the class to come to my ice skating party on Friday. My parents have a lot of money and they are paying for the whole rink for just my party."

**STOP.** Is Della bragging? What is she bragging about? (parents' money)

**(Picture 2)** The kids in the class are excited about the party. But they are not excited about hearing Della talk about her skating. "I am a really good skater," she tells her classmates. "I'm sure you would like to see my skating trophies, but there are too many to bring to school. You'll have to see them at the ice rink on Friday. But here are some photographs of my trophies." She passes them around.

**(Picture 3)** Mindy looks at the pictures. "You must be a really good skater, Della. These are really nice pictures and they look like nice trophies." "They are, Mindy," says Della. "These are professional pictures taken with a really good camera. I have had lessons for years, and I am really good. It's the truth, I'm not bragging."

**STOP.** Is Della bragging? What was the compliment Mindy gave her?

**(Picture 4)** Finally Friday comes and it is time for the skating party. Della is wearing a new skating outfit that her parents bought for her. "You look adorable, little birthday girl," says one of the mothers who dropped off her child. "You are so pretty and you look so nice!" Della gives the mom a big smile. "I know," she says smiling, and she skates off.

**STOP.** What compliment was Della given? How did she handle it?

**(Picture 5)** "You skate really well," says a little boy. "I can skate backwards," Della says, bumping into someone behind her. "Not everyone can skate backwards. It's kind of hard to do." The boy she bumps into gets up. "Would you like me to teach you how?" Della offers, trying to be polite. "I'm a really good teacher of backwards skating." The boy shakes his head. "No, I think I'll just skate the way I want to." Della shrugs. "Well, OK."

**STOP.** What compliment was she given now? Why do you think the boy didn't take her up on her offer?

**(Picture 6)** Finally it is time to open presents. Della gets all kinds of toys, games, clothes, and candy. "Thank you so much," she says to everybody. "Thank you for coming to my party. You made this a really special day for me. Don't forget to come to my skating contest next weekend, if you can make it. I'll probably win so it will be fun for you to come! Goodbye!"

**STOP.** What compliment did Della give to her guests? Did you think she was going to get one more opportunity to brag? What was it this time? Do you think anyone will show up?

# I-7C. Accepting a Compliment

1.

2.

3.

4.

5.

6.

# Lesson I-8: Recognizing Humility

**The contents of Lesson I-8 include:**
- Worksheet I-8A, Which One Shows Humility?
- Worksheet I-8B, Using Gestures
- Worksheet I-8C, When Someone Brags about You

## Worksheet I-8A, Which One Shows Humility?

1. Pass out the worksheet to students. Have them complete the review section at the top.
2. Directions for this worksheet ask students to circle the person in each pair who better shows humility.

**Answers**

1. second; 2. first; 3. first; 4. first

**Discuss**

1. How did the person in situation 1 show good sportsmanship?
2. Why was it important for the person in situation 4 to give credit to someone who helped him?

## Worksheet I-8B, Using Gestures

1. Pass out the worksheet to students and have them complete the review section at the top.
2. Directions for this worksheet involve having the students finish drawing the incomplete person to indicate a gesture that, in turn, communicates humility.

**Answers**

1. a wink; 2. a smile; 3. thumbs up; 4. touching friend on arm

**Discuss**

1. What are some other gestures you can show a person to acknowledge his or her comments or praise without being boastful about it? *("OK" sign)*
2. Do you think communicating with gestures rather than words can be a powerful way to let someone else know what you are thinking and feeling?

## Worksheet I-8C, When Someone Brags about You

1. Pass out the worksheet to students and have them complete the review section at the top.
2. Directions involve having students read the situations in which someone else is bragging about a person. They should discuss how that person could tactfully handle this situation without being rude or bragging.

**Discuss each situation**

*Possible answers*

1. "I'm a good student, but certainly not the smartest."
2. "Oh, Dad, I'm sure they don't want to look at all that stuff."
3. "I'm just lucky!"
4. "I don't know if it's a great example, but I'd love to read it."

# I-8A. Which One Shows Humility?

**Review**

Humility means _____ _____ about _____.

**Directions:** Which person in each pair is better at showing humility? Circle that person.

---

1.

---

2.

---

3.

---

4.

---

# I-8B. Using Gestures

**Review**

Humility means _____ _____ about _____.

**Directions:** These people are using gestures to show humility. Read each item and finish drawing the blank person to show how each is using a gesture, rather than words, to show humility.

1. Marcus went to a professional basketball game and saw his favorite player walking in the building. He went up to him and asked for his autograph. While the player was writing his name on a piece of paper, Marcus said, "You are my favorite player! You are so good! You are the best player on the team!!!" The player handed the autograph to Marcus and gave him a wink to show that he appreciated the compliment.

2. Sharon decorated a birthday cake to look like a golf course. Everyone at the party gathered around to tell her how cute the cake was and how creative she was. Sharon smiled and handed pieces of the cake to people.

3. Devon played in the tennis finals for the weekend intramural team. Lots of people were cheering as he hit the ball and won the match. A friend came up to him and said, "You were awesome! You really clobbered that guy!" Devon looked at his friend and quietly gave him the thumbs-up sign.

4. Sandra built a beautiful doll house for an art project. She spent hours and hours painting it, making furniture for it, and decorating the house. Her friend Alison came up to her and said it was the best project in the class and Sandra was a wonderful artist. Sandra quietly said, "ooh," and touched her friend on the arm.

Name _____ Date _____

# I-8C. When Someone Brags about You

**Review**

Humility _____ not _____ about _____.

**Directions:** The person in each situation below is not bragging, but someone else is bragging about him or her. How could the person handle the situation with humility?

_____

1.

This is my little nephew, Johnny. He is the brightest boy in the whole class, aren't you, Johnny?

_____

2.

Welcome to our home. Would you like to come in the basement and look at all of my daughter's bowling trophies? We have about 100 of them! It will only take an hour or two.

_____

3.

This is my friend Janie. She is going to be a super-model in Europe. She has already been on the cover of a teen magazine. Isn't she beautiful?

_____

4.

Alex, this is about the best written play I have ever received from a student! Why don't you read a little bit of it for your fellow classmates? I'm sure they would like to hear a good example of how to do it right!

_____

# Lesson I-9: Applying Humility

**The contents of Lesson I-9 include:**
- Worksheet I-9A, Ways I Can Show Humility
- Worksheet I-9B, Models of Humility
- Quiz on Part 3: Humility
- Role-play activity

## Worksheet I-9A, Ways I Can Show Humility

1. Pass out the worksheet to students and have them complete the review section at the top.
2. Directions for the remainder of the worksheet ask the student to think of times when he or she may have wanted to brag about himself or herself, and then to think of appropriate ways to acknowledge this with humility.

**Discuss**

1. Have you ever heard of anyone bragging about being humble?
2. Do you think it is better or more accepted if someone else talks about your achievements than if you do?
3. Have you ever been really embarrassed by someone else who was bragging about you?

## Worksheet I-9B, Models of Humility

1. Pass out the worksheet to students and have them complete the review section at the top.
2. The rest of the worksheet asks students to look for examples or models of humility around them. This could be in the lives of other people they know, celebrities, or other examples found in the media. Just as important as the example, however, is the student's reaction to that example. Have them record (in the third column) how the example made them feel. Were they impressed? Did they think it was phony? Were they pleased? etc.

**Discuss**

1. The first column requests the source of the model of humility. Compare sources among your classmates. Were primary sources the family? school? religious figures?
2. The second column requests the specific example of humility. Did you select words? gestures?
3. Share your feelings and new appreciation for this character skill of humility.

## Quiz on Part 3: Humility

This quiz can be used as a follow-up for the lessons in Part 3.

**Answers**

1. (*definition*) Humility means not bragging about yourself.

2. (*examples*) a. first; b. second; c. first (winking)

3. (*applying*) Answers will vary.

## Role-Play Activity for Part 3

Directions for this activity and sample role-playing cards are at the end of this lesson.

# I-9A. Ways I Can Show Humility

**Review**

Humility means _____

_____.

The opposite of humility is _____.

**Directions:** Think of times when you wanted to brag about something or had someone else brag about you. What are ways that you could show humility?

| Things I Could Brag About... | Ways I Could Show Humility... |
| --- | --- |
|  |  |

Name _____ Date _____

# I-9B. Models of Humility

**Review**

Humility means _____

_____.

The opposite of humility is _____.

**Directions:** Look around for examples of people who demonstrate humility by what they say, their tone, gestures, or how they accept compliments. You might observe classmates, people interacting with each other, articles in newspapers and magazines, or interviews on television. What is your reaction to each example?

| Source | Example of Humility | My Reaction |
| --- | --- | --- |
| | | |

Name _____ Date _____

# Quiz on Part 3: Humility

1. What is meant by humility?

_____

_____

2. Circle the response that shows humility in each situation below.

a.

b.

c.

3. How could you show humility if your grandmother started bragging in front of all of your friends about how you won a prize for being the most important player on your team?

_____

_____

_____

_____

# Role-Play Activity for Humility

**Materials:**

You need role-play cards. (Samples are given here to help you get started.)

**Objective:**

To give students opportunities to practice generating and evaluating expressions of humility

**Directions:**

Divide students into groups of 2 or 3. Explain that each group will be given a situation to role-play in front of the class to demonstrate the character skill of humility. Allow each group about 2–3 minutes to choose roles and rehearse their lines. Select volunteers to perform their role-plays in front of the class. Discuss how well the character skill of humility is portrayed in each role-play.

**Variation:**

For fun, role-play each situation two times. The first time, demonstrate the "wrong" way (showing extreme bragging). The second time, tone it down to show a more appropriate way (with humility).

| | |
|---|---|
| You just got your picture in the local newspaper for winning the schoolwide handwriting contest. Your mother is walking around all over town handing out copies of the picture to everyone. | You returned a lost wallet that had no money in it and suddenly people are calling you a hero and wanting to take your picture. |
| You made the winning touchdown/basket/goal for your sports team. Everyone on your team is telling you how great you are. | Your rich aunt took you shopping and bought you a lot of new clothes. Now your friends think you are stuck-up and different because you don't look like them anymore. |
| A major magazine called you to ask if you would pose on the cover to advertise their new line of clothing because you have "the right look" that everyone admires. | You got the highest score on the math test and saw that your teacher hung your paper in the hallway for everyone to see. |
| Your cat won first prize at the cat show. Mostly it was because your little sister brushed her and took care of her, but you were the one to get the praise. Your sister is watching while people come up to you and tell you what a wonderful cat you have. | You bought your sick neighbor a bouquet of her favorite flowers and she is going on and on about how you are the most thoughtful person on the planet. |
| You wrote a song on your new guitar and are playing it at the mall. People start coming up to you to tell you how wonderful it is. | You know you are the best player on your soccer team, but you have been helping one of the other players improve his/her skills, and now he/she is almost as good as you. A reporter from the school newspaper wants to interview one of you for the school paper. |

# Lesson I-10: Defining Responsibility

**The contents of Lesson I-10 include:**

- Journal Ideas
- A Pre-/Posttest on situations involving responsibility
- Worksheet I-10A, Understanding Your Job
- Worksheet I-10B, Completing the Job
- Worksheet I-10C, The Lemonade Stand

## Journal Ideas

These questions and ideas can be used for daily or occasional writing activities. Have students share their responses with each other.

## Pre-/Posttest

Pass out the pre-/posttest to students and explain that they are to choose the response to each situation that best shows responsibility.

**Answers**

1. d; 2. a; 3. b; 4. c; 5. b

## Worksheet I-10A, Understanding Your Job

1. Write the definition of *responsibility* on the board or in a place where students can easily see it. *"Responsibility means understanding your job and then doing it."*
2. Pass out the worksheet to students and have them complete the review section at the top. On the remainder of the worksheet, students are to consider the examples and decide whether or not the person understands the job, and then write yes or no.

**Answers**

1. no (bed is not properly made); 2. yes; 3. no (can't read the handwriting); 4. yes; 5. no (doesn't know what he needs to take)

**Discuss**

1. Why did some of the characters on the worksheet have trouble taking responsibility?
2. Was it their fault that they did not understand what to do?
3. How could they have clarified what their responsibility was?

## Worksheet I-10B, Completing the Job

1. Review the definition of responsibility.
2. Pass out the worksheet and have students complete it by answering the questions that follow each situation.

**Answers**

1. yes, no, forgot; 2. yes, no (not according to the directions she was given), she gave out two instead of one; 3. yes, yes, might have forgotten about the toys; 4. yes, yes, practice

**Discuss**

1. Why is it important for someone to follow the directions when given a job?
2. What could Xena have done (in situation 2) to find out if she could give out two ice cream bars?

# Worksheet I-10C, The Lemonade Stand

1. Review the definition of responsibility.

2. Pass out the cartoon section of the worksheet to students.

3. Explain that you are going to read them a short story about two children who are taking responsibility to run a lemonade stand and some of the problems they encounter.

**Answers**

See the teacher's script.

# Journal Ideas: Responsibility

1. *Rate yourself:* How well do you take responsibility?

   0—I'm not very responsible.

   1—I'm usually not responsible.

   2

   3 -Sometimes I am responsible.

   4

   5—I am always responsible.

2. What jobs or chores are you responsible for at home? at school? in the community?

3. How does it make you feel when someone says, "I know (you) can do the job." What if you aren't sure you can do the job?

4. What jobs or careers do adults have that require a lot of responsibility? For what things does a doctor or medical person have to be responsible for? What about an office worker?

5. What job or task do you wish someone would trust you with, but hasn't yet? Why do you think you haven't been given this responsibility yet?

6. What are some things (jobs or tasks) that adults can do, but children are not allowed to do? Why do you think children have to wait until they are older to do things like drive a car, hold a job, etc.? What does AGE have to do with responsibility?

7. Think about a person you know (don't name names) who is very responsible. What does this person do or say that makes you think he or she can be trusted to do the job?

8. Have you ever let someone down who was counting on you to be responsible? How did it make you feel? What happened? What could you do to change things?

9. Why do you think some people don't want jobs that require responsibility? Would you rather have an easy job that didn't require much (but didn't pay well) or would you rather have a job that required a lot of responsibility but had some rewards? What are some examples of these kinds of jobs?

10. Have you ever heard someone say, "Remind me to stop and get —"? What other kinds of "back-up" plans do people create to help them remember to take responsibility?

© 2002 by The Center for Applied Research in Education

# Responsibility: Pretest/Posttest

Read the situations below and choose the response that best shows responsibility.

1. Elana was supposed to take out the garbage every night after dinner. One night her friends called and wanted her to go out with them to the basketball game. She was in a hurry and wanted to get going. She could…

   a. Take the garbage out when she gets home.

   b. Ask her brother to take the garbage out for her.

   c. Ask her mother if she could take it out later.

   d. Have her friends wait while she takes out the garbage.

2. Jeffrey has a big math test coming up on Monday. His teacher told him to take his practice sheets home and study them over the weekend. He could…

   a. Put his sheet in a folder to take home.

   b. Take his math book home in case he has time to open it.

   c. Get to school early on Monday to study.

   d. Call a friend to come over to do homework together if there's time.

3. Denisha has piano lessons every Thursday at 5 o'clock, but to get there on time she needs to leave by 4:30. It always takes her awhile to find her music, get the money to pay the teacher, and walk three blocks to the lesson. She knows she will be busy after school this Thursday. She could…

   a. Call her father at the office to give her a ride so she won't be late.

   b. Make sure she has her piano materials packed and ready the night before.

   c. Run the three blocks as fast as she can.

   d. Call the piano teacher and ask if she can switch lessons with someone else.

4. Clarie got some new pajamas from her Aunt Carol for her birthday. Her mother told her to be sure to send a thank-you note. Clarie could…

   a. Write her aunt's address on a piece of paper.

   b. Plan to tell her aunt "thank you" when she sees her in 4 months.

   c. Get a cute card and write something in it for her aunt.

   d. Wait until she gets a Christmas present from her aunt and send a note then thanking her for both gifts.

5. Zeke's neighborhood friends want to play soccer the next day. Zeke says he will get two more people to come, bring the soccer ball, and meet everyone at the park at noon to play. Zeke could…

   a. Bring a football instead and say that it would be more fun.

   b. Call some friends the night before to make sure they can come.

   c. Decide that he doesn't want to play after all.

   d. Show up at 1:30, but have several people with him.

# I-10A. Understanding Your Job

**Review**

Responsibility means under_____ your j_____, and then

do _____ _____.

**Directions:** The first part of the definition involves understanding what you are responsible for. Read each example below and write YES if the person understands the job and NO if he or she does not.

1.

_____

2.

_____

3.

_____

4.

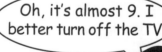

_____

5.

_____

# I-10B. Completing the Job

**Review**

Responsibility means un_____ your j_____,

and then d_____ _____.

**Directions:** The people in the examples below have been given a job to do, but some of them have not completed the job. Answer the questions that follow each situation.

1. Ted is supposed to take his cough medicine every morning and every night. He remembered in the morning, but at night he was sleepy and went to bed without taking it.

   Did he understand his job? _____

   Did he do his job? _____

   What was the problem? _____

2. Xena was supposed to pass out one ice cream bar to every student in the cafeteria as they went past the lunch ticket desk. She saw a friend of hers come up to her and ask if she could have an extra one. Xena thought there would be enough left over, so she gave her friend two of them.

   Did Xena understand her job? _____

   Did she do her job? _____

   What was the problem? _____

3. Barbara was babysitting for her neighbors' twin boys. The mother asked if Barbara would make sure the toys were cleaned up before they came home. After Barbara put the boys to bed, she started watching TV and realized that there was a really good movie on. She quickly put the toys away and sat down to watch the movie.

   Did Barbara understand her job? _____

   Did she do her job? _____

   What might have happened if she started watching the movie and didn't put the toys away? _____

4. Mrs. Thompson's class was doing a poetry show in front of the whole school. Robert had a long poem to memorize. Every night he practiced saying his lines to his parents, to his grandmother, and to his stuffed animals. When it was time for the show, he said his poem without making a mistake.

   Did Robert understand his job? _____

   Did he do his job? _____

   What helped him get the job done? _____

# For the Teacher
## (Script for Worksheet I-10C, The Lemonade Stand)

Follow along with the pictures as I read you a short story about two children who want to start a little business. Every once in awhile I will stop and ask you some questions about the story.

**(Picture 1)** April and Danny want to have a lemonade stand in the summer. It is a really hot week and they think they can make some money. Besides, it would be fun. They decide they will each get what is needed, work together to sell the lemonade, and split the money. April tells Danny, "Get some money from your mom and then I'll go buy the lemonade mix. I can get a big cardboard box for our stand." "OK," says Danny, "and I will make a big sign to hang up, too." The children hurry off to get what they need.

**STOP.** What is April's responsibility? *(get lemonade mix)* What is Danny's responsibility? *(get money and a sign)*

**(Picture 2)** Danny's mother gives him some money, but she tells him he has to replace it when they are done with their sales. He says OK. He goes into the garage and finds a board to make a sign. His mother says he may have it, but if he uses paint, he has to work outside and be sure to put the covers back tightly on the can so the paint does not dry out.

**STOP.** What is Danny's job now? *(replace the money; put paint can lids on tightly)*

**(Picture 3)** Meanwhile, April gets a big cardboard box and sets it up in front of her house. Her mother says they should have a trash can for the empty paper cups so people won't throw them on the ground. "It's OK if you have a stand here," she says, "but don't let it get messy. Pick up all the trash."

**STOP.** What is April's job now? *(get a trash can; clean up all trash)*

**(Picture 4)** Finally, they are ready for business. The sign is up, the lemonade is made, cups are filled, and they are ready to go! It is a hot day, and people are coming from all over to have a glass of nice cold lemonade. But look at what people do with their cups….

**STOP.** What problem do you see? *(cups all over the yard)* Whose responsibility is it to keep the yard clean? *(April's)*

**(Picture 5)** One of the customers is Danny's older brother. "Boy are you in trouble," he tells Danny as he gulps down the lemonade. "Why?" asks Danny. "Because you didn't put the lids on the paint can, my dear little brother," he tells Danny. "Dad's going to be mad when he gets home!" Danny looks at April. "I better get home right now," he tells her. "If I stir the paint and get the lids on, it might be all right." Before she can open her mouth, Danny is gone.

**STOP.** What's the problem now? *(Danny didn't take care of the paint cans and he left April to run the stand)*

**(Picture 6)** April makes a lot of money that day because everyone likes her lemonade. When it is afternoon, she closes up shop. She picks up the paper cups and puts them in the trash can. She puts away the sign.

**(Picture 7)** Then Danny shows up. "Where's my half of the money?" he asks. "I need to pay back my mom." April shakes her head. "You didn't work all afternoon like I did. You ran home to take care of that paint thing. I did all the work."

**(Picture 8)** April and Danny glare at each other. How can they ever work this out?

**STOP.** What do you think should happen next? How could these two work out the problem? Is one person entirely right and the other wrong? Did they each take responsibility? What are some possible solutions?

Name _____     Date _____

# I-10C. The Lemonade Stand

1.

2.

3.

4.

5.

6.

7.

8.

# Lesson I-11: Recognizing Responsibility

**The contents of Lesson I-11 include:**
- Worksheet I-11A, Is This Responsibility?
- Worksheet I-11B, Responsibility with Common Sense
- Worksheet I-11C, Which One Is Showing Responsibility?

## Worksheet I-11A, Is This Responsibility?

1. Pass out the worksheet to students. Have them complete the review section at the top.
2. Directions for the rest of the worksheet ask students to write Yes or No to indicate if the character in each example is showing responsibility.

**Answers**

1. no; 2. yes; 3. no; 4. yes; 5. yes; 6. no; 7. yes

**Discuss**

1. Why didn't the people in situations 1, 3, and 6 show responsibility?
2. Do you think those individuals understood their jobs?

## Worksheet I-11B, Responsibility with Common Sense

1. Pass out the worksheet to students and have them complete the review section at the top.
2. Directions for the remainder of the worksheet ask students to read situations and discuss the problem encountered by a character in each.

**Answers**

1. this was an unusual situation—not Dave's fault; 2. the storm was beyond her control; 3. the broken machine was not her fault; 4. Dick did not know how to complete this job because he didn't have enough information; 5. Abby attempted to get what she needed, but unfortunately the store was out of it; 6. this was an accident; 7. she did not know how to complete the task because she missed the instruction the day she was absent

**Discuss**

1. Most of the problems encountered were beyond the person's control, so we can understand why their jobs were not completed. What could each person do next in order to complete his or her job?
2. When you are given a new responsibility, when is a good time to ask questions about how to do it and what to do if you run into problems?

## Worksheet I-11C, Which One Is Showing Responsibility?

1. Pass out the worksheet to students and have them complete the review section at the top.
2. Directions for the remainder of the worksheet ask the student to read each situation, circle the character who is showing responsibility, and cross out the one who is not.

**Answers**

1. circle first, cross out second; 2. circle first, cross out second; 3. cross out first, circle second; 4. cross out first, circle second; 5. circle first, cross out second; 6. cross out first, circle second

**Discuss**

1. What are the problems with the characters who did not show responsibility?

2. Are these common responsibilities that you have heard someone say to you?

# I-11A. Is This Responsibility?

**Review**

Responsibility means _____ your _____,

and then _____ _____.

**Directions:** Read each example below. Write YES if it describes someone taking responsibility and write NO if someone is not.

1. George was supposed to change the cat's litter box every other day. He cleaned it on Monday and Friday. _____

2. Suzy's mother asked her to set the table for the family so that when the parents got home from work, it would be all ready for them. Suzy got home from school, put her books away, and got out the plates and dishes and put them on the table for everyone. _____

3. Mrs. Taylor has a class rule about sharpening all pencils before she begins to talk, and making sure that students have at least two pencils. Jamal broke the lead on his pencil when Mrs. Taylor began talking and then realized that he didn't have any other pencils. _____

4. The principal of the school passed out permission slips to all of the students in the third grade so that they could go on a field trip. The slips had to be returned the next day or students could not go. Every student in the class returned a signed permission slip. _____

5. Carlos had to go to speech class three times a week for help on pronouncing some of his letter sounds. He wrote the times on a card and taped it to his desk. Then he made sure he looked at the card every morning so he would know when to get up and leave for speech. _____

6. A few of the neighborhood kids wanted to get together to play cards. Debbie said she had three decks of cards and would bring them over to Tom's house so they could play. She not only forgot the cards, but she also forgot to go to Tom's house. _____

7. Stevie and Sandy were supposed to meet at 5 o'clock to help their neighbor rake her leaves. Stevie got the rake and Sandy got the leaf blower and they went over on time. _____

Name _____ Date _____

# I-11B. Responsibility with Common Sense

**Review**

Responsibility means _____

_____ _____, and

then _____ _____.

**Directions:** The people in the examples below have been given responsibility to do something, but they are not completing their jobs. Read each example and discuss the problem and how each could be solved.

1. Dave's mother said it is his responsibility to get his homework done before bedtime. One night they had unexpected company—Dave's cousins—and he had to spend time with them. He did not get his homework done.

2. One of Alyssa's chores to do is to walk to the post office each day and get the mail from the family's mailbox there. There was a big snowstorm and many of the community buildings were closing early, so Alyssa did not go to get the mail.

3. Stella was supposed to gather everyone's dirty laundry, sort it, and begin doing the wash. She noticed that there was a broken dial on the washing machine and she could not get the machine to start.

4. Dick's teacher asked him to take a message to each teacher in the building who coached a basketball team. Then Dick's teacher left the room. Dick realized he did not know which teachers were coaches.

5. Abby wanted to get her ears pierced. Her mother said it would be OK as long as she took care of them by keeping her ears clean and following all of the instructions to prevent infection. Abby agreed and went to the pharmacy to get the hydrogen peroxide to keep her ears clean. The store was all out of it.

6. Lars's father said that it was Lars's responsibility to clean the lawn mower carefully and put it in the garage when he was finished mowing the lawn. Lars was almost finished mowing the yard when he heard a "clunk" and the mower stopped. He could not get it to move.

7. Kara's teacher said that the students should all complete page 74 in their math book by the next day. Kara took her book home and realized that she did not understand how to do any of the problems on that page because she was absent the day before.

# I-11C. Which One Is Showing Responsibility?

**Review**

Responsibility means _____ your _____,

and then _____ it.

**Directions:** Read each situation below and decide which character is showing responsibility. Circle the one who is showing responsibility and cross out the one who is not.

# Lesson I-12: Applying Responsibility

**The contents of Lesson I-12 include:**
- Worksheet I-12A, My Responsibilities
- Worksheet I-12B, How Responsible Am I?
- Quiz on Part 4: Responsibility
- Maze Activity: Take Out the Garbage
- Monitoring Your Responsibility: Making a Chart

## Worksheet I-12A, My Responsibilities

1. Pass out the worksheet to students and have them complete the review section at the top. Remind them that the opposite of responsibility is irresponsibility, or not doing the job they were given to do.
2. Directions for the remainder of the worksheet require students to list some of their responsibilities around home, school, and other places. They are to draw a picture of a person (probably an adult) who gives them their responsibilities, and to write what that person might say.

**Discuss**

1. Do you enjoy being given responsibilities?
2. Which ones do you like? Which ones do you dislike?
3. Why do you think these people have given you the particular jobs that they have given you? (why you and not your brother or another classmate?)

## Worksheet I-12B, How Responsible Am I?

1. Pass out the worksheet to students and have them complete the review section.
2. Students are to think about a specific responsibility they have been give and then to complete the questions on the worksheet by interviewing the adult or person who has given them the job. They can write their answers on another sheet of paper.
3. Discuss the questions on the worksheet.

## Quiz on Part 4: Responsibility

This quiz can be used as a follow-up for the lessons in Part 4.

**Answers**

1. (*definition*) Responsibility means knowing your job and then doing it.
2. (*example*) a, c
3. (*applying*) Answers will vary.

## Maze Activity: Take Out the Garbage

Directions for this activity are at the end of this lesson.

## Monitoring Your Responsibility: Making a Chart

Directions for defining a specific responsibility and making an appropriate chart are at the end of this lesson.

Name _____ Date _____

# I-12A. My Responsibilities

**Review**

Responsibility means _____

_____.

The opposite of responsibility is _____.

**Directions:** What are some of your responsibilities? Think of jobs you are expected to do around the house, at school, in your community, at places you might work, and any other places where you are given responsibility. Draw a person who is giving you the job and write what he or she might tell you.

(teacher)

(parent)

(coach)

(other)

Name _____  Date _____

# I-12B. How Responsible Am I?

**Review**

Responsibility means _____

_____.

The opposite of responsibility is _____.

**Directions:** Think about a responsibility or job that you have been given. Think about what is involved in that responsibility. Then interview the person who has given you that responsibility.

My responsibility is _____

_____.

A person involved in giving me this responsibility is _____.

**Interview Questions**

1. What is involved in completing this job properly? (list steps, materials needed, etc.)

2. Do I understand the job?

3. Can I do the job? (Any reasons why you can't do it?)

4. Do I usually or always do this job without reminders?

5. What problems might happen if I don't do this job correctly?

6. Have I ever forgotten to do the job or done it incorrectly?

7. What are some ways I can improve my job performance?

8. How would I rate myself on this job?

9. How would the person I am interviewing rate me?

10. Do I agree or disagree with the person? Why or why not?

Name _____ Date _____

# Quiz on Part 4: Responsibility

1. What is meant by responsibility? _____

_____

_____

2. Circle each person below who is showing responsibility.

a.
I promised Marge I would get her sweater dry-cleaned after I borrowed it. I will take it to the cleaners right now.

b.
The report on Italy is due tomorrow. I forgot to write down the books we were supposed to read.

c.
I will take off my good sweater before I go out to play in the leaves.

d.
I'm supposed to unplug the space heater when I leave the room. I'll be coming back in a few minutes. I'll just leave it on.

3. "It's YOUR responsibility!" Who has said that to you? What was your job? How did you do?

_____

_____

_____

_____

_____

_____

# Maze Activity for Responsibility: Take Out the Garbage

**Materials:**

You need a copy of the maze and a pencil for each student. You might want to laminate the maze for repeated use.

**Objectives:**

To complete the activity by using the maze to connect the garbage can at the beginning of the maze to the street at the end of the maze

To take responsibility for "talking" another person (who has not seen the maze) through the correct passage of the maze by using his or her own completed maze (hidden from the other person) and by giving verbal clues using the small pictures at intersections throughout the maze.

**Directions:**

1. Pass out a blank maze to each student. Explain that their first job is to "take out the garbage" by following the path that leads to the street. They should use a pencil to lightly draw their path and erase the false moves. When they have completed this task, they have successfully "taken out the garbage." (They may want to highlight this path with a colored marker.)

2. The second task is for students to assist another person in completing this task. The second person should follow the instructions of the student who has already figured out the correct path. The first student should hide his or her completed maze from the second person and should only give hints, Hints could include something like: "When you get to the tree at the bottom, turn right immediately and go straight up," or "Go through the butterfly."

**Discuss:**

1. Did you understand the job?
2. Were you able to do it?
3. How did it go?
4. What problems did you run into?
5. If you were given this job to do with a different student, would you do it even better the second time?

# Take Out the Garbage

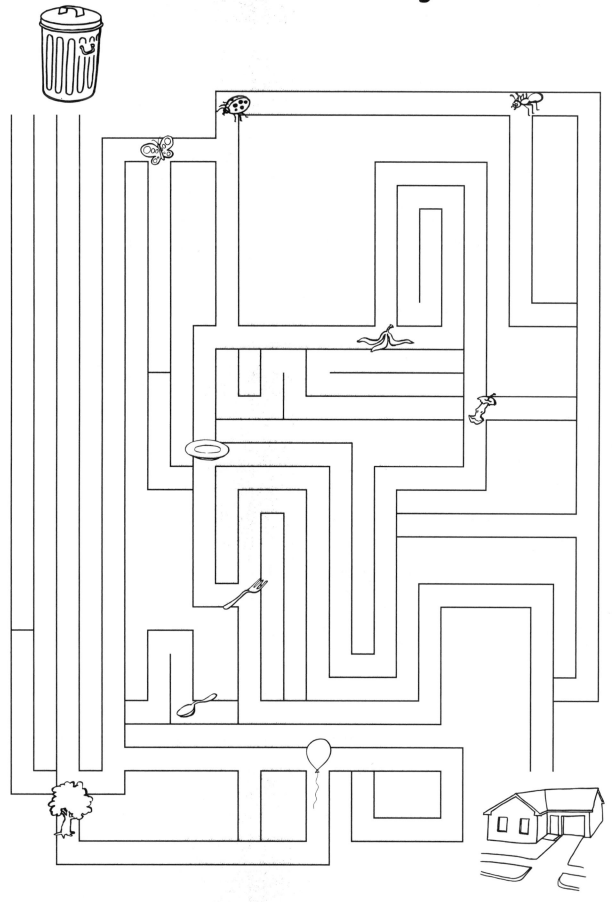

Name _____ Date _____

# Monitoring Your Responsibility: Making a Chart

This is my responsibility: _____

_____

Do I understand the job? Yes ____ No ____

Am I able to do the job? Yes ____ No ____

**Directions:**

Design a chart that will help you remember to take responsibility for this job.

This might include a **calendar** (e.g., mark off each day that you complete your homework).

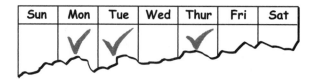

**Circles** to cross off (e.g., cross one off every time you practice a certain piece on the piano).

A **list** of smaller tasks that you need to do to complete the bigger task (e.g., all the things you need to do to have a surprise party ready at a certain time).

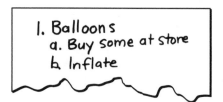

A **sticker** (on a calendar or assignment sheet) to remind you that it is time to keep an appointment or work on your job (e.g., test coming up, report due, the day you are supposed to clean your bedroom).

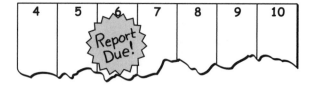

What else can you think of?

_____

_____

_____

_____

_____

# Lesson I-13: Defining Best Effort

**The contents of Lesson l-13 include:**

- Journal Ideas
- A Pre-/Posttest on situations involving effort
- Worksheet I-13A, Knowing What You Can Do
- Worksheet I-13B, Important Jobs or Ordinary Jobs
- Worksheet I-13C, The Pen-Pal Letters

## Journal Ideas

These questions and ideas can be used for daily or occasional entries into a journal. Opportunities to share students' responses should be given at appropriate times.

## Pre-/Posttest

Pass out the pre-/posttest to students and explain that they are to choose the response that shows someone putting forth the best effort in that situation.

**Answers**

1. c; 2. d; 3. a; 4. a; 5. c

## Worksheet I-13A, Knowing What You Can Do

1. Write the definition of *best effort* on the board or in a place where students can easily see it. *"Best effort means working your hardest on something that is important to do right."*

2. Briefly discuss the idea of working hard and achievement. Mention that even if a person wants to work hard at something, if he or she doesn't possess the skills or talents to do a task, he or she may not be able to accomplish it. The task has to be realistic for the person to accomplish.

3. Pass out the worksheet to students and have them first complete the review section at the top. The remainder of the worksheet requires students to write yes or no to indicate whether the jobs are probably possible for the person to accomplish.

**Answers**

1. no (that is a very fast time); 2. no (too much to memorize); 3. yes; 4. yes; 5. no (too many questions); 6. no (she may not possess the skills); 7. yes; 8. no (cutting down a tree would be unlikely for a costume)

**Discuss**

1. Why would the situations to which you responded with a *no* be unlikely or impossible for an ordinary person to accomplish? *(we all have normal limits)*

2. Why do you think some people really do accomplish unlikely things, even when people say they can't? Does hard work make the difference?

3. What would be more realistic situations for 1, 2, 5, 6, and 8?

## Worksheet I-13B, Important Jobs or Ordinary Jobs

1. Review the definition of best effort.

2. Briefly discuss how some jobs, though they may be important, simply do not require excellence. People have to be somewhat selective in where they direct their energy. You might use the terms "important jobs" and "ordinary jobs" to help make a distinction.

3. Pass out the worksheet and have students complete it by putting a check mark in front of the jobs that would probably require "best effort."

**Answers**

(Answers may vary. Allow students to explain their answers.) Check mark in front of 1, 4, 5, 7, 8, 11, 12, 15.

**Discuss**

1. In some situations, you might do a job in a hurry (e.g., frosting a cupcake) and it would be fine. In a slightly different situation (a special birthday party), more care might be required to do a good job (e.g., frosting the cupcake very carefully and adding decorations to it). Go through the examples and discuss how each might be a very important job in some situations.

2. Why can't people put forth their best effort on everything they do?

## Worksheet I-13C, The Pen-Pal Letters

1. Review the definition of best effort.

2. Pass out the cartoon section of the worksheet to the students.

3. Explain that you are going to read a short story about two boys who become pen-pals. You will stop the story after some of the pictures to ask students questions about best effort.

**Answers**

See the teacher's script.

# Journal Ideas: Best Effort

1. *Rate yourself:* How often do you give your best effort?

   0—I usually don't put forth much effort.

   1—I sometimes put forth effort.

   2

   3—Usually I show my best effort.

   4

   5—I always put forth my best effort.

2. Here are some careers that depend on someone putting forth a lot of effort. What might happen if these people didn't care about their effort?

   doctor   car mechanic   hairdresser   house painter

3. How are people recognized or given praise for showing good effort on something at school? in sports? for contests? at home?

4. What is something you know you can do well and have proof of it?

5. Sometimes getting a reward like a sticker or money or even an A+ at the top of a paper can help someone work harder. Why? What are some other incentives?

6. Write about a time when you worked hard and did a really good job on something.

7. Why would someone work hard for something that no one else might comment about or even notice? In other words, if you weren't going to get praise or money or another type of reward, why would you do a good job?

8. List 10 things you do on a typical day that you know you could do better if you just put forth more effort. Put a ★ by the top three you think you should work harder on.

9. Do you think that just spending more time on a project would make it better or does it depend on what you do with that time? Explain.

10. How would it make you feel if you worked really hard on something, gave it your best effort, and then someone criticized it and pointed out all of the mistakes? Has this ever happened to you or someone you know? Write about it.

Name _____   Date _____

# Best Effort: Pretest/Posttest

Read the situations below and choose the response that shows someone who is putting forth the best effort.

1. Dorothy is supposed to copy the list of assignments written on the chalkboard onto her assignment sheet. She could…
   a. Copy every word as written on the board.
   b. Copy just the assignments she hasn't finished.
   c. Copy the assignments but use abbreviations when possible.
   d. Use her best handwriting and take a long time writing it carefully.

2. Steve is a good basketball player, but his team is struggling at halftime. Steve's coach tells him to go in and do his best to help the team catch up. He could…
   a. Grab the basketball every time he gets a chance to try to make baskets.
   b. Yell at the other players to play harder.
   c. Give the ball to other players, even if they aren't good players.
   d. Look for good plays for himself and teammates to make.

3. Mrs. Clark lets her children get a puppy, but she tells them they have to train the dog. The children could…
   a. Spend time every day working with the puppy to be obedient.
   b. Read a book on dog training.
   c. Take the dog for walks every day.
   d. Play with the puppy every day.

4. Jo Ellen wanted to get 100% on her spelling test. She could…
   a. Take the list home all week and practice writing the words.
   b. Look at the list the night before the spelling test.
   c. Get a sharp pencil and make sure it is in good shape.
   d. Do homework every night for an hour.

5. Donald has a button fall off his favorite shirt. He picks up the button off the floor and takes it home. He could…
   a. Give the button and shirt to his mother to sew back on.
   b. Pin the button on the shirt with a safety pin.
   c. Carefully sew the button back onto the shirt.
   d. Use tape to close his shirt.

# I-13A. Knowing What You Can Do

**Review**

Best effort means w_____ your hardest

on s_____ that is i_____

to do right.

**Directions:** These people want to give their best effort on these jobs. Are these jobs realistic for these people? Write yes or no.

1. Ricardo wants to win the 100-yard dash for his track team. He tells the coach that he will run as hard as he can and finish in 3 or 4 seconds. _____

2. Sandi is studying for a vocabulary test she is having tomorrow morning. She wants to do well so she is taking home the dictionary and going to study every word in the whole book. _____

3. Mark is supposed to make a poster of the parts of a flower for his science project. He is planning to copy some pictures of different kinds of flowers, draw some color pictures himself, and gather some real flowers to put on the poster. _____

4. It snowed three inches last night. Ami promises her grandmother that she will shovel the sidewalk in front of the house. _____

5. Alex wants to interview the principal for an article in the school newspaper, and he really wants to do a thorough job. He makes an appointment to talk to the principal and has a list of 94 questions to ask him. _____

6. Mandy is just learning how to play soccer. Her team practices every Saturday morning at the park. She promises her mother that she will score three goals for her team if her mother comes to watch the game. _____

7. Danielle is planning to bake special cookies for her birthday party. She finds an easy recipe, gets all of the ingredients, and plans to follow the directions step-by-step to make them just right. _____

8. Antonio's class is going to put on a play about a talking dinosaur, and the kids are supposed to make their own costumes. Antonio is supposed to be a tree, so he plans to cut down a real tree, hollow out the middle, and use that for his costume. _____

Name _____ Date _____

# I-13B. Important Jobs or Ordinary Jobs

**Review**

Best effort means w_____ your h_____ on something that is
im_____ to do right.

**Directions:** Some jobs are ordinary and do not require "best effort." Others need more of an
effort to do well. Put a check mark in front of the jobs that need more of an effort to do correctly.

_____ 1. making sure all of the words are spelled right on a letter

_____ 2. brushing your dog

_____ 3. putting on nail polish

_____ 4. cutting out cardboard shapes to make stencils for art class

_____ 5. wallpapering your room to make the patterns line up right

_____ 6. making lemonade

_____ 7. trying out for the basketball team

_____ 8. riding your bicycle on a busy street

_____ 9. wiping your muddy feet on a mat

_____10. decorating the top of a cupcake

_____11. installing a new program on your computer

_____12. copying a poem to give to your mother

_____13. pouring dog food into a bowl for your puppy

_____14. tying your shoes

_____15. lining up the numbers in a large math problem

# For the Teacher
## (Script for Worksheet I-13C, The Pen-Pal Letters)

Follow along with the pictures as I read you a story about two people who become pen-pals. After some of the pictures, I will ask you a few questions about the story and about effort.

**(Picture 1)** Mrs. Davidson's class is excited about having pen-pals. Each boy and girl in her class is going to write a letter to a student in a classroom in another school. Fernando is very excited. He finds out that his pen-pal is a boy named Mike. He gets out his pencil and paper and begins writing a long letter to Mike.

**STOP.** What is the task that Fernando has to do? *(write a letter)*

**(Picture 2)** Fernando is in such a hurry that he doesn't bother to write neatly. In fact, he writes so fast that he cannot even read back what he has written—but he figures Mike will have fun trying to figure it out.

**STOP.** Is Fernando putting his best effort into this job? *(no—writing hurridly)* Is this an important job to do right? *(yes—otherwise Mike won't be able to read it)*

**(Picture 3)** When Mike gets the letter, he holds it upright, then turns it upside-down— but he cannot read more than a few words. He thinks Fernando's name is just "Fern," so he thinks he has a girl for a pen-pal. He is not thrilled about that.

**STOP.** What mistake is caused by Fernando's lack of effort? *(Mike can't read the letter and mistakenly thinks the sender is a girl)*

**(Picture 4)** Mike is a good sport, so he writes back to "Fern" and asks her all kinds of questions about her interests. He asks if "Fern" likes to go shopping, if she has slumber parties, and if she has any brothers who would like to write back to him.

**(Picture 5)** When Fernando gets the letter, he is puzzled by the questions. He answers them by writing: No, No, Yes. He writes the words very carefully so that Mike will have no trouble reading them. Then he sends the letter.

**STOP.** How is the mistake growing? *(Mike is writing confusing questions back to Fernando)* Is Fernando putting effort into his next letter? *(he's writing neater, but he's answering the questions with one-word answers)*

**(Picture 6)** The two classes get together so that the children can meet their pen-pals. When they are all matched up, Mike and Fernando are the only ones left without pen-pals. Mike says, "Since my pen-pal isn't here, do you want to be pen-pals? My pen-pal is supposed to be some girl named Fern who doesn't write very good letters." Fernando laughs and says, "I think I know what happened to your pen-pal."

**STOP.** What do you think will happen next? *(Fernando will clear up the mystery)*

# I-13C. The Pen-pal Letters

1.

2.

3.

4.

5.

6.

# Lesson I-14: Recognizing Best Effort

**The contents of Lesson I-14 include:**
- Worksheet I-14A, Is This Showing Best Effort?
- Worksheet I-14B, Using Common Sense
- Worksheet I-14C, When to Do Your Personal Best

## Worksheet I-14A, Is This Showing Best Effort?

1. Pass out the worksheet to students and have them complete the review section at the top.
2. Directions for the rest of the worksheet require students to circle the person in each situation who is showing best effort.

**Answers**

1. second; 2. first; 3. first; 4. second

**Discuss**

1. In situation 1, why does it show more effort to use harder words even though it requires more work?
2. In situation 2, do you think the person should have given up if he knew he wasn't going to win anyway?
3. When you give something to someone else, do you think that person looks at how it is wrapped or presented and connects it with how you feel about that person?

## Worksheet I-14B, Using Common Sense

1. Pass out the worksheet to students and have them complete the review section at the top.
2. Directions for the remainder of the worksheet ask students to read the situations on the worksheet and discuss why the people in the examples may not be using common sense on their tasks.
3. Discuss each item and why it may not require best effort.

**Answers**

*(may vary)* 1. taking too long; 2. she's not varying her workouts and not keeping the rest of her life in balance; 3. a rough draft means you don't have to be perfect, and copying by hand is inefficient; 4. this might be OK for a play, but for a one-minute skit it is too much work; 5. a quick list would have been enough; 6. he won't finish in time

## Worksheet I-14C, When to Do Your Personal Best

1. Pass out the worksheet to students and have them complete the review section at the top.
2. Directions for the rest of the worksheet ask students to put a check mark in front of the tasks that would probably require best effort.

**Answers**

Check mark in front of 1, 3, 6, 8, 11, 12, 14, 15.

**Discuss**

1. Why shouldn't you do your very best on every job?
2. Do you think some jobs get easier to do well the more you practice doing them?

Name _____ Date _____

# I-14A. Is This Showing Best Effort?

**Review**

Best effort means _____ your _____ on something that is

_____ to do right.

**Directions:** Circle the person in each situation who is showing the best effort on the job.

1.

 I will use only little words that I know how to spell so I won't have to correct anything.  I will use this dictionary to help me spell the long words right.

2.

Only one more hurdle—I can do it, I can do it, faster... faster!!   Oh, I'm going to get second place anyway.

3.

I want this room to be really clean—I'll move the chair and vacuum behind it.  Good enough!

4.

This is a present for my dad. He won't care what it looks like.   I'll put the tape on the ends so it won't show.

# I-14B. Using Common Sense

**Review**

Best effort means _____ your

_____ on _____ that

is _____ to do _____.

**Directions:** Why aren't these students using common sense in these situations? Why shouldn't they put forth their best effort?

1. Mary is writing a thank-you note to her aunt for the sweater. She is spending about two hours on the computer doing research on sweater-making so she can let her aunt know that she is interested in the gift.

2. Allie is trying to do her best on the cross-country team. The coach told her to practice and to vary her workouts. Every day she goes out and runs three miles as fast as she can. She has been skipping meals, church, and time with friends and family to run every day.

3. Bob is writing a school play. He is supposed to turn in a rough draft by the next day. He is copying each word carefully by hand and writing five copies for all of the performers in the play.

4. Suzon and the girls in her group are supposed to do a funny skit in front of the class that should last one minute. Suzon arranged for the members of her group to come over to her house for rehearsals and to sew costumes for their performance.

5. Clark's mother asked him to write down everything he needs for school, as she is going to the store that night. Clark sat down and numbered his paper from 1 to 50. Then he used his black pen to list every item and where it was located in the store.

6. Charlie's grandmother is dropping in for a quick visit, so Charlie was supposed to clean up his room. He has 5 minutes before his grandmother will arrive! He got down on his hands and knees and began to pick out every single dog hair on the rug.

# I-14C. When to Do Your Personal Best

**Review**

Best effort means _____ your

_____ on _____ that is

_____ to do right.

**Directions:** Sometimes it is not so important to do an excellent job on a task; other times, it is very important that you give your best effort. On which situations below should you give your best effort? Put a check mark in front of those items.

_____ 1. trying out for the school basketball team

_____ 2. making paper airplanes with your little brother

_____ 3. taking a final spelling test

_____ 4. writing in your personal journal

_____ 5. taking the dog for a walk

_____ 6. interviewing for a job after school

_____ 7. painting with watercolors at home on scrap paper

_____ 8. decorating a get-well card for your favorite aunt who is in the hospital

_____ 9. bowling with your friends after school

_____10. making a clay bowl for your cat to eat out of

_____11. making a clay bowl to enter in an art contest

_____12. taking a picture to be used in the school newspaper

_____13. doing a back flip in your back yard

_____14. painting a mural on the wall at school for art class

_____15. singing with the choir for a school performance

# Lesson I-15: Applying Best Effort

**The contents of Lesson I-15 include:**
- Worksheet I-15A, How Do I Do?
- Worksheet I-15B, Outstanding Effort
- Quiz on Part 5: Best Effort
- Puppet Show: I Can Do It Better!

## Worksheet I-15A, How Do I Do?

1. Pass out the worksheet to students and have them complete the review section at the top. Remind them that the opposite of best effort is low effort or poor effort.
2. Directions for the remainder of the worksheet require students to think about tasks that they typically are asked to perform at school, at home, or other places. In the first column, they should think about how they do (as far as effort) on that job. In the second column, they should write ways they could improve their effort.

### Discuss

1. What are some tasks that are just naturally easier for you to do well?
2. What are some tasks that are really difficult for you to do well?

## Worksheet I-15B, Outstanding Effort

1. Pass out the worksheet to students. Have them complete the review section at the top.
2. Directions for the rest of the worksheet ask students to select a task (they may choose from the list or come up with their own ideas) and write down very specific ways they could show outstanding effort on this task.

### Discuss

1. Why did you choose the task that you selected?
2. What are ways you are going to do an outstanding job?
3. Is there a particular person who you are going to try to impress?

## Quiz on Part 5: Best Effort

This quiz can be used as a follow-up for the lessons in Part 5.

### Answers

1. (*definition*) Best effort means working your hardest on something that is important to do right.
2. (*examples*) c, d
3. (*applying*) Answers will vary.

## Puppet Show: I Can Do It Better

Directions for this activity and the puppet show script are at the end of the lesson.

# I-15A. How Do I Do?

**Review**

Best effort means _____

_____.

The opposite of best effort is _____.

**Directions:** Consider each of these tasks that you may have to do. Write how you presently perform these jobs. Then think of ways you could improve your performance, if necessary, to show best effort.

|  | **Right Now** | **Best Effort** |
|---|---|---|
| 1. writing a paragraph |  |  |
| 2. making your bed |  |  |
| 3. organizing your desk or closet |  |  |
| 4. participating in a sport |  |  |
| 5. making a card or gift for someone |  |  |
| 6. washing your bike or your parent's car |  |  |
| 7. taking care of your hair |  |  |
| 8. doing a project for school |  |  |

# I-15B. Outstanding Effort

**Review**

Best effort means _____

_____.

**Directions:** On some tasks, you may want to do the most outstanding performance that you can. You may work so hard on this task that people can't help but notice that it is outstanding. Choose a task below (or add to the list) and make a plan for how you will give an OUTSTANDING effort!

1. making a poster (include drawings, charts, examples, colored pictures)

2. cleaning your room (include good-smelling carpet cleaner, dusting in the corners, all shoes put away, etc.)

3. writing a paragraph (check for spelling mistakes, good handwriting, correct headings, more than 3 sentences, etc.)

4. cheerleading (wearing a smile, leading cheers loudly, encouraging others on your squad)

5. taking care of someone's plants while he or she is away (make sure there is no water or dirt on the table, arrange them so they get sunlight, etc.)

6. making cookies (use cookie cutters and decorations, put people's names on them)

My own ideas:

_____

_____

_____

_____

_____

_____

_____

_____

_____

_____

# Quiz on Part 5: Best Effort

1. What is meant by best effort?

_____

_____

2. Circle each person below who is showing best effort appropriately.

a.

> I am supposed to write a paragraph about what I liked about our trip to the zoo. I will ask if I can take this home so I can go to the museum to do more research on the history of bats.

b.

> A clean room means everything ugly should be out of sight!

c.

> Our stories are supposed to be at least one page long, but I think I will add another character and put some cartoon drawings to go with my story.

d.

> When you shovel, you have to get the steps and the sidewalk, too.

3. When did you show your best effort on something? What was the task and how did you show best effort?

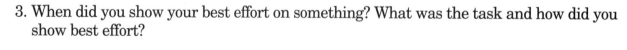

_____

_____

_____

_____

# Puppet Show for Best Effort:
# "I Can Do It Better"

## Characters:

| | |
|---|---|
| Slinky Skunk | Mrs. Dolphin |
| Barney Bear | Mrs. Zebra |
| Charlie Cheetah | Fairy Goodworker |
| Coach | Super Slinky (Slinky with a red cape) |
| Slinky's Mom | Teacher |
| Slinky's Sister Selina | Other Students |
| Mr. Tiger | |

**Synopsis:** Slinky Skunk is a talented, but rather lazy skunk. He sees no reason to try hard at anything until he is visited by a magical fairy who lets him see what a day in his life would be like if he gave more effort. He sees the effect that more effort has on other people.

**Narrator:** Here is a story for you about a lazy skunk who didn't put much effort into anything, until one day… well, something important happened.

## Scene I: The Playground

*Background scene:* school, swing set, other characters

**Narrator:** We are first going to visit the Animal School playground where we see Slinky Skunk, Barney Bear, and Charlie Cheetah in the middle of a game of tag.

*(Slinky and his friend are playing tag.)*

**Barney Bear:** You're it! Run!

**Slinky:** *(tagging Charlie)* Hee hee—you're it!

**Charlie Cheetah:** You can't catch me… you can't catch me!

**Barney Bear:** Whew…! I'm tired. Let's rest.

**Slinky:** Oh, come on, you can't be tired already.

**Charlie:** Well, not everyone is so fast as you.

**Barney:** Look, our coach is here! Hey, it's time for the races! Come on, Slinky—I know you can win. You are the fastest runner on the playground.

*(The characters line up.)*

**Coach:** Line up, everybody. Are you ready? When I say "GO," you're going to run to the big rock. First one there is the winner. Ready?

**Barney:** *(jumping up and down)* Ready! Ready!

*(Puppet Show for Best Effort, page 2)*

**Charlie:** *(swaying sideways)* Yeah, let's go, baby!

**Slinky:** *(yawning)* Ho hum. Let's get this over with.

**Coach:** Ready… set… go!

*(The three run in one direction while the background moves in the other—simulating speed!)*

*(The three take turns taking the lead, first one, then another.)*

**Charlie:** I'm ahead! I can't believe it!

**Slinky:** Oh, I'm just going to quit. *(stops)* If I can't win, I'm not even going to try.

**Barney:** *(passing him)* Oh, come on, Slinky! You can beat ME!

**Coach:** Charlie, you're the winner! Slinky, what happened to you?

**Slinky:** *(shrugs)* Awww, I don't care.

**Coach:** I guess not!

*(Bell rings.)*

**Charlie:** Come on, let's go in.

*(They leave.)*

**Coach:** What a shame. That Slinky could be a winner if he tried harder!

**Narrator:** Slinky didn't put much effort into his school work either. Let's take a peek at what happens when he studies for a spelling test at home.

## Scene 2: Slinky's Kitchen

*Background scene:* kitchen window, refrigerator, tables, etc.

**Mother:** Now, Slinky, sit down and let's practice your spelling words. You know there is a big test tomorrow.

**Slinky:** Aww, Mom, I don't want to. I'll pass it.

**Mother:** Sit down. *(bops him in the head with a list)* Here's the first word. DOG. Now spell it for me.

**Slinky:** D… O… *(leans head forward with each letter)*

**Mother:** D… O…

**Slinky:** *(scratches head and mumbles)* I don't know… Gee, I don't know… gee…

**Mother:** YES! G! D-O-G ! Now let's try CAT.

**Slinky:** C… A… *(leans head forward with each letter)*

*(Slinky's sister Selina comes into the kitchen with a cup.)*

**Mother:** What do you have there, dear?

**Slinky:** Tea?

**Mother:** *(excited)* YES! T! C-A-T! Good job, Slinky!

**Selina:** *(flustered)* Mom! Slinky doesn't know how to spell those words! He's just guessing!

**Slinky:** I'll get you!!! *(He chases Selina around the kitchen, while Mother throws her hands up and finally leaves.)*

**Narrator:** Things weren't any better on the job. Slinky has a paper route after school. He's supposed to deliver a paper to everyone in the neighborhood.

## Scene 3: The Neighborhood

*Background scene:* a row of houses

**Slinky** *(whistling)*: Good afternoon, Mr. Tiger. *(tosses a paper over his head)*

**Mr. Tiger:** Well, it's about time you got here! I would like to know what's on TV for the evening sometime before the evening is over!

**Slinky:** Am I late? Sorry. I stopped to talk to my friends.

**Mr. Tiger:** Hmmmmmfph. Can't you get here on time? *(leaves)*

*(Slinky goes to the next house and tosses the paper through the window.)*

**Slinky:** OOPS!! I hope they're not home!

*(He goes to the next house.)*

**Mrs. Zebra:** Slinky, you have been tossing my paper in the bushes. When we open it up, leaves fall out!

**Slinky:** No extra charge for the leaves, Mrs. Zebra.

**Mrs. Zebra:** That isn't the point, Slinky. Please put the paper on the front porch!

**Slinky:** Yeah, yeah, whatever.

**Narrator:** But one day, something happened! Slinky had a special visitor.

*(Dramatic music or chimes to indicate something important is going to happen.)*

## Scene 4: Magical Scene

*Background scene:* brilliant colors and designs

*(A magical fairy suddenly pops up in front of Slinky as he is walking along with his newspaper pouch.)*

**Fairy:** Shazam!!

**Slinky:** Whoa!! What are you?

**Fairy:** I am your Fairy Goodworker.

**Slinky:** Huh?

**Fairy:** Fairy Goodworker. I am going to show you how important it is to show good effort when you have things to do.

**Slinky:** Do I have to do anything?

**Fairy:** No, Slinky. Just sit there and let's go through your day all over again, but this time let's see what could happen if you gave a little more effort on things.

**Slinky:** Well, can I sit down and eat ice cream while you're showing me all this?

**Fairy:** No. Now pay attention or I'll have to bop you on the head with my magic wand. They don't give us these wands just for looks, you know.

**Narrator:** So, while Slinky sat down to watch, Fairy Goodworker replayed the whole day for him. This time he saw Super Slinky giving his best effort.

## Scene 5: The Playground

*(Charlie and Barney are playing on the playground. Suddenly Slinky joins them, wearing a red cape.)*

**Charlie:** Want to race with us?

**Super Slinky:** Sure, I'll give it a try.

*(The friends line up.)*

**Coach:** Ready, guys? Ready… set… go!

*(The race sequence begins again with the three taking turns being in the lead.)*

**Slinky:** I'm… *(puff, puff)* getting tired… *(puff, puff)*… I want to quit… *(puff, puff)*… but I'll keep going!

*(He finishes in second place.)*

**Coach:** Charlie, you're first! Good job! And YOU, Slinky… *(he comes over to Slinky)* I was very impressed with your effort! You didn't give up. I like that attitude. I expect to see you at track tryouts.

**Super Slinky:** Yes, Sir!

**Charlie:** Good job, Slinky! *(gives him a "high five")*

**Barney:** *(patting him on the back)* Nice job! You ran well, buddy!

**Fairy:** *(to Slinky)* What do you think?

**Slinky:** I didn't know I could do that well.

**Fairy:** Come on. I have more to show you.

*(dramatic music)*

**Narrator:** Next, Fairy Goodworker took Slinky to the classroom where he had his spelling test.

© 2002 by The Center for Applied Research in Education

## Scene 6: The Classroom

*Background scene:* chalkboard, desks, flag

**Teacher:** Well, I hope you all studied for your spelling test.

**Super Slinky:** Ready! Bring it on, baby!

**Teacher:** *(arms crossed)* Excuse me?

**Super Slinky:** Uhh, I mean… yes, Ma'am.

**Teacher:** Take out a sheet of paper and number it from 1 to 20.

*(Super Slinky is furiously working.)*

**Teacher:** The first word is "amphibian."

**Super Slinky:** *(writing, then looks up)* Got it.

**Teacher:** *(amazed)* You're done?

**Super Slinky:** Yes, Ma'am.

*(Teacher peeks over his paper and nods her head.)*

**Teacher:** The next word is "dinosaur."

**Super Slinky:** *(writing furiously)* Got it.

**Teacher:** *(peeking again)* Well, Slinky, I must say… your handwriting is beautiful. I can read every word and you spaced it so nicely. Lovely, just lovely. I think I may cry.

**Slinky:** *(to Fairy)* I think I made her day. She said that my last spelling test made her want to cry, too, but I don't think she was happy.

**Fairy:** Come, we have another place to visit. *(takes him by the hand)*

**Narrator:** Fairy Goodworker took Slinky back to the neighborhood where he was delivering newspapers. Let's watch.

## Scene 7: The Neighborhood

*Background scene:* row of houses

**Fairy:** Sit over here, Slinky. Then we'll be out of the way.

*(Super Slinky enters with his newspaper pouch and newspapers.)*

**Mr. Tiger:** Slinky! I must be late if you're here already!

**Super Slinky:** Oh no, Mr. Tiger, you're not late. I'm right on time.

**Mr. Tiger:** You didn't have to talk to anyone today?

**Super Slinky:** I decided to get my job done and then I'll go play with my friends. Bye!

*(He goes to the next house.)*

*(Puppet Show for Best Effort, page 6)*

**Super Slinky:** I am placing the newspaper neatly on the porch. Oh, good afternoon, Mrs. Dolphin.

**Mrs. Dolphin:** Good afternoon, Slinky. *(to herself)* What a nice young skunk he is.

*(He goes to Mrs. Zebra's house.)*

**Super Slinky:** I am placing the newspaper neatly on the porch. Hi, Mrs. Zebra.

**Mrs. Zebra:** On the porch!? Slinky, are you all right?

**Super Slinky:** Yes, Mrs. Zebra. I'm just taking a little more time to do it right.

**Mrs. Zebra:** Well, how nice of you! No leaves in the classified ads tonight. Thank you so much! *(to herself)* I must give him a big tip when it's time to pay for the papers. What a good worker!

**Fairy** *(to Slinky):* Well, have you seen enough, Slinky?

**Slinky:** Yes. Yes, I believe I have.

*(dramatic music and change of scene)*

**Narrator:** Slinky learned something very important that day.

## Scene 8: Magical Scene

*Background scene:* brilliant colors and designs

**Fairy:** Well, Slinky? Did you learn anything from our little trip today?

**Slinky:** This was a very important day for me. You will see a new Slinky from now on!

**Fairy:** I'm so glad to hear that. *(Slinky starts to leave.)* Hey, where are you going?

**Slinky:** I've gotta get a CAPE like that! It's so cool!!!! SUPER SLINKY!!! *(He flies off stage.)*

*(Fairy turns to the audience and hits herself on the head with her wand.)*

## The End

# Lesson I-16: Defining Personal Health

**The contents of Lesson l-16 include:**

- Journal ideas
- A Pre-/Posttest on situations involving personal health
- Worksheet l-16A, Healthy Body, Healthy Mind
- Worksheet l-16B, What Is Healthy?
- Worksheet l-16C, All About Tomás

## Journal Ideas

The journal ideas can be used for daily or occasional entries in student notebooks. Opportunities should be given for students to periodically share their ideas.

## Pre-/Posttest

Pass out the pre-/posttest to students and explain that they are to choose the response that indicates someone demonstrating good personal health in each situation.

**Answers**

1. c; 2. d; 3. b; 4. a; 5. c

## Worksheet I-16A, Healthy Body, Healthy Mind

1. Write the definition of *personal health* on the board or another place where students can easily see it. "Personal health means doing good things for your body and mind."

2. Briefly discuss that healthy things for your body might include exercise, nutrition, and avoiding things that are known to be unhealthy (smoking, drinking, etc.). Also discuss how your mind can be treated in a healthy way by filling it with good things. Some examples might be reading materials that are educational, positive in nature, or just different from what the person normally reads (to promote expanding the mind and growing in knowledge). Other activities healthy for the mind might be making positive self-statements instead of putting yourself down, trying to see the good in a situation rather than dwelling on the negative, and avoiding situations in which your mind is exposed to unhealthy things (violence, hatred, etc.).

3. Pass out the worksheet to students and have them complete the review section at the top. The remainder of the worksheet requires the student to write **B** if the example demonstrates a way to have a healthy body or **M** if it demonstrates a way to have a healthy mind.

**Answers**

1. B; 2. B; 3. M; 4. B; 5. B (and maybe M); 6. M; 7. M; 8. B; 9. M; 10. M

**Discuss**

1. Do you think that having a healthy body helps you have a healthy mind, and the other way around? In other words, does having one mean you have the other?

2. Some people get very caught up in having a great physical appearance or spending a lot of time being concerned about their body (bodybuilders, models). Do you think this could be bad if someone "cares too much"?

3. If you had to pick one, do you think it would be more important to have a healthy body or a healthy mind?

4. What are some educational programs that are fun and interesting as well as good at teaching something? How do those programs make learning fun?

5. Can you think of some activities that are healthy for the mind and the body at the same time? *(running in the park while talking to a friend about how you feel!)*

## Worksheet I-16B, What Is Healthy?

1. Review the definition of personal health.

2. Briefly discuss why healthy things are good for your body or mind. What are some reasons why people should try to achieve these goals? *(helps you look better, feel better, be more knowledgeable, more fun to be around, etc.)*

3. Pass out the worksheet and have students complete the review section at the top. The rest of the worksheet requests students to sort through the examples of healthy behavior and decide which category it goes with.

### Answers

(may vary—allow students to explain their answers) *Column 1:* a, c, e, h; *Column 2:* a, d, f, i; *Column 3:* a, b, c, g

### Discuss

1. What are some things you do in your family or for yourself that might be helpful for other people to try?

2. Why is it important to read about things you don't know?

3. What does getting a good night's sleep have to do with performing well later? Can't some people get by on a little sleep or erratic sleep?

4. Do you have to eat perfectly well all of the time? What about having candy once in a while? *(moderation is a good goal)*

## Worksheet I-16C, All About Tomás

1. Review the definition of personal health.

2. Pass out the cartoon section of the worksheet to the students.

3. Explain that you are going to read a story about a boy named Tomás whose family is from Mexico. Students should listen to find out some healthy things about his family. You will stop after the pictures to ask questions about what you just read.

### Answers

See the teacher's script.

# Journal Ideas: Personal Health

1. *Rate yourself* using the scale: 0 = never; 1 = almost never (not very often); 2 = a couple of times; 3 = sometimes; 4 = usually; 5 = all the time. How often do you:

   - exercise? ____
   - read? ____
   - eat healthy food? ____
   - get a good night's sleep? ____
   - spend time with friends? ____
   - have a new idea? ____
   - smoke? ____
   - drink alcohol? ____
   - do illegal drugs? ____
   - sing or hum? ____

2. Before you meet someone new (for example, an adult friend of your parents), what do your parents expect you to do? How do they expect you to dress? What do they expect you to say to the new person? How well do you follow what you think they want you to be like?

3. Why is your appearance important? In what places or situations is it more important than others?

4. What are some reasons why kids smoke or drink? What do you think of these reasons?

5. What foods are healthy to eat and what foods are not? How could you find out?

6. List 10 different ways to exercise. List 5 indoor ways and 5 outdoor ways.

7. Write down how many hours a week you think you spend watching television. Then keep track of how much time you spend watching TV for one week. List the programs that you watch. Did you spend more or less time than you guessed?

8. Do you have a hobby? What? How long have you been doing this activity? Why does it appeal to you?

9. Do you have any pets? Why do you think caring for pets is part of a healthy lifestyle?

10. What are some of your favorite books to read? Do you have a favorite author or favorite series of books?

Name _____ Date _____

# Personal Health: Pretest/Posttest

Read the situations below and choose the response that shows someone who is doing things
for his or her personal health.

1. Bruce went to a party where kids were passing around cigarettes. He thinks smoking
   is not something he wants to do. He could…

   a. Take a cigarette and then casually toss it away.

   b. Light the cigarette and pretend to smoke it, but then move away where no one can
      see him and throw it away.

   c. Say, "No, thanks."

   d. Say, "Smoking is really bad for you. I have some literature that I can read to you
      about the horrible long-term effects."

2. Charlese thinks she is gaining too much weight. She could…

   a. Quit eating entirely until she loses the weight she wants to lose.

   b. Skip meals to eat less.

   c. Learn how to throw up what she eats after every meal.

   d. Eat foods that are low-calorie and healthy.

3. Randy is with friends who want to see a really popular movie with a lot of blood, killing,
   and violence. He is not sure he wants to see that kind of movie. He could…

   a. Suggest that they all rent it on video and fast-forward through the bad parts.

   b. Suggest that they go see a different movie that is still interesting.

   c. Tell his friends that he is more mature than they are.

   d. Tell his friends that he can't go because he's busy that night.

4. Shelli has a very important test in three days. It counts for half of her grade in social
   studies for the grading period. She could…

   a. Start studying now and get a good night's sleep before the test.

   b. Spend every second studying until it's time for the test.

   c. Wait until the night before the test and then stay up all night to study.

   d. Not study at all and just try her hardest on the day of the test.

5. Kurt loves to read comic books, but that is pretty much all he reads. His older brother
   tells him that he should learn about some other things, because he might find them
   interesting, too. Kurt could…

   a. Go to the library and read his mother's favorite romance novel.

   b. Try another brand of comic books.

   c. Ask a friend to recommend a good book that the friend enjoyed.

   d. Ask his teacher what books are good for extra credit.

# I-16A. Healthy Body, Healthy Mind

**Review**

Personal health means doing g_____ things for your b_____

and m_____.

**Directions:** Read the items on this list of ways to have a healthy body or healthy mind. Write **B** if it goes with a healthy body. Write **M** if it goes with a healthy mind.

_____ 1. eating vegetables

_____ 2. taking a walk through the park

_____ 3. reading a library book

_____ 4. playing outside

_____ 5. getting enough sleep

_____ 6. watching educational TV

_____ 7. saying positive things about yourself

_____ 8. brushing your teeth

_____ 9. listening to the news to find out what is going on in the world

_____10. going to church

Name _____ Date _____

# I-16B. What Is Healthy?

**Review**

Personal health means doing g_____ things for your b_____

and m_____.

**Directions:** Read each example below of something healthy for your body or mind. Why are these considered healthy things? Write the letter of each in the appropriate column below.

| Makes you stronger | Helps you think more clearly | Makes you look better |
|---|---|---|
|  |  |  |

a. getting a good night's sleep

b. washing your hair

c. jogging

d. reading about other people

e. eating carrots and beans

f. listening to someone talk about something you don't know about

g. wearing clean clothes

h. taking vitamins

i. asking questions if you don't understand something

# For the Teacher
## (Script for Worksheet I-16C, All About Tomás)

Follow along with the pictures as I read a story about a boy named Tomás. He does many things that show good health for his body and mind. See if you can find them as we go through the story.

**(Picture 1)** Tomás has three brothers and sisters. All of them go to church on Sunday morning, along with their mother and father. This is something they enjoy doing together as a family. Everyone in the family thinks it is important because it helps them learn how to treat other people.

**STOP.** What is something this family does together? What are some reasons why this shows personal health? *(it is something that brings the family together; it teaches them how to treat other people)*

**(Picture 2)** One day Tomás's aunt and uncle come from Mexico to visit the family. They do not speak much English, and they want to go to night school to learn to read and write this language since they will be visiting often. Tomás says he will help them if they have trouble, since he is able to speak both languages very well. In fact, Tomás is interested in learning to speak beginning Japanese when it is offered as an after-school course.

**STOP.** Why do Tomás's relatives want to learn a new language? How could Tomás help them? What else does Tomás want to learn that is new? Do you think it will be hard for each of these people to learn new languages? Do you think it is important?

**(Picture 3)** At school, the children are giving reports about something they enjoy doing. Tomas brings some of his Little League trophies to school and holds up some pictures that were taken of him hitting the ball. He passes around his ribbon that he received for being "Most Valuable Player." He tells the class that he loves baseball and someday wants to be a professional baseball player—maybe even in Japan.

**STOP.** How do you think Tomás feels about his hobby? *(he is proud of how well he did in baseball)* How good is he? *(he has won some trophies and a ribbon)* Do you think he is bragging about his accomplishment? *(he is fulfilling a school assignment, he is proud of himself)* Do you think playing sports is important to Tomás? *(yes, he wants to make it his career)*

**(Picture 4)** One day Evan comes home with Tomás after school. He is surprised at how much work Tomás is expected to do. "Your room is so clean," he says. "Don't you get tired of picking things up all the time?" Tomás just laughs. "It's not so hard. I want my room to look nice," he says. "Also, Mama insists that we keep our rooms in good shape in case people come over. So I do it partly because I want Mama to be pleased with me."

**STOP.** Does Evan think Tomás has a lot of work to do? *(yes)* Does Tomás think he has a lot of work to do? *(not really; he is used to it)* How is Tomás showing personal pride? *(he is proud of his room and he wants his mother to be proud of him)*

**(Picture 5)** The boys hear the door open and Mrs. Romirez comes in. "Well, hello, boys!" she calls to them. "Why aren't you outside playing on a nice day like this?" Tomás looks at Evan. "We could either play some computer games… or we could go outside and play baseball with my brother and some of his friends. What would you like to do?" Evan reaches into his backpack and pulls out his mitt. "Guess?"

**STOP.** What does Mrs. Romirez think the boys should do? *(go outside and play)* What choices do the boys have for activities? *(play computer games, do something outside)*

**(Picture 6)** After the boys play baseball for an hour, they enter the kitchen and are greeted by wonderful smells! "Ahhh, hamburger casserole!" sings Tomás. "My mother is a great cook." Mrs. Romirez laughs and pats Tomás on the head. "Don't forget there is chocolate cake for dessert—after you finish your vegetables, of course." Evan says, "I don't like beans. I just want to eat cake." Tomás looks at Evan. "Don't you want to be a pro baseball player someday? Like me? Well, to play on my team, you better be strong and that means…" Evan laughs. "I know, I know. Eat my vegetables." Mrs. Romirez gives him a very small helping of beans and a large piece of chocolate cake.

**STOP.** How does Tomás feel about his eating habits? *(wants to eat healthy)* Why? *(he understands the connection between eating right and being strong)* What are some of the examples of personal health that you see in Tomás's life? *(doing family things, learning new things, excelling in baseball, taking care of his body by exercising and eating healthy, taking pride in his room)*

# I-16C. All About Tomás

1.

2.

3.

4.

5.

6.

# Lesson I-17: Recognizing Personal Health

**The contents of Lesson I-17 include:**

- Worksheet I-17A, Healthy or Harmful?
- Worksheet I-17B, Making a Better Choice
- Worksheet I-17C, Using Common Sense

## Worksheet I-17A, Healthy or Harmful?

1. Pass out the worksheet to students and have them complete the review section at the top.
2. The rest of the page asks them to write yes or no on the line to indicate whether or not the person is doing something healthy for his or her body or mind.

**Answers**

1. no; 2. yes; 3. yes; 4. no

**Discuss**

1. What's wrong with eating potato chips and watching a couple of movies? *(it's not "wrong," but there are healthier things to eat and it sounds as though this person has been watching TV for quite a long time)*
2. What are some other activities that kids could do outside that are fun? *(inline skating, skateboarding, etc.)*
3. Why is going to church or synagogue or other places of worship a healthy activity? *(teaches values, how to get along with others, opens mind to better lifestyle)*

## Worksheet I-17B, Making a Better Choice

1. Pass out the worksheet to students and have them complete the review section at the top.
2. Directions for the rest of the page require students to circle the person in each row who is doing something healthy.

**Answers**

1. second; 2. first; 3. first; 4. second

**Discuss**

1. In situation 1, the boy says he doesn't like to exercise, but he doesn't mind walking with the dog. How can this be a good activity for both of them?
2. In situation 2, what's unhealthy about not taking a bath for a week?
3. In situation 3, why should a person be careful about getting anything pierced on his or her body? *(health regulations, possibility of infection)*
4. How do you take care of your teeth in your family?

# Worksheet I-17C, Using Common Sense

1. Pass out the worksheet to students and have them complete the review section at the top.
2. Directions for the rest of the worksheet ask students to read and discuss each situation in which a person says he or she wants to do something healthy, but he or she is not using common sense.

**Discuss:**

1. What might wearing a gas mask really be saying to Sam's grandparents? *(that they are repulsive to him; overexaggerates, etc.)*
2. How can alcohol have a positive benefit? *(for medicinal purpose)*
3. Is Randi overreacting in situation 3? *(she seems to be avoiding going on the walk; she might truly be afraid of snakes or perhaps she just doesn't want to participate)*
4. What do you think about Mickey in situation 4? *(he's just being silly)*
5. What doesn't make sense about Alisha's situation in number 5? *(if she knew she was going to babysit, she should have gone to bed earlier)*
6. What do you think about Carlos's report? *(he's just being silly)*

Name _____ Date _____

# I-17A. Healthy or Harmful?

**Review**

Personal health means doing _____ things for your _____

and _____.

**Directions:** Write yes or no to show whether each person below is doing something healthy for his or her body or mind.

1. _____

I think I'll eat one more bag of potato chips while I watch the next movie of the week.

2. _____

Let's ride our bikes to school today instead of taking the bus. It's a nice day!

3. _____

Would you like to come to church with us? There is a special program for kids.

4. _____

My brother has some marijuana in his bedroom. I know how to use it.

Name _____ Date _____

# I-17B. Making a Better Choice

**Review**

Personal health means doing _____ things for your _____

and _____.

**Directions:** Which person in each row is choosing something that is healthy for his or her body or mind? Circle that person.

1.
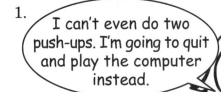
*I can't even do two push-ups. I'm going to quit and play the computer instead.*

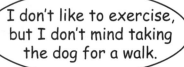
*I don't like to exercise, but I don't mind taking the dog for a walk.*

2.
*I know Dad wants to make a good impression on the new neighbors, so I'll comb my hair before we go over.*

*Aunt Julie's going to stay with us for a week while Mom and Dad are gone, so I won't have to take a bath for days!*

3.

*Let's get our ears pierced. There is a place at the mall that will do it if we have our parents' permission.*

*I want to get a tattoo on my arm. My friend's brother knows how to do it. He has a big eagle on his back.*

4.

*Oh! Chocolate chip cookies! I love cookies! I will eat them all! I don't have to go to the dentist for at least 6 more months.*

*I know that too many sweets aren't good for you. I'll just take one cookie and make sure I brush my teeth really well!*

# I-17C. Using Common Sense

**Review**

Personal health means doing _____ things for your _____

and _____.

**Directions:** These people have the opportunity to do healthy things. Why aren't they using common sense? Discuss your answers.

1. Sam has decided that he is not going to smoke cigarettes. Both of his parents smoke, his grandparents smoke, and his older brother smokes. To show that he is going to take pride in being healthy, he has decided to wear a gas mask when he is in the house.

2. Cynthia thinks it is wrong to drink alcohol. She has a bad cold and her mother gets her some medicine that contains alcohol. She refuses to take it because she does not want to take a drink.

3. Randi wants to learn more about the outdoors and the environment, so she joins a Saturday youth group that takes nature walks. When the group decides to take a walk through the park, she thinks there might be a snake out there so she tells them she doesn't want to go outside.

4. Mickey does not swear or use rude language because he thinks it is not good for someone who wants to take pride in his language. He overhears someone talk about a beaver dam and he reports to the teacher that the other person is using bad language.

5. Alisha is supposed to babysit for twins on Saturday, but she went to a friend's slumber party on Friday night and stayed up all night. She goes to the babysitting job, but tells the kids that they have to leave her alone and let her take a nap because she is very tired.

6. Carlos's class goes on a field trip to a museum to learn about customs in other countries. Carlos wants to do his report on how to say "You are so ugly" in other languages.

# Lesson I-18: Applying Personal Health

**The contents of Lesson I-18 include:**
- Worksheet I-18A, What Do You Think?
- Worksheet I-18B, My Health Goals
- Quiz on Part 6: Personal Health
- Games: Hop for Health and Touchdown

## Worksheet I-18A, What Do You Think?

1. Pass out the worksheet to students and have them complete the review section at the top. Remind them that the opposite of healthy is unhealthy.
2. Directions for the rest of the page ask students to write their personal opinion about each topic listed.

### Discuss

1. What are some things on the list that aren't really bad for you unless you spend way too much time doing them or neglect doing something else that you should be doing (like homework) and choose to spend time on another activity instead?
2. Why shouldn't you be able to eat anything you want to if it tastes good? Why is it so important to eat fruits and vegetables?
3. What are some things on this list that are hard for you? What are some things that are easy for you?

## Worksheet I-18B, My Health Goals

1. Pass out the worksheet to students. Have them complete the review section at the top.
2. Directions for the rest of the page ask students to write one personal goal that they could work on to try to have better health.

### Discuss

1. What goals will be hardest for you? What goals will be easiest for you?
2. What will you do to try to start reaching these goals? Who can help you?

## Quiz on Part 6: Personal Health

This quiz can be used as a follow-up for the lessons in Part 6.

### Answers

1. *(definition)* Personal health means doing good things for your body and mind.
2. *(examples)* b, c
3. *(applying)* Answers will vary.

## Games: Hop for Health and Touchdown

Directions for these games are at the end of the lesson.

Name _____  Date _____

# I-18A. What Do You Think?

**Review**

Personal health means _____

_____

_____.

The opposite of healthy is _____.

**Directions:** What is your opinion on the following topics or ideas? Write a brief answer next to each item on the list.

1. videogames _____

_____

2. using the computer _____

_____

3. movies _____

_____

4. cleaning your room _____

_____

5. head lice _____

_____

6. taking showers _____

_____

7. eating fruits and vegetables _____

_____

8. staying up late _____

_____

9. getting up early _____

_____

10. reading _____

_____

Name _____  Date _____

# I-18B. My Health Goals

**Review**

Personal health means _____

_____.

The opposite of healthy is _____.

**Directions:** Write one goal that you can work on to achieve better personal health in each area below:

Exercise                                        Learning something new

_____            _____

_____            _____

_____            _____

Your appearance                            Getting enough sleep

_____            _____

_____            _____

_____            _____

Eating healthy                               Your teeth

_____            _____

_____            _____

_____            _____

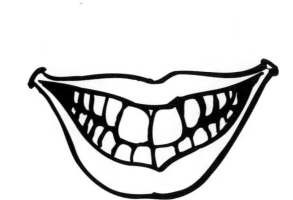

# Quiz on Part 6: Personal Health

1. What is meant by personal health?

_____

_____

_____

2. Circle each person below who is showing personal health.

a.

b.

c.

d.

3. What are three ways you can do healthy things for your body and mind?

a. _____

_____

b. _____

_____

c. _____

_____

# Game for Personal Health: Hop for Health

**Materials:**

You need 5 blue squares and 5 red squares (construction paper).

**Players:** 4

**Objective of the Game:**

To be the last player remaining

**How to play:**

1. Arrange the squares randomly on the floor (leaving enough room that players can "hop" to each). You may want to tape each square to the floor if players hop too vigorously.

2. Have players start on any square.

3. Call out an example of healthy/unhealthy behavior. After you read the example, say "Go!" and students must hop to either a blue (healthy) or red (unhealthy) square.

4. After five examples, begin removing one red and one blue square after each turn, so that there are fewer and fewer squares. One player (who didn't make it to a safe square) leaves the playing field after each turn.

5. The winner is the last player on the floor.

**Healthy Examples:**

taking vitamins

taking the dog for a walk

swimming

eating an apple

riding your bike

reading a book

lifting weights

getting a good night's sleep

**Unhealthy Examples:**

playing hours of video games

smoking a cigarette

eating lots of candy

skipping meals to lose weight

drinking alcohol

smoking marijuana

taking someone else's medicine

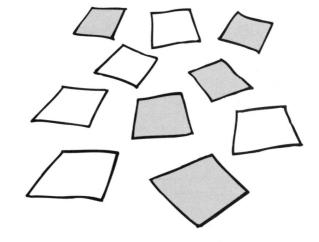

# Game for Personal Health: Touchdown

**Materials:**

You need a football gameboard, a "football" marker, 1 die, and list of healthy/unhealthy examples (see ideas for Hop for Health).

**Players:** 2 teams

**Objective of the Game:**

To score the most touchdowns within a given time limit

**How to Play:**

1. Start with the "football" at the 50-yard line. Toss a coin to determine which team goes first.

2. The winning team has to answer a healthy/unhealthy situation. If they answer correctly, one player from the team rolls the die and moves the "football" accordingly (rolling a 1 = 10 yards, 2 = 20 yards, and so on).

3. Play then goes to the opposite team. A player from that team will respond to the example, roll the die, and move the football in *their* direction.

4. Play continues back and forth until a touchdown is scored and 7 points is awarded to that team. The football goes back to the 50-yard line and play continues.

5. The game is over at a predetermined time—either when 10 minutes are up, or one team scores 5 touchdowns, or one team makes it to 50 points first, etc.

# Section II
# Having Respect for Others

We defined respect in Section I as *being careful with something because it is important.* Not only is it important to develop positive individual characteristics, it is also important to develop characteristics that affect our interactions with others. By showing respect for others, individuals may find that they are receiving unexpected benefits themselves! We can show respect for others by demonstrating these qualities:

- **peace-seeking**—finding peaceful ways to solve problems
- **generosity**—sharing what you have
- **compassion**—caring about the needs of others
- **forgiving**—letting bad feelings for someone go
- **understanding others**—knowing how someone else would feel or act
- **loyalty**—being a friend to someone all of the time

# Lesson II-1: Defining Peace-Seeking

**The contents of Lesson II-1 include:**

- Journal Ideas
- A Pre-/Posttest on situations involving being peace-seeking
- Worksheet II-1A, Is This Peace-seeking?
- Worksheet II-1B, Looking for Trouble
- Worksheet II-1C, All Kinds of Arguments

## Journal Ideas

This is a list of topics and situations for students to write about in a personal journal. Opportunities should be given for students to periodically share their ideas with each other.

## Pre-/Posttest

Pass out the pre-/posttest to students and explain that they are to choose the answer to each question that shows a peaceable person.

**Answers**

1. b; 2. d; 3. a; 4. c; 5. c

## Worksheet II-1A, Is This Peace-Seeking?

1. Write the definition of *peace-seeking* on the board or other place where students can easily see it. *"Peace-Seeking means finding peaceful ways to solve problems."*
2. Briefly discuss that this definition means people who are peaceable don't go directly to arguing and fighting to handle difficulties; they search for peaceful ways to solve their problems without hurting anyone or stirring up trouble.
3. Pass out the worksheet to students and have them complete the review sentence at the top. On the rest of the worksheet, students are to write yes or no to indicate whether or not the people on the worksheet are solving problems in a peaceful way.

**Answers**

1. no; 2. yes; 3. yes; 4. no; 5. yes; 6. no

**Discuss**

1. In situation 1, why is the boy being argumentative? *(he wants a window seat)* How could he resolve this peacefully? *(trade on the way back)*
2. In situation 2, how is this girl being peaceable? *(she's offering the shirt to the other girl)*
3. In situation 3, what does the boy think at first about writing his name the way the teacher said? *(he doesn't think it's important)* What might have happened if he had argued about it? *(made the teacher mad)*
4. In situation 4, why is the man so angry? *(his order was wrong)* Is he going to get what he wants anyhow? *(yes, the clerk will redo the order)* Was it necessary for him to get so upset about a hamburger? *(probably not)*
5. In situation 5, why is the woman impatient? *(she's in a hurry today)* How is the woman in front of her helping to make this a peace-seeking situation? *(letting her go first)*
6. In situation 6, how could the man in the chair get what he wants without yelling? *(tell the boy that he is in the way, because he probably doesn't know)*

# Worksheet II-1B, Looking for Trouble

1. Review the definition of peace-seeking.
2. Pass out the worksheet and have students complete the review section at the top. The rest of the worksheet asks students to draw a picture that shows a peaceful way to resolve each situation.

**Answers**

(may vary) 1. Barbara could ask her sister to put the wet towel in a hamper; 2. Don could come in quietly; 3. Alex could let the coach handle the problem; 4. Bea could avoid Denise for awhile; 5. Charlie could eat something else or wait until his brother gets home and ask if they could split it

**Discuss**

1. How could each person in the examples be thought of as someone looking for trouble? *(other people made their lives complicated or unhappy)*
2. How could each have reacted in a way that would cause more problems?

# Worksheet II-1C, All Kinds of Arguments

1. Review the definition of peace-seeking.
2. Pass out the cartoon section of the worksheet to the students.
3. Explain that you are going to read a story about a girl who has all kinds of arguments for trying to get out of doing a chore. They are to listen to the story and then discuss the girl's different approaches.

**Answers**

See the teacher's script.

# Journal Ideas: Peace-Seeking

1. *Rate yourself:* How much of a peacemaker are you?

    0—I look for trouble.

    1—I usually look for trouble.

    2—I am peaceable but not very often.

    3—Sometimes I am peaceable.

    4—I am usually a peace-seeking person.

    5—I am always a peace-seeking person.

2. Who is someone who almost always looks for peaceful solutions to problems? Give an example of how he or she tries to be peace-seeking in working things out.

3. Who is someone famous (a celebrity, sportsperson, etc.) who is often in the news for getting into arguments or problems with others? What kinds of problems is he or she involved with?

4. What is the most ridiculous argument you have ever had with someone? What was it about? How did you resolve it?

5. What is the last argument you had with a friend? How long did it take for you to become friends again?

6. What would you do if you had two tickets to a game that you really wanted to see and two friends who didn't like each other, but both of them wanted you to ask them to go?

7. What are some ways that cartoon or comic superheroes keep peace among the villains they encounter? If you created a new superhero, what special powers would you give him or her to help keep peace?

8. List 10 things that really make you angry. Which ones are the most difficult for you to resolve peacefully?

9. What are some things that you *should* get angry about? (for example, if something wrong is happening to someone you care about)

10. Observe how people handle these situations:

    a. being in a waiting room at a doctor's office

    b. being in a hurry at the checkout line at a supermarket

    c. getting a mixed-up order at a fast-food restaurant

    d. accidentally being knocked into in a crowded place

© 2002 by The Center for Applied Research in Education

# Peace-Seeking: Pretest/Posttest

Read the situations below and choose the response that shows a peace-seeking person.

1. Trevor had to get up from the computer to answer the phone. Meanwhile, his brother slipped into his seat while he was gone and erased the game he was playing. His brother said that he needed to use the computer for "something important." Trevor could…

    a. Tell him to move, that he was there first.

    b. Offer to let his brother have the computer after he finished his game in about 5 minutes.

    c. Call Mom to settle the argument

    d. Wait until his brother typed a page, then erase it.

2. Cammie came into the classroom to find that two kids were arguing about a fight that happened in the hallway. The teacher asked Cammie if she saw what happened since she was right there. Cammie could…

    a. Say she didn't see anything and not get involved.

    b. Say that they were both at fault.

    c. Say that the bigger kid was right.

    d. Tell exactly what she saw without blaming anyone.

3. The principal was upset that the third-grade class was rude and noisy on the field trip. He wants everyone to write a letter of apology. David was quiet the whole way, reading a book. David could…

    a. Write a letter saying that he understands how this behavior is a problem.

    b. Tell the principal who the troublemakers were.

    c. Refuse to write the letter because he didn't do anything.

    d. Argue that the kids were just having fun and there was no damage done.

4. Jessica's neighbor complains when the kids play baseball in the front yard and the ball rolls into her flower bed. Jessica could…

    a. Tell the neighbor that they live there too and they have a right to play baseball.

    b. Play ping-pong in the basement instead.

    c. Play at the park down the street.

    d. Try not to hit the ball in her flowers.

5. Andy is building a model car for fun because he just likes to make models. His little sister wants to "help" him but she just gets in the way. Andy could…

    a. Let his sister ruin his model to keep her happy.

    b. Tell her to go find something else to do.

    c. Let his sister put a sticker on the model so she thinks she's helping.

    d. Yell at her for bothering him.

# II-1A. Is This Peace-Seeking?

**Review**

Peace-seeking means finding p_____ ways to s_____

p_____.

**Directions:** Are these people following the definition of being peace-seeking? Write yes or no in the box.

# II-1B. Looking for Trouble

**Review**

Peace-seeking means f_____

p_____ ways to solve

p_____.

**Directions:** These people are looking for trouble by not finding peaceful ways to solve their problems. On another sheet of paper, draw what you think will happen next in each situation. On the lines, write how each person could act peaceable in each situation.

1. Barbara is mad at her sister for leaving a wet towel on the bathroom floor, so she put the wet towel on her sister's bed.

   _____

   _____

2. Don comes into the classroom late while the class is quietly taking a science test and makes the announcement: "I'm here, everybody!"

   _____

   _____

3. Alex thought he made a touchdown but the referee called him out of bounds. He told the ref that he needed glasses because obviously he was blind.

   _____

   _____

4. Bea was really angry at her former friend Denise, so she told all of her other friends that they better not talk to Denise either or they could forget about coming to Bea's birthday party next week.

   _____

   _____

5. Charlie's brother wanted Mom to save him a piece of chocolate cake for when he got home from school. Charlie got home first and was hungry, so he ate the piece, even though he knew his brother wanted it.

   _____

   _____

# For the Teacher
## (Script for Worksheet II-1C, All Kinds of Arguments)

Follow along with the pictures as I read you a story about a girl who is asked to do something for her mother. You will see that she comes up with all kinds of arguments for why she cannot do this task. After you listen to the story, we will discuss your analysis of her reasons.

**(Picture 1)** It is a busy morning in the Miller household. Mrs. Miller fixes breakfast for herself and her four children: Christa, the oldest; Johnny and Stevie, the twins; and Angela, the baby. Mrs. Miller is in a hurry to get to work because she has an important meeting, so before she leaves, she says to Christa: "I would like you to wash the breakfast dishes as soon as you get home from school."

**(Picture 2)** Christa comes up with all kinds of arguments for why she does not want to do this chore. First of all, she says, "It's not my turn to do the dishes. It's Johnny's turn. I did the dishes last night and I did them the night before."

**(Picture 3)** Mom crosses her arms. Christa decides to try another argument. "I'm too busy, Mom. You know that I have a big Social Studies test. When I get home from school, I have to STUDY!"

**(Picture 4)** Mom begins tapping her foot. Christa tries another approach. She holds up her little finger. "Look," she said, pointing to her finger. "I hurt my finger this morning when I cut it on that butter knife. Look—it broke the skin and I think it's still bleeding. You can't expect me to wash dishes with an injury like that!"

**(Picture 5)** Mom begins putting on her coat. Christa holds up a plate. "I didn't even eat very much," she insists. "Look! Look! I used only one plate—everybody else dirtied two or three plates and glasses! I did not make all this mess!"

**(Picture 6)** Mom yawns and reaches for her purse. "I hate washing dishes!" Christa cries, following her mother. "It's soooo boring! It's such an awful job! I don't want to do it! I'll sweep the floor! I'll vacuum! I just don't want to wash dishes!"

**(Picture 7)** Mother picks up the baby and waves goodbye to the older children as she sees the school bus approaching to pick them up. "Have a nice day!" she calls to them. Christa pouts and gets on the bus. Life is so unfair.

**STOP.** Let's make a list of Christa's arguments and discuss her reasons.
- Picture 2—not her turn (fairness issue)
- Picture 3—something more important to do (priority issue)
- Picture 4—hurt herself (ability issue)
- Picture 5—not her mess (fairness issue)
- Picture 6—boring (priority issue)

Her mother does not answer Christa at all. Do you think she is affected by Christa's arguments? *(probably not)* Why or why not? *(not very good reasons)*

What do you think will happen next? Do you think Christa will do the dishes when she gets home? *(probably)*

Do you think it is unfair for Mother to ask Christa to do this chore? *(no, everyone has to help out in a family)*

If Christa was seriously hurt or was panicking about the test, do you think Mother would have had someone else do the dishes? *(probably)*

What could Christa have done to avoid the argument and be a peaceable person? *(quit keeping track of whose turn it is and just help out)*

# II-1C. All Kinds of Arguments

1.

2.

3.

4.

5.

6.

7.

# Lesson II-2: Recognizing Peace-Seeking

**The contents of Lesson II-2 include:**

- Worksheet II-2A, Recognizing Peace-Seeking People
- Worksheet II-2B, Giving Up Something for Someone Else
- Worksheet II-2C, Is This Peace-Seeking?

## Worksheet II-2A, Recognizing Peace-Seeking People

1. Pass out the worksheet to students and have them complete the review section at the top.
2. The rest of the worksheet asks students to write yes or no on the line to indicate whether or not the people are solving a problem in a peaceable way.

**Answers**

1. yes; 2. no; 3. no; 4. yes; 5. yes

**Discuss**

1. In situation 2, is it fair for the teacher to ask the boys to help get the balls if they didn't even use them? *(sure—it's a class cooperative effort)*
2. In situation 3, what if it really was not a strike? What if the umpire made a mistake? *(have to respect his calls)*
3. In situation 4, what other ways could the people have resolved this problem? *(go to one movie one night, the other one the next night)*

## Worksheet II-2B, Giving Up Something for Someone Else

1. Pass out the worksheet to students and have them complete the review section at the top.
2. Directions for the rest of the worksheet ask students to read each situation and decide what is being given up and for whom.

**Answers**

1. (a) pizza, (b) a boy; 2. (a) loud music, (b) his aunt; 3. (a) playing time, (b) Jamal

**Discuss**

1. In these examples, is it a "big deal" to give up something for someone else?
2. In situation 1, what if the person hated liver? Should he still have given up the pizza for the other person? *(no, perhaps the boy behind you also likes liver)*
3. In situation 2, what other choices to hear music does Tommy have? *(he could listen somewhere else, at another time, etc.)*
4. In situation 3, would it have been a big deal if the team was losing 4–0 instead of winning? *(yes, then the coach probably should have left Rex in if they wanted to win the game)*

# Worksheet II-2C, Is This Peace-Seeking?

1. Pass out the worksheet to students and have them complete the review section at the top.

2. Directions for the rest of the worksheet ask students to draw a smile or a frown on the face to indicate whether it is a peaceable situation or not.

**Answers**

1. frown; 2. smile; 3. smile; 4. frown

**Discuss**

1. In situation 1, what did Anthony do that made him unpleasant? *(grumbled)*

2. In situations 2 and 3, the people did not argue, but they changed their behavior to please someone else. Do you think these will be long-lasting changes? *(Barb is supposed to be wearing her glasses, so it should be; Lila probably should write carefully all the time so maybe this will help her learn to slow down)*

3. In situation 4, how do you think the other people in the class felt about Charles and his blurting out answers? *(annoyed)* How could he let the teacher know he knows the answers in a peaceful way? How would others respond to him if he were more peaceable? *(probably less annoyed)*

Name _____  Date _____

# II-2A. Recognizing Peace-Seeking People

**Review**

Peace-seeking means _____ _____ ways to solve

_____.

**Directions:** Read each example below. Decide whether or not the people involved are solving a problem in a peaceable manner. Write YES or NO on the line.

1.

*Please be home at 5 o'clock.*

*OK, Mom.*

_____

2.

*There are still some balls left on the playground. Mike and Steve, would you please get them?*

*We didn't even play with those balls!*

*They are way over by the fence.*

_____

3.

*STRIKE!*

*It was not!!!*

_____

4.

*Let's see this movie!*

*No, I want to see the other one.*

*Hey, let's just flip a coin.*

_____

5.

*Someone moved the TV program guide off the TV set. How will I know what's on?*

*Oops, that was me. Sorry, I'll just go get it.*

*Why is he so mad about that??*

_____

# II-2B. Giving Up Something for Someone Else

**Review**

Peace-seeking means finding _____

ways to _____

_____.

**Directions:** Read the situations below. For each, decide (a) what is being given up and (b) for whom.

## Situation 1

There is only one slice of pizza left in the cafeteria serving line. You know that the boy behind you wants it. You would like it, too, but you also like liver, which is the other choice. You decide to take liver.

(a) What is given up? _____

(b) For whom? _____

## Situation 2

Tommy likes to play his music LOUD!!! When his aunt comes to visit for a week, she asks if he could turn it down so she can take her afternoon nap. Tommy decides to use earplugs so it won't bother her.

(a) What is given up? _____

(b) For whom? _____

## Situation 3

Rex is captain of the soccer team and he gets to play a lot. He knows that Jamal really wants to play, but he doesn't get much playing time because he's not that good. Rex's team is ahead 4–0 in the last quarter. Rex asks the coach if Jamal could take his place to finish the game. The coach says that would be fine.

(a) What is given up? _____

(b) For whom? _____

Name _____ Date _____

# II-2C. Is This Peace-Seeking?

**Review**

Peace-seeking means _____ peaceful

_____ to _____

problems.

**Directions:** Draw a smile on the face if it shows a peaceable situation. Draw a frown if it does not.

1. Anthony decides that the program on TV is boring, so he changes the channel even though other people are watching. They start to complain about it, so he grumbles and says they can watch their boring program.

2. Barb does not want to wear her glasses to school so she puts them in her backpack. When she gets to school, she remembers that she has promised her mother she would wear them, especially because she has a doctor's appointment after school, so she puts them on.

3. Lila's teacher cannot read Lila's handwriting, so the teacher asks her to copy it over more clearly. Lila wants to go to the puzzle table instead, but she says OK and carefully copies her assignment so that the teacher can read it.

4. Charles blurts out the answers in math without ever raising his hand when he knows the answers. The teacher asks him to please raise his hand. Charles says, "But I know the answer! You asked the question, and I am answering it for everybody!" The other kids laugh and wait to see what the teacher will do.

# Lesson II-3: Applying Peace-Seeking

**The contents of Lesson II-3 include:**

- Worksheet II-3A, What Would You Do?
- Worksheet II-3B, This Makes Me Mad!
- Quiz on Part 7: Peace-Seeking
- Activity: Peace Posters

## Worksheet II-3A, What Would You Do?

1. Pass out the worksheet to students and have them complete the review section at the top. Remind them that the opposite of peaceable is argumentative or looking for trouble.
2. Directions for the rest of the worksheet ask students to draw or write their response that indicates what they might do if they were the indicated person in each situation.

**Discuss**

1. In situation 1, the person has a choice whether or not to redo the poster. What if he didn't want to do it over, but didn't argue about it? Would that be OK if he didn't care? *(it wouldn't be showing best effort)*
2. What are several different reactions that the person could have in situation 2? What might be the most effective way to stop her from poking? *(try ignoring, redirect her to doing something fun)*
3. In situation 3, if the girl really wanted the pink or red marker, why should she have to take the black one just to be a peacemaker? Should she stand up for what she wants and grab for the other colors? *(if it doesn't matter to her, she could be a peacemaker in this situation; depends on how important it is to her. Also, she could negotiate—they could trade markers after 5 minutes, etc.)*
4. In situation 4, what is a bad reaction that the girl could have? What is a peaceable reaction? How would it affect the reaction if the first girl did it on purpose? *(might handle it differently, tell the girl that she didn't appreciate that happening)*
5. What is the first reaction you might have to situation 5? *(punch him!)* What is a peaceable response? *(ignore; say "good job this time")*

## Worksheet II-3B, This Makes Me Mad!

1. Pass out the worksheet to students. Have them complete the review section at the top.
2. The rest of the worksheet asks students to complete the sentences to indicate things that annoy them, upset them, and that they think are unfair, etc. They can add to the list at the bottom.

**Discuss**

1. What things bother you that don't bother other people?
2. Do you find that you react differently to annoyances depending on how you feel, who you are with, or how important it seems at the time?

## Quiz on Part 7: Peaceable

This quiz can be used as a follow-up for the lessons in Part 7.

### Answers

1. *(definition)* Peace-seeking means finding peaceful ways to solve problems.

2. *(examples)* d

3. *(applying)* Answers will vary.

## Activity: Peace Posters

Directions for this activity are at the end of the lesson.

Name _____ Date _____

# II-3A. What Would You Do?

**Review**

Peace-Seeking means _____
_____.

The opposite of peace-seeking is _____.

**Directions:** Read each situation and think about what you might do if you were the person in the story. Draw or write your response.

1.
"This is not your best work. These posters are going to be displayed in front of the whole school. Why don't you come in during recess and lunch break to do it over?"
"I don't want to give up all that time..."

2.
"poke, poke, poke"
"Sally, please stop bothering me."

3.
"I don't want the black marker; I want the pink one."
"I don't want the black one either; I want the red one."
"There are only 3 markers..."

4.
"Oops, I spilled ketchup on your food. It was an accident!"
"I hate ketchup!!"

5.
"Nah, nah, nah! Our team beat your team!!"
"Grrrr! He is so annoying!"

Name _____ Date _____

# II-3B. This Makes Me Mad!

**Review**

Peace-seeking means _____

_____.

The opposite of peace-seeking is _____.

**Directions:** What makes it hard for you to be a peace-seeking person? Complete these sentences.

1. I get really angry when _____

_____

2. It really bothers me when someone _____

_____

3. I can't stand it when I see _____

_____

4. It's unfair when _____

_____

5. I would be upset if _____

_____

6. I usually argue about _____

_____

7. It's too hard for me to _____

_____

8. I don't like to _____

_____

Add your own list of things that upset you:

_____

_____

_____

Name _____   Date _____

# Quiz on Part 7: Peace-Seeking

1. What does peace-seeking mean? _____

_____

2. Which of these examples show peace-seeking people?

3. What could you do if you are very tired and want to go to bed, but your brother/sister shares your room and wants to leave the light on to finish reading a book?

_____

_____

_____

_____

_____

_____

_____

# Activity for Peace-Seeking: Peace Posters

**Materials:**

You need posterboard, magazines, markers, and other art supplies.

**Directions:**

Divide students into pairs or small groups. Using the theme "peace," have them design a poster or collage in which they work together to form a visual project that demonstrates peace. Students might select magazine pictures, add their own drawings or photographs, and cut out words or phrases from magazines to illustrate "peacefulness."

**Follow-up:**

Have students share their peace posters with each other. They may wish to explain how they came up with their ideas. Display them in a prominent place for all to see!

# Lesson II-4: Defining Generosity

**The contents of Lesson II-4 include:**

- Journal Ideas
- Pre-/Posttest on situations involving generosity
- Worksheet II-4A, What Are You Sharing?
- Worksheet II-4B, Giving Away, But Not Generous
- Worksheet II-4C, The Garage Sale

## Journal Ideas

This is a list of questions and situations for students to think about and write about. Give students the opportunity to share their thoughts with each other.

## Pre-/Posttest

Pass out the pre-/posttest to students and explain that they are to read each item and write yes or no in front of each to indicate whether or not it shows generosity.

**Answers**

1. no (it has no value to you since you are full anyway); 2. yes (costs you time and money); 3. yes (you give up time that you could have been working on homework); 4. yes; 5. no (it is broken!); 6. no (it may be her generosity, not yours); 7. no (many people don't want puppies, free or not); 8. no (this is a business deal); 9. yes; 10. no (it doesn't mean anything to you, not much value)

## Worksheet II-4A, What Are You Sharing?

1. Write the definition of *generosity* on the board or other place where students can easily see it. *"Generosity means sharing what you have."*

2. Briefly discuss the definition. Students are probably familiar with the idea of sharing, but truly being generous is more than giving things away or passing things around. Tell students that true generosity also involves sharing things that are meaningful or have value. This will become clear as they work through the various worksheets. To keep it simple, use the definition above.

3. Pass out the worksheet to students and have them complete the review section at the top. On the rest of the worksheet, students should read the examples and try to figure out what exactly is being shared with others (e.g., time, talent, possessions, or money).

**Answers**

1. money; 2. time; 3. possession; 4. talent; 5. time; 6. talent

**Discuss**

1. What are some other examples of generosity that involve money? time? talents or skills? possessions?

2. Do you think it is harder to be generous with money rather than one of the other types of generosity?

# Worksheet II-4B, Giving Away, But Not Generous

1. Review the definition of generosity.
2. Pass out the worksheet and have students complete the review section at the top. On the rest of the worksheet, students are to read each situation and discuss why the examples do not show generosity.

**Answers**

1. the person wants attention for his good deed; 2. the cookies are of little value; 3. the second girl gave away clothes that were not even hers; 4. the boy is taking the little kids to the zoo, but he is being paid for it

**Discuss**

1. In situation 1, what is more important to that boy, giving money to help someone else or getting attention for it?
2. In situation 2, the girl is being nice to take food to school, but is it anything of value? What is it costing her?
3. In situation 3, the girls are both giving away clothes that they don't want or need anymore. What would be a better example of generosity if someone needed clothes?
4. In situation 4, the lady assumed that the boy was being generous with his time to take the kids to the zoo. Why would this not be considered generosity?

# Worksheet II-4C, The Garage Sale

1. Review the definition of generosity.
2. Pass out the cartoon section of the worksheet to the students.
3. Explain that you are going to read a story about a class that has a garage sale to earn some money. The students will find some examples of generosity. You will be stopping to ask questions.

**Answers**

See the teacher's script.

# Journal Ideas: Generosity

1. How generous are you? *Rate yourself* 0–5 on the following items (0 = not generous at all, 5 = extremely generous):

    a. with my "stuff"

    b. with my time

    c. with my friends

    d. with my money

2. If you had $100 to give away, what would you do with it?

3. What is the best or nicest thing someone has given you?

4. What is the best or nicest thing someone has done for you?

5. What is your most prized possession? Why is this important to you? Would this be hard for you to part with or to give away?

6. Who are some adults who have been generous with their time? (coaches, teachers, relatives) Why do you think they share their time with you and others?

7. Would you rather have someone give you their money, time, or possessions? Why?

8. If you needed help with someone, who are the top three people you would ask for help? Why?

9. Make a list of skills you have that you could teach or share with others.

10. Who are some famous characters in books or movies who are very generous? Who are very stingy? Give examples.

Name _____ Date _____

# Generosity: Pretest/Posttest

Read each situation below and write **yes** or **no** if it shows generosity.

_____ 1. You have a big candy bar and are full after eating half, so you give half to a friend.

_____ 2. You babysit for free for a young couple who don't have a lot of money so they can go out for the evening.

_____ 3. You read a story to your little brother before you do your homework.

_____ 4. You are working on a poster and a friend needs help with his, so you stop working on yours to help him.

_____ 5. A friend asks if he can have your broken computer keyboard and you say OK.

_____ 6. Your mother sends cookies to school with you to pass out to your whole class.

_____ 7. Your dog had lots of puppies so you ask your neighbors if they will take them for free.

_____ 8. You lend $10 to a friend, but he has to pay you back $12 including interest.

_____ 9. You stay after school to pick up homework assignments for a sick friend.

_____10. You get your old sweatshirt out of the bottom of your closet to give to a friend who needs one.

# II-4A. What Are You Sharing?

**Review**

Generosity means sh_____ what you h_____.

**Directions:** There are many types of things to share (time, talent, possessions, money, etc.).
What is each person below sharing with others?

1. *I still need another $5 to have enough money to go to camp this summer.*  *Here, take some of my babysitting money. I have enough.*

_____

2. *Will you help me study for my test?*   *Yes, I will. I can finish practicing on the piano later.*

_____

3. *I'm cold.* *Let me get you another blanket.*

_____

4. *It would be really fun to write a play for our class. I know that you are a really good writer.* *It's a lot of work... but I'll help you.*

_____

5. *It's Wednesday night! Time for our Boy Scout meeting!* *Hello, boys! I'm not late, am I?*

_____

6. *Can you teach me how to do that?*    *It's not so easy as it looks. But I'll teach you if you want to try.*

_____

Name _____ Date _____

# II-4B. Giving Away, But Not Generous

**Review**

Generosity means sh_____ what you h_____.

**Directions:** These people are giving things or time away, so it seems that they are sharing with others, but they would not really be considered generous. Why? Read each situation and discuss your thoughts.

---

1. Oh, that poor person needs money. I will give her some! Is everybody watching? See how generous I am!! Be sure to spell my name correctly for the paper...!

---

2. Look! These cookies are just about old enough to throw out. I'll take them to school and pass them out for treats.

---

3. Here are some clothes I don't want anymore. But they are in good shape and I bet someone could use them.

Oh, I'll take them.

Here! I have some clothes for you! They are my really special clothes, but I know you need them so I will sacrifice for you.

---

4. No! I don't want to take my sister and her little friends to the zoo! It's boring!

I'll pay you $20.

Awww, it's nothing.

You are so kind to spend your Saturday with the kids!

It's a deal.

# For the Teacher
## (Script for Worksheet II-4C, The Garage Sale)

Follow along with the pictures while I read the story about a class that is trying to be generous. I will stop along the way and ask you questions, so listen carefully.

**(Picture 1)** Mrs. McIntyre's class wants to raise money to help buy a new computer for their classroom. She tells the kids that they will have a garage sale that weekend, so they should bring in items that they could sell to raise money. Everyone thinks it is a great idea.

**STOP.** What is the purpose of the fund-raising? *(to get money for a computer)* How are they going to get money? *(have a garage sale)* At this point, do you observe anyone being generous? *(no)*

**(Picture 2)** The kids go home and tell their parents that they need to bring in things to sell. Jamie finds a lot of toys that are still good, but are not needed at his house anymore. Aimee brings in some clothes. Carla brings in a pair of roller skates. All kinds of things are piling up in Mrs. McIntyre's garage.

**STOP.** Were people being generous yet? *(possibly—they were donating items that they didn't need anymore)*

**(Picture 3)** Ellen's father drives up in his truck. He says, "I love to make things. I heard that you need to raise money, so I built some wooden rocking chairs for you to sell." Everyone crowds around to look. The chairs come in different sizes, but they are all really nice and everyone has to try them out.

**STOP.** Do you see any generosity yet? *(yes—Ellen's father is donating chairs that he spent time, talent, and money on)*

**(Picture 4)** One of the other parents is there and sees the beautiful chairs. She says, "How nice of him to do that. I would like to buy a couple of them. I am going to talk to my daughter who does stained glass. I bet she would make some stained-glass windows that you could have at the sale."

**STOP.** What do you think will happen next? *(she will bring in stained-glass windows)*

**(Picture 5)** As the week goes on, more and more people begin bringing in unusual things to sell at the garage sale. Susan's grandpa brings in some model cars that he has made. Jeremy's dad, who owns a shoe store, brings in several pairs of brand-new running shoes. "I'm happy to do it," he says. "They should bring you some money!" Before long, Mrs. McIntyre's garage looks like a department store.

**STOP.** What examples of generosity do you find in this picture ? *(car models, shoes, other items)*

**(Picture 6)** Mr. Miller looks at all the stuff in the garage. "Would you like me to help you organize this?" he asks. "My wife and I will be glad to help take in money during the sale." Mrs. McIntyre says, "Oh, that would be wonderful!" They begin putting things in order.

**STOP.** What examples of generosity do you find now? *(time to organize and time to help sell)*

**(Picture 7)** A big truck drives up. It is Mr. Allen and his wife. They own a big computer retail store in town. In the back is a big cardboard box. "We want to donate something to your sale," Mr. Allen announces. "It's a new computer." Mrs. McIntyre laughs. "Well, that's great," she says. "This is why we are having a sale in the first place!" Mrs. Allen smiles and said, "Well, if you want… you can just keep it and you'll have two."

**(Picture 8)** The kids run up to Mrs. McIntyre. "We don't even need to have a garage sale now, do we?" they ask. "Oh yes we do," says Mrs. McIntyre. "My husband would like to park his car in the garage again and besides… we need to save up money for TWO computer tables! Everybody start tagging the merchandise! We open for business in an hour!"

**STOP.** How are Mr. and Mrs. Allen being generous? *(donating a computer)* What did it cost them? *(the wholesale price of a new computer)* Do you think this garge sale will be a success? *(probably, everyone is already being very helpful and generous)*

# II-4C. The Garage Sale

1.

2.

3.

4.

5.

6.

7.

8.

# Lesson II-5: Recognizing Generosity

**The contents of Lesson II-5 include:**

- Worksheet II-5A, Is This Generosity?
- Worksheet II-5B, Common-Sense Generosity
- Worksheet II-5C, Which One Is Being Generous?

## Worksheet II-5A, Is This Generosity?

1. Pass out the worksheet to students and have them complete the review section at the top.
2. Directions for the rest of the worksheet ask students to circle yes or no to indicate if the example shows generosity.

**Answers**

1. yes (gave up computer); 2. no; 3. no (motive was to get rid of overripe tomatoes); 4. yes; 5. yes; 6. yes (you can live without dessert); 7. no (should have made room for her at your table); 8. yes (giving time and skills)

**Discuss**

1. When should you just give helpful advice to someone rather than actually helping him or her do a task or solve a problem? *(when they need to learn how to do it, such as solving math problems)*
2. In situation 2, what would a generous person have done? *(given the girl some paper)*
3. In situation 4, how did this person show generosity? *(gave extra time, went beyond the basic job of feeding the dog)*
4. In situation 6, what if the friend wanted to buy dessert too? Should this person have felt obligated to give the friend money? *(no—in this case the person wanted to buy milk, not dessert)*
5. In situation 7, how could the person have made the new girl feel welcome? *(included her at the lunch table, made sure she knows her way around)*

## Worksheet II-5B, Common-Sense Generosity

1. Pass out the worksheet to students and have them complete the review section at the top.
2. Directions for the rest of the worksheet ask students to read each item and decide why the person should not share what is in the example.

**Answers**

1. now the person has no money for lunch; 2. this is an extremely valuable item, so should check with mother first; 3. this doesn't belong to the person and it was something that was going to be thrown away; 4. don't share a comb, especially if you've had head lice; 5. some people would not appreciate a free kitten; 6. he should check with his father first

**Discuss**

1. In situation 1, why shouldn't the girl share her lunch money? *(her parents probably gave it to her, intending that she should eat; dessert is not essential)*

2. In situation 2, what's wrong with giving away something very valuable? *(it's a family heirloom; might not mean much to the person who gets it, but it would mean a lot to the family)*

3. In situation 4, why isn't he being generous? *(don't share head lice!)*

4. In situation 5, what is a problem with giving away animals? *(should check with the family, make sure there are no allergies, can afford to maintain a pet, etc.)*

5. In situation 6, the boy is being generous with his dad's time. What's the problem with that? *(should check with his dad who may have plans)*

## Worksheet II-5C, Which One Is Being Generous?

1. Pass out the worksheet to students and have them complete the review section at the top.

2. The rest of the worksheet asks students to circle the person in each situation who is being generous.

**Answers**

1. first; 2. first; 3. second; 4. second; 5. second

**Discuss**

1. In situation 1, what if a family cannot afford to feed another person on Thanksgiving? Does this mean they are not generous? *(no, if you do not have the money, you are unable to help someone financially; there are other ways to be generous—time, etc.)*

2. In situation 2, how does "keeping the change" show generosity? *(the person is not expecting to get every penny back)*

3. In situation 3, is anything wrong with just sending a card? *(no, a card would certainly be appreciated, but the second person wants to give time that would probably help Grandma more than good wishes)*

4. In situation 4, if the person does not have time right at that moment to help out, what else could he do? *(schedule a more convenient time)*

5. In situation 5, why is it more generous to bring treats for everyone rather than just the winners? *(it shows that everyone's participation was appreciated)*

# II-5A. Is This Generosity?

**Review**

Generosity means _____ what you _____.

**Directions:** Read each item listed below. Circle YES if it shows generosity. Circle NO if it does not. Remember that generosity costs something of value.

1. You just got a new computer. A friend comes to visit and wants to use it, so you turn off the game you are playing and let him pick what he wants to play.                                         **YES     NO**

2. You have a new pad of paper. You notice that the girl sitting next to you doesn't have any paper, so you tell her that the teacher has some in the front of the room.                                   **YES     NO**

3. You have a lot of extra tomatoes from your garden. Some are starting to get pretty ripe so you need to do something with them soon. You take several to your neighbor.                                   **YES     NO**

4. You are supposed to feed and water your neighbors' dog while they are on vacation. While you are there, you realize that the dog is lonely, so you brush him and take him for a walk besides feeding him.   **YES     NO**

5. It's a really hot day for your soccer team to play, so you check with your Mom and bring enough flavored ices for the whole team to enjoy after the game.                                                **YES     NO**

6. A friend wants to borrow some money to buy an extra milk at lunch. You realize that you don't have enough to buy an extra dessert if you give him your money, but you decide to give it to the friend.   **YES     NO**

7. There is a new girl in your classroom who doesn't know anyone else. At lunchtime, you think about asking her to sit at your table, but there aren't extra chairs so you figure she'll find somewhere else to sit. **YES     NO**

8. Your dad coaches a basketball team for little kids. You would like to help out after school because you enjoy working with kids, so you ask if you can come to the gym after school and help them.        **YES     NO**

# II-5B. Common-Sense Generosity

**Review**

Generosity means _____ what you _____.

**Directions:** These people want to be generous by sharing, but what is the problem in each case? Write your answers on the lines after each item.

1. *Would you like that extra ice cream dessert? Here, you can take my lunch money.*

_____

_____

_____

2. *I thought you would like this pretty necklace. I got it out of my mother's closet. I think it's worth a lot of money because it's an old family heirloom.*

_____

_____

_____

3. *Happy Birthday, Sue! I got this from my neighbor's basement. They were going to throw it away, but I thought you would like it.*

_____

_____

_____

4. *You want to borrow my comb? Here, just take it. I think I am probably rid of the head lice by now.*

_____

_____

_____

5. *My cat has kittens. Take one, they are free. I know you're allergic to cats, but isn't this one sooooo cute????*

_____

_____

_____

6. *Do you need parents to drive on the field trip? Oh, my dad will drive. He won't mind taking off work and borrowing his brother's van and going with us for a whole day.*

_____

_____

_____

Name _____ Date _____

# II-5C. Which One Is Being Generous?

**Review**

Generosity means _____ what _____ _____.

**Directions:** Circle the person in each situation who is being generous.

1. Here is a list of needy people who could use a meal on Thanksgiving. / Here's our address. Come on over. / I will help you find a good cheap restaurant.

2. Would you like to buy some cookies for our fund-raiser? / Here, keep the change. / They don't look very fresh.

3. Grandma is sick. What should we do? / Send an expensive card. / Let's help clean her apartment for her.

4. I need help with division. Will you help me? / I am busy right now. Ask me some other time. / Sit at the table with me and I'll help you while I'm waiting for my hot chocolate to cool.

5. We are having a class party after the game. / I'll bring treats for the winners. / I'll bring treats for everyone.

# Lesson II-6: Applying Generosity

**The contents of Lesson II-6 include:**

- Worksheet II-6A, What Do You Have to Offer?
- Worksheet II-6B, What Could You Do?
- Quiz on Part 8: Generosity
- Game: Give It Away

## Worksheet II-6A, What Do You Have to Offer?

1. Pass out the worksheet to students and have them complete the review section at the top of the page. Remind them that the opposite of generosity is being stingy or greedy.

2. Directions for the rest of the worksheet ask students to think about their own resources and to list their possessions, time commitments, and talents that they could share with others.

### Discuss

1. Should you share everything with others, or should you put some limits on what you share? For example, should you share something of great value with someone whom you know is careless?

2. How can you share your talents with others? What if you aren't good at explaining how to do something?

3. How can you use your time to help others?

## Worksheet II-6B, What Could You Do?

1. Pass out the worksheet to students. Have them complete the review section at the top.

2. Directions for the rest of the worksheet ask students to draw a picture to show a way that they could demonstrate generosity in each situation.

### Answers

(Will vary) 1. have a party and invite everyone in the class; 2. wait for your brother and walk him home; 3. give your friend the sweatshirt; 4. make cookies and bring them in for the class; 5. go around to neighbors and collect toys; 6. quietly offer to bring in an extra book for Tommy

### Discuss

1. What are some situations that you can tell about in which you were generous with someone else?

2. What are some situations in which someone was generous to you?

# Quiz on Part 8: Generosity

This quiz can be used as a follow-up for the lessons in Part 8.

**Answers**

1. *(definition)* Generosity is sharing what you have.

2. *(examples)* b, c

3. *(applying)* Answers will vary.

# Game: Give It Away

Directions, sample game cards, and gameboard can be found at the end of this lesson.

# II-6A. What Do You Have to Offer?

**Review**

Generosity means _____
_____.

The opposite of generous is _____.

**Directions:** Think about ways that you could be generous by sharing what you have.

POSSESSIONS: What are things you have that you could share with others?

_____

_____

_____

TIME: How could you spend time helping someone else?

_____

_____

_____

TALENT: What are some things you are able to do that you could share with others?

_____

_____

_____

Name _____ Date _____

# II-6B. What Could You Do?

**Review**

Generosity means _____

_____.

The opposite of generous is _____.

**Directions:** On another sheet of paper, draw a picture to show what you could do in each situation to show generosity.

1. Your favorite aunt gives you $100 for your birthday and tells you to "have fun."

2. Your dad has to work late and can't pick up your little brother from his music lesson after school.

3. A friend wants to borrow your new sweatshirt.

4. Your teacher asks who can bring in treats for the party.

5. The student council is asking for donations of toys to give to poor kids during the holidays.

6. Everyone in the class is supposed to bring in books for a book exchange, but you know that Tommy doesn't have any books at his house.

Name _____  Date _____

# Quiz on Part 8: Generosity

1. What does generosity mean? _____

_____

_____

2. Which of these examples shows generosity?

3. What could you do if you found out that one of your classmates didn't have enough money to buy a school sweatshirt, but was very self-conscious about being given things?

_____

_____

_____

_____

_____

_____

# Game for Generosity: Give It Away

**Materials:**
You need a gameboard (see example), 48 cards (12 each of these categories: time/money/skills/stuff), tokens to move around the board, and spinner or die.

**Objective:** To get rid of all your cards

**Players:** 2–4

**How to play:**
1. Shuffle the cards and pass them out to players (12 each if there are 4 players).
2. Players should keep the four categories of cards separated in front of them.
3. Roll the die (or spinner) to see who goes first (highest number goes first).
4. Players move tokens around the board after rolling the die.
5. Each space indicates a category (time/money/skills/stuff). Players get rid of a card that matches the category by reading the generous comment and putting the card down.
6. Play continues until one player is out of cards.
7. Follow the instructions on "special spaces."

## Sample card comments:

**TIME**
Help brother with homework.

Walk a neighbor's dog.

Read a story to a little kid.

Listen to a friend.

Stay after school to help work on a project.

Clean up the kitchen for your dad.

Get up early to walk to school with a friend.

Explain how to write a story to your sister.

Wash the dishes for your mom.

Practice playing catch with a friend.

Show a new classmate around the school.

Sit down and watch TV with your little brother.

**MONEY**
Give extra change to someone selling candy.

Work a car wash to earn money for a good cause.

Give a friend extra money to buy school supplies.

Donate $1 to the animal shelter.

Buy a book for a classmate who doesn't have extra money.

Babysit for free.

Collect money for sick kids at a hospital.

Put in money for flowers for your school secretary on her birthday.

Buy treats for everyone on your team.

Put some change in a jar to treat diseases.

Help collect money for a fund-raiser for your team.

Do odd jobs for people to get money to send to the Red Cross.

## SKILLS

Teach a friend how to throw a football.

Show a classmate how to draw horses.

Practice going over lines with a classmate for a play.

Spend time helping a friend learn to do a cartwheel.

Let your brother watch you play and win a videogame.

Tell a friend how you run so fast.

Show someone how to saddle a horse.

French-braid your sister's hair.

Explain how your digital camera works.

Work with a partner on putting together a model car.

Share a book on cartooning with someone else.

Invite a friend to take a bowling lesson with you.

## STUFF

Let your sister borrow your new sweater.

Work with a friend to put a puzzle together.

Bring in some games to play with friends for indoor recess.

Share your new markers with classmates.

Let a friend borrow a CD.

Bring in candy for the whole class.

Bring your favorite book to school and put it on the show-and-tell table.

Trade baseball cards with a friend.

Pass out stickers.

Take stuffed animals to kids in the hospital.

Make T-shirts for your soccer team.

Make an interesting necklace for your aunt on her birthday.

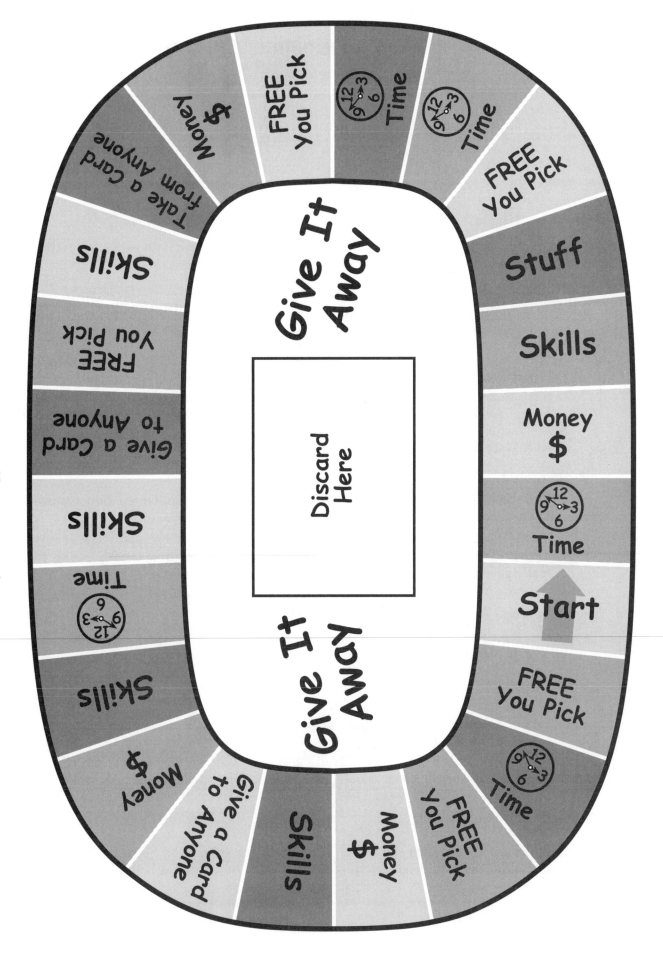

# Lesson II-7: Defining Compassion

**The contents of Lesson II-7 include:**

- Journal Ideas
- Pre-/Posttest on generosity
- Worksheet II-7A, Needs or Wants?
- Worksheet II-7B, Type of Need
- Worksheet II-7C, Choose Your Ending

## Journal Ideas

Have students select topics that they would like to record in their journals. Share entries periodically with others.

## Pre-/Posttest

Pass out the pre-/posttest to students and explain that they are to circle the letter of the answer that best shows compassion in each situation.

### Answers

1. c (if you are physically able to help); 2. d (this response is actually doing something to help the situation other than just expressing sympathy; answer **a** might be OK but your hands will get cold too; in **d**, you are caring for her by trying to resolve the problem); 3. a (showing sympathy); 4. d; 5. c (the intentions for **b** are good, but it's changing the focus to your problems and situations)

## Worksheet II-7A, Needs or Wants?

1. Write the definition of compassion on the board or other place where students can easily see it. *"Compassion means caring about the needs of others."*

2. Briefly discuss the situation. Explain that just feeling sorry for someone else is only a part of compassion. Actually being compassionate implies that you are willing to really do something to help take care of the other person's needs.

3. Pass out the worksheet to students and have them complete the review section at the top. They are to circle N (need) or W (want) for each item.

### Answers

1. W; 2. N; 3. N; 4. W; 5. W; 6. N; 7. N; 8. N; 9. W; 10. W

### Discuss

1. How often do you hear people say "I need—" when they really mean "I want—." What's the difference? *(question of if they can live without it or if it is essential to completing a job they have to do)*

2. Do you think that a "need" depends on someone's situation? For example, an athlete might "need" special shoes or equipment to effectively do his or her job, while you who are not competing but just playing for fun or sport could do with a lesser quality shoe or equipment. Why, then, would the athlete "need" something that you wouldn't? *(that is his or her job, task, goal, etc.)*

3. What are some things you want? What are some things you need in order to do specialized things such as play sports, accomplish a personal goal, help you in a hobby, etc?

# Worksheet II-7B, Type of Need

1. Review the definition of compassion.
2. Pass out the worksheet to students and have them complete the review section at the top. For the remainder of the worksheet, have students decide what type of need (money, learning/skill, social, or physical) is described in each example. More than one type of need might apply.

**Answers**

1. physical (too short); 2. learning/skill; 3. physical, social; 4. physical; 5. social; 6. physical/social; 7. money; 8. physical (medical); 9. physical, learning/skill; 10. learning/skill

**Discuss**

1. Of the four types of needs discussed, which ones do you think are the most important or powerful? If you have unlimited money, would that take care of a deadly disease or brain damage from an accident? If you had perfect health, does that mean you could make a lot of money or learn how to do brain surgery?
2. Do you think more people are willing to help others by giving money or by doing physical work to help out?

# Worksheet II-7C, Choose Your Ending

1. Review the definition of compassion.
2. Pass out the cartoon section of the worksheet and have students complete the review section at the top.
3. Explain that you are going to read a story that has two different "paths" it will take. The story starts with a woman who oversleeps and explains how this affects the people in her family and how what happens to them affects others. There are two ways the story evolves, however. One is filled with uncompassionate people; the other, with compassion. Students are to listen to the story and answer the questions.

**Answers**

See the teacher's script.

# Journal Ideas: Compassion

1. How compassionate are you? *Rate yourself* 0 (not caring about others at all) to 5 (always concerned about the welfare of others) on the lines below.

    0 _____ 1 _____ 2 _____

    3 _____ 4 _____ 5 _____

2. What ads have you seen on TV or in magazines that try to make people aware of how to help those in need? For example, sponsoring a child in a foreign country, disaster relief, etc. How do the ads make you feel? Do you think they are effective?

3. What disastrous events have occurred lately (e.g., earthquake, hurricane, fire) that put a large number of people in need?

4. What is the Red Cross? What is Habitat for Humanity? How do they help people? Do you know of other organizations that try to help people in specific ways? Which ones?

5. What are some occupations that show a lot of compassion for people? How must these people show compassion to others?

6. Have you ever encountered someone begging on a public street, asking for money or food? What goes through your mind? What do your parents tell you to do or not do?

7. Some people need more than just money for relief. What are other needs that people might have? What type of service or person would be best able to help them?

8. Have you ever been to a nursing home or hospital? What type of needs do you think you would encounter there?

9. Who is a person you know (famous or local) who you think of as being very compassionate? Why? What has he or she done that makes you think this way?

10. Is it easier to help someone by just writing a check (if you had the money) or actually putting in time to help them? Or does it "just depend"? On what?

Name _____ Date _____

# Compassion: Pretest/Posttest

Read each situation. Choose the answer that best shows compassion.

1. A boy is having trouble lifting a heavy box in the trunk of a car. You…
   a. Agree that it sure is a heavy box!
   b. Ask if he would like you to call someone at home to help.
   c. Ask if he would like you to try to help.
   d. Tell him your dad is very strong and will do it for you when he gets home from work.

2. It's really cold out and a girl in your class has no mittens to wear for outside recess. You…
   a. Take yours off and give them to her.
   b. Tell the teacher that everyone needs to bring in money to buy her some mittens.
   c. Tell her you're very sorry that she doesn't have any mittens.
   d. Ask if she'd like you to go with her to check lost and found for an extra pair.

3. Annie missed an easy word on the oral spelling test and the kids are laughing at her. You…
   a. Tell Annie you missed an easy word too and it's not a big deal.
   b. Laugh, but very quietly.
   c. Hit the kids who are laughing at her.
   d. Tell Annie that there are tutors available who can help her after school.

4. A little boy is crying because he is lost in the supermarket. You…
   a. Take him home with you.
   b. Yell for his parents.
   c. Tell him to stay where he is until his parents realize he is missing.
   d. Stay with him until his parents or a responsible adult come by.

5. A friend's father is dying of cancer. You…
   a. Tell him you will make everything all right.
   b. Tell him about when your uncle broke his leg and how hard it was on the family.
   c. Spend time with him so he knows you are available when he needs help.
   d. Tell him you will be glad to help in any way you can, as long as it's not during soccer practice or Saturdays or after school on Wednesdays.

# II-7A. Needs or Wants?

**Review**

Compassion means c_____ about the n_____ of

o_____.

**Directions:** Which of these are things a person needs? Which are things a person might want, but could do without? Circle N (need) or W (want).

1. nails manicured at a beauty salon      N    W

2. breakfast before school      N    W

3. special soft-soled shoes for gym class      N    W

4. a set of encyclopedias from the
   book cart      N    W

5. extra dessert at lunch      N    W

6. $1 for bus fare to get to work      N    W

7. glasses to see the board at school      N    W

8. medication for a very bad cough      N    W

9. a maid to clean up your room      N    W

10. a new bike if you get a flat tire      N    W

# II-7B. Type of Need

**Review**

Compassion means c_____ about the

n_____ of o_____.

**Directions:** There are different types of needs that people have. Read each example below and write if it is a money need, a learning/skill need, a social need (from another person), or a physical need. It could be more than one!

1. I can't reach the stuff on the top shelf!

   _____

2. I don't understand why this story problem doesn't come out to the same answer that the teacher got.

   _____

3. There's my neighbor. He's an old man who can't rake his leaves anymore.

   _____

4. That poor little girl is shivering—I'll get her a sweater.

   _____

5. That boy is new to this school. He doesn't have any friends yet.

   _____

6. Grandma can't drive to the store anymore to buy food.

   _____

7. We don't have enough money to fix the leaky roof.

   _____

8. I can't stop coughing! Cough! Cough!

   _____

9. Don't make fun of Timmy because he missed catching the ball. He feels badly enough so leave him alone.

   _____

10. This wheel on my skateboard came loose. I think it just needs to be tightened, but I don't know how to fix it.

   _____

# For the Teacher

## (Script for Worksheet II-7C, Choose Your Ending)

The picture at the top of the worksheet shows a bad day for Mrs. Ohime. She oversleeps and the rest of the day is filled with things to deal with. Pictures 1 through 6 show the rest of her day when she is with people who are not compassionate. Pictures 7 through 11 show her day with compassionate people. Take a look at each picture while I read the story. I will ask you questions about compassion—caring about the needs of others.

**Top picture:** Mrs. Ohime had a very busy day on Thursday, so she got to bed late at night. Unfortunately, she overslept on Friday morning. Let's go through this day two different ways to see how compassionate people can make a difference in our lives.

**(Picture 1)** Mrs. Ohime scrambles out of bed and realizes that she hasn't made lunches for the little kids. She asks her daughter Karen if she would make lunches for them. Karen, who is also running late because no one woke her up, replied: "I didn't finish my math from last night. I don't have time. Now we are all late. Thanks, Mom."

**(Picture 2)** The little kids are grouchy because they don't get breakfast before the bus comes. They are pouting and moving slowly. The bus driver yells at them for moving too slowly. "Hurry up," she says. "Get moving, I can't wait all day." They get on the bus and start pushing each other because they don't have enough room.

**(Picture 3)** At school, Karen goes to her math class and has most of the answers wrong. "It's not my fault," she complains to the teacher. "My mom was too busy to help me last night and she overslept this morning." The teacher says, "You each have study partners. Why didn't you call your partner?" Karen says, "I went shopping last night. I thought I would have time to do it later." The teacher says it is just too bad, and she collects the papers anyway. Karen knows she will get a bad grade.

**(Picture 4)** Meanwhile, Mrs. Ohime still feels rushed because she has to meet a couple to show them a house she is trying to sell. She doesn't have her make-up on and her hair is messy. "I am sorry I don't have all the paperwork with me," she tells the people. "If you like, I could run back to the office to get it." The people just say they are in a hurry and will get back to her later. Mrs. Ohime knows what that means—forget it!

**(Picture 5)** Back at the office, Mrs. Ohime's boss wants to know if the people bought the house. She says they haven't made up their minds. The boss says she needs to be more organized before she takes people to a house and he expects her to look professional. He begins raising his voice in front of the other people in the office, who try to look busy.

**(Picture 6)** Finally, the day is over and the family meets back at home. The little kids have gotten in trouble at school for fighting, Karen is still upset about her math assignment, and Mrs. Ohime just wants to jump in the bathtub and forget about the day.

**STOP.** Do you see any examples of compassion in this side of the story? Do you see examples of people who have an opportunity to show compassion? What? *(Picture 1: Karen could have helped make lunches. Picture 2: Bus driver could have been nicer. Picture 3: The teacher could have given her extra time. Picture 4: The people could have overlooked her messy appearance. Picture 5: The boss could have been kinder and not yelled at her in front of the whole office.)*

© 2002 by The Center for Applied Research in Education

Now let's go through the day with some compassionate people in this family's lives. Start the day at the top with Mrs. Ohime oversleeping. Now follow the other pictures.

**(Picture 7)** Mrs. Ohime asks her daughter Karen if she would pack lunches for the other children. Karen says, "Here you go, kids, and I threw in extra potato chips so you can share with somebody at lunch." Mother thanks Karen for helping and says they could all plan on going out for pizza tonight.

**(Picture 8)** The little kids are late to the bus stop, and some of the bigger kids in the back are yelling at them to hurry up. The bus driver turns to them and says, "My goodness! You really want to get to school today! I didn't know you loved school so much!" That makes everybody laugh.

**(Picture 9)** At school, Karen tells her math teacher that she didn't get her assignment done because she didn't allow enough time last night and this morning was a chaotic mess at her house. The teacher asks the rest of the class if anyone else had trouble with the assignment and almost everyone raises their hands. She says, "Why don't we take today's lesson time to go over it together to make sure everyone knows what to do?" Everyone votes yes to that!

**(Picture 10)** At the office, Mrs. Ohime has a woman waiting to fill out the paperwork to sell her house, but she is so rushed she can't find the forms she needs. She keeps apologizing to the woman who finally says, "Just relax and get a cup of coffee, dear. I'm not going anywhere and you just take your time." Mrs. Ohime takes a deep breath and goes to look for the forms. Another employee stops her by the file cabinets and says, "Here is what you're looking for. I have an extra one right here in my hand, all filled out and ready to go. Just take it."

**(Picture 11 )** The family gets together at the end of the day and decides they will call for a pizza to be delivered. Karen offers to go pick up a movie so they can watch something together and just take it easy that night.

**STOP.** In this version, what examples of compassion do you find? How does it affect the stressed people? *(Picture 7: Karen gave the kids extra treats in their lunch. Made for a better mood. Picture 8: Bus driver made a joke, calmed everybody down. Picture 9: The teacher realized that a lot of people had trouble with the assignment, so was flexible on her schedule for that day. Picture 10: The woman did not pressure Mrs. Ohime; the other office worker helped her find a form.)*

# II-7C. Choose Your Ending

1.

2.

3.

4.

5.

6.

7.

8.

9.

10.

11.

# Lesson II-8: Recognizing Compassion

**The contents of Lesson II-8 include:**

- Worksheet II-8A, Is This Compassion?
- Worksheet II-8B, Compassion with Common Sense
- Worksheet II-8C, Caring and Doing

## Worksheet II-8A, Is This Compassion?

1. Pass out the worksheet to students and have them complete the review section at the top.
2. Directions for the rest of the worksheet ask students to circle the person in each example who is showing compassion.

**Answers**

1. second; 2. second; 3. second; 4. first; 5. second; 6. first

**Discuss**

1. In situation 1, what if the person who offered to help gave a big sigh and acted like it was a big deal to help? Would that change how you felt about his offer of help? *(probably wonder if he was sincere or not)*
2. In situation 2, what are other ways to make a person from a different place feel welcome? *(do things that don't have a language barrier—playing, eating, drawing)*
3. In situation 3, even if you didn't have the skills to be able to help someone fix something, how could you show compassion? *(offer to walk with him, have him wait at your house, call someone for him)*
4. In situation 4, why shouldn't the girl just be tough about her injury? *(it actually might be serious and it certainly hurts!)*
5. In situation 5, the person offered to help fix the project. Do you think a person might always want help or might he just want to work on his own? *(ask the person to find out)*
6. In situation 6, what do you think of the second person's response? *(self-centered)*

## Worksheet II-8B, Compassion with Common Sense

1. Pass out the worksheet to students and have them complete the review section at the top.
2. Directions for the rest of the worksheet ask students to discuss why each situation is not showing compassion.

**Answers**

1. this is a business deal; 2. this person needs an audience to be compassionate; 3. help is not wanted; 4. he is embarrassing the person; 5. she gave away things that weren't hers to give

**Discuss**

1. If a person needs an audience to show compassion, is that person really interested in helping someone?

2. What do you think of the person in situation 2 who has the skills to help someone, and is offering to help, but still needs recognition for that?

3. How is the person in situation 3 being too helpful? How could he have gone about this in a better way? *(checked with dad, worked with dad)*

4. Does everyone who appears to be in need really be needy? Do you think some people would rather work out their problems or needs on their own? *(probably!)*

5. Have you ever been in a situation such as situation 4, where someone embarrassed you? How did you feel?

6. In situation 5, the girl wanted to help, but what do you think about the way she got the money? *(it wasn't hers to give—mother will be very surprised to find her empty closet)*

## Worksheet II-8C, Caring and Doing

1. Pass out the worksheet to students and have them complete the review section at the top.

2. Directions for the rest of the worksheet ask students to draw a picture or use words to show how the people in each situation could show compassion.

**Answers**

1. go get Aunt Rose a glass of water; 2. go see Pete and find out if he needs anything; 3. give helpful comments, don't yawn, be polite; 4. help the girl look for her kitten, don't bring up the possibility of death; 5. get some friends together and go to Ryan's party

**Discuss**

1. Is it sometimes good enough to just say "I feel really sorry for you" or "I know how you must feel"? How would you know whether to try to do something or to just leave it at that? Are words enough? *(depends on situation—if you don't know the person well, verbal condolences are probably fine; if you are good friends, you should be available to do whatever is needed and helpful)*

2. Some people are willing to "go an extra mile" to help others. For example, the girl with the lost kitten would probably really appreciate the boy going on a hunt for the missing kitten rather than just saying he would tell her if he saw the kitten. Can you think of other ways to "go the extra mile" for someone?

3. What could the boy in situation 5 do to help make Ryan's birthday party a success? *(bring his friends and show up for awhile)*

# II-8A. Is This Compassion?

**Review**

Compassion means _____ about the _____ of

_____.

**Directions:** Read each situation and circle the person who is showing compassion.

1. I can't get this backpack on. It's too heavy for me. / Try harder. / I'll help.

2. That girl just moved here from another country. She doesn't even speak our language. / Too bad. / Maybe she could play a game with us.

3. My tire popped on my bike. / There's a gas station down the road about a mile. / I know how to fix it. Wait here.

4. Ow! I really cut my arm! / You might need stitches. I'll get the nurse. / Be tough. And don't bleed on my book.

5. My science project is falling apart. It's just terrible. / Yes, it's pretty bad. / You had a good idea. I bet we can still fix it.

6. It's hard for Grandma to walk up all these steps. / Take my arm, Grandma. We'll go slowly. / Does that mean we have to go outside in the cold to talk to her?

# II-8B. Compassion with Common Sense

**Review**

Compassion means _____ about

the _____ of

_____.

**Directions:** Read each situation. Discuss why this
is not showing compassion.

1.

> I know you need $5 for the field trip.
> Here, I have $5 for you right in my pocket. You can pay
> me back next week, but I will need to charge you $2 interest, so
> pay me back $7. If you can't pay me, then I'll charge you more
> late fees. But enjoy your field trip!

2.

> Tommy is a lousy player, but I can help him!
> Hey, guys, let me give Tommy some tennis lessons. I feel
> really sorry for him and I know I can help him. We even have our
> own tennis court at my house. I'll help him! You can come
> over and watch me if you want to.

3.

> Here, Dad, I cleaned up
> your messy office for you while you
> were gone. I put everything in files and
> threw out all of the empty paper and files
> that were crumpled. Now you have time
> to relax when you get home.

> But... where is my
> report? Where are my checks? You
> threw out my important memos and notes
> from the meetings. Everything was organized
> the way I wanted. I know you were trying
> to help, but you should have
> asked me first.

4.

> I know we're supposed to
> take turns reading out loud and that
> you are a really bad reader, so we'll just
> skip over you. Don't even worry about it!
> Hey—SKIP JOHN!!! He doesn't
> have to read!!!

5.

> It's a really good cause
> to raise money to help support children in a
> foreign orphanage, so I went into my mom's closet and sold
> her fur coat, all of her new shoes (she has way too many
> anyhow), and I found $100 in her wallet! Here! Now
> those little kids can eat and eat!!

Name _____ Date _____

# II-8C. Caring and Doing

**Review**

Compassion means _____ about the _____ of

_____ .

**Directions:** These people are not being compassionate. On another sheet of paper, draw a picture or use words to show how each person could show compassion.

1.

Welcome to our house, Aunt Rose. Are you thirsty? The kitchen is right in there.

2.
Pete's mother just died of cancer. He is very upset. Let's go play.

3.
I'll be glad to listen to you practice giving your speech. Go ahead.

Yawn... Wow, are you ever BAD! This is so boring!

4.
You lost your kitten somewhere in the neighborhood? It probably got hit by a car on that busy street. If I see it, I'll tell you.

5.
I don't think anyone is going to show up at Ryan's birthday party. He's not very cool. I sure don't want to be the only one there, so I'm not going either.

# Lesson II-9: Applying Compassion

**The contents of Lesson II-9 include:**
- Worksheet II-9A, An Exercise in Observing
- Worksheet II-9B, Individual and Group Projects
- Quiz on Part 9: Compassion
- Game: First to 50

## Worksheet II-9A, An Exercise in Observing

1. Pass out the worksheet to students and have them complete the review section at the top. Remind them that the opposite of compassion is uncaring.
2. Directions for the rest of the worksheet ask students to actually spend some time observing people and their actions in several situations. After completing some time observing people, they should record their observations of acts of compassion that they have seen.

**Discuss**

1. Were you surprised at the acts of compassion (or lack of compassion) that you observed?
2. Did you find that there is less compassion at home than among strangers?

## Worksheet II-9B, Individual and Group Projects

1. Pass out the worksheet to students and have them complete the review section at the top.
2. The rest of the worksheet lists ideas for conducting an individual and/or a group project that emphasizes demonstrating compassion toward others. Students can select their own individual project. You may wish to involve all students in a class project.

**Discuss**

1. What individual projects did you find appealing?
2. How did you carry out your compassion project?
3. Do you feel you made a difference?

## Quiz on Part 9: Compassion

This quiz can be used as a follow-up for the lessons in Part 9.

**Answers**

1. *(definition)* Compassion is caring about the needs of others.
2. *(examples)* a, c
3. *(applying)* Answers will vary.

## Game: First to 50

Directions for this game are found at the end of this lesson.

Name _____ Date _____

# II-9A. An Exercise in Observing

**Review**

Compassion means _____

_____.

The opposite of compassion is _____.

**Directions:** Spend some time doing field research. What are some examples of compassion that you have observed?

| Place | Date | Compassion Observed |
|---|---|---|
| 1. Home | | |
| 2. School | | |
| 3. Neighborhood/Community | | |
| 4. Sports/Clubs | | |
| 5. Friends | | |
| 6. Other | | |

Name _____  Date _____

# II-9B. Individual and Group Projects

**Review**

Compassion means _____
_____.

The opposite of compassion is _____.

**Directions:** Choose an individual goal that you will make to practice showing compassion in some way. Some ideas may include:

- finding out the specific needs of someone in your family or neighborhood
- working extra to make money to donate to a worthy cause
- writing letters to someone who is in need
- visiting a nursing home or hospital
- organizing a yard sale or other fund-raiser to get supplies for a charity
- spending time with an elderly person who is lonely
- making a quilt (or other project) to give as a gift to a needy group

## Group Projects

Organize a classroom project to undertake showing compassion in some way. Some ideas may include:

- volunteering at the Red Cross or other charitable organization (duties might include stuffing envelopes, assisting with mailing, cleaning and organizing supplies, etc.)
- raising money for a local project (Humane Society, fire victims, etc.)
- inviting a speaker to come to the school to talk about disaster relief experiences (perhaps someone from the Peace Corps or a medical missionary group)
- visiting a homeless shelter and finding out what specific needs they have and how they try to help people
- getting information about a Ronald McDonald house or a children's hospital to see what needs they have

## Specific Things You Can Do:

- sing, visit, play games, share
- send cards
- give money
- give time
- raise money
- make the community aware of this agency

# Quiz on Part 9: Compassion

1. What does compassion mean? _____

_____

2. Which of these examples show compassion? Write **yes** or **no** on the line.

a. I can't draw a house. It's for an art project.

I can show you how I draw houses. Maybe you can try the way I do.

_____

b. Will you stop by Robbie's class after school and pick up his books? He's been sick with the flu for three days.

I can't carry all of his books and mine, too! They are too heavy!

_____

c. Laura tries hard, but she just does not know how to write very well. This is supposed to be a group project and I'm the leader, so I think I'll ask her if she would like to be the illustrator. I know she would like to do that and it would be helping our project.

_____

d. We're taking a collection of money and supplies for Sherry's family. Their house was destroyed in a fire.

Sherry was never very nice to me. Don't they have insurance anyway?

_____

3. What is one way you could show compassion to someone in need in three different settings or situations?

_____

_____

_____

_____

_____

_____

# Game for Compassion: First to 50

**Materials:**
    You need a scoreboard, 50 compassion playing cards, and 10 random point cards (+ and -). Each compassion card is given a point value (3 to 10 points). The random point cards are given positive 5 and negative 5 points.

**Players:** 2–4 or 2 teams

**Objective:** To be the first player to reach 50 points

## How to play:

1. Shuffle all 60 cards and place in the middle of the playing area.

2. Dealer goes first. Turn over the top card, read the sentence, and collect the number of points assigned.

3. Each player keeps track of his or her own score.

4. Play continues with each player taking the top card, reading the sentence, and adding (or subtracting) points.

5. The first player to reach 50 points after all have had a turn is the winner.

## Sample Compassion Cards

**10-point cards**

- Build a hospital for sick children.
- Donate $5,000 to build a library in an inner-city area.
- Spend a year building houses for people in a third-world country.
- Climb a tree to rescue a kitten.
- Dive into a river to save a drowning boy.

**5-point cards**

- Bake cookies for a sick friend.
- Babysit for a neighbor who is very busy.
- Help a child build a model.
- Help someone look for a lost wallet in the park.
- Go shopping for an elderly neighbor.
- Assist in a car wash to raise money for a burn victim.

**3-point cards**

- Compliment a teammate even when he (or she) misses a goal.
- Read a story to your sister.
- Send a card to a discouraged friend.
- Take your neighbors' dog for a walk to help them out.
- Open a door for a person whose arms are full.

# Lesson II-10: Defining Forgiving

**The contents of Lesson II-10 include:**

- Journal Ideas
- Pre-/Posttest on situations involving forgiving
- Worksheet II-10A, Mean, Unpleasant, Unfair
- Worksheet II-10B, Holding a Grudge
- Worksheet II-10C, The Softball Game

## Journal Ideas

These questions and ideas can be used for daily or occasional writing activities. Have students share their responses periodically with each other.

## Pre-/Posttest

Pass out the pre-/posttest to students and explain that they are to circle the letter of the answer that best shows forgiveness.

**Answers**

1. b; 2. d; 3. c; 4. a; 5. b

## Worksheet II-10A, Mean, Unpleasant, Unfair

1. Write the definition of *forgiveness* on the board or other place where students can easily see it. "Forgiving means letting bad feelings for someone go."

2. Pass out the worksheet to students and have them complete the review section at the top. On the remainder of the worksheet, inform students that some examples of bad feelings can result from situations that involve meanness, an unpleasant situation (which may not be the result of someone's intended unkindness), or an unfair situation. They are to read each example and write what type of example each is.

**Answers**

1. mean (calling him lazy); 2. unpleasant (probably an accident); 3. mean (tattling); 4. unfair (if it's true); 5. unpleasant (but probably accident); 6. mean (telling him he is fat); 7. unfair (not his turn, but got yelled at anyway); 8. mean; 9. unfair; 10. unpleasant (but really no one's fault)

**Discuss**

1. Why is it difficult to forgive people who are mean? *(it is personal and you might be quite sensitive)*

2. Is it easier to forgive unpleasant situations? *(possibly, you still might feel angry, but if no one intended to hurt you it might be easier)*

3. What, if anything, can you do about feeling angry about unfair situations? *(try to talk to someone else to prevent it from happening again)*

## Worksheet II-10B, Holding a Grudge

1. Review the definition of forgiving.

2. Pass out the worksheet and have students complete the review section at the top.

3. Directions for the rest of the worksheet ask students to circle the person in each situation who is holding a grudge.

### Answers

1. first; 2. second; 3. first; 4. first; 5. second

### Discuss

1. In situation 1, why is the boy angry at his father? *(embarrassing him over a silly nickname)*

2. Why is this hard to forgive? *(hurts his feelings, embarrasses him)*

3. In situation 2, the teacher has criticized Rick's report. How is the second person holding a grudge? *(going to do a bad job on purpose)* Who does this hurt? *(the boy)*

4. In situation 3, why was the waitress late with the water? *(busy)* How is the first boy going to get back at her? *(no tip)*

5. In situation 4, why is the first girl mad at the birthday girl? *(she didn't come to her birthday party)* Why should she forgive the girl for that? *(maybe the girl was busy and couldn't make it, maybe it wasn't personal at all)*

6. In situation 5, how do you know the boy has not forgiven the girl for getting paint on his shirt? *(he still wants to get even)*

## Worksheet II-10C, The Softball Game

1. Review the definition of forgiving.

2. Pass out the cartoon section of the worksheet to students.

3. Explain that you are going to read a story about two girls who have bad feelings for each other during a softball game. You will be asking students questions as you go.

### Answers

See the teacher's script.

# Journal Ideas: Forgiving

1. *Rate yourself:* How forgiving are you?

    0 = holds grudges

    5 = forgives easily

2. What is something that has been really hard for you to forgive and forget? Why do you think it has been so difficult for you? Are you still wrestling with this?

3. What's the quickest way to get you upset? What thing or things really trigger you to get mad or upset? (e.g., name-calling, being gossiped about, etc.)

4. How does holding a grudge make you feel inside? Do you feel like you want to get even?

5. Think of a person who has hurt you (no names, please). Describe what the person did and how it made you feel. Now describe it through *their* words—what would this person say and how would he or she describe what happened?

6. Did you and a good friend ever have a fight or argument over something that now seems silly? List your silliest arguments.

7. Sometimes death or divorce can be an extremely painful event that causes anger and hostile feelings, but it's hard to direct these feelings at someone you love. Has this been something you have ever had to deal with? How did it make you feel? How did you deal with it?

8. Have you ever done something that you thought was so awful you could not ever forgive yourself? Describe what you went through.

9. What if you did something to really hurt someone else and wanted to make things right, but the other person refused to even talk to you? What could you do? How do you know when to stop trying?

10. How far would you go to prove that you were right or to have the last word in an argument? Would you get a lawyer? A witness? A tape recorder? What?

Name _____ Date _____

# Forgiving: Pretest/Posttest

Read each situation and circle the letter of the answer that best shows forgiveness.

1. Your bus driver is angry because you made him wait. He sounds rude to you as he tells you to hurry up and get on the bus. You…

   a. Glare at him.

   b. Say, "Good morning, sorry about the wait," and sit down.

   c. Walk as slowly as you can to your seat.

   d. Explain that it's not your fault.

2. The team is picked for the Math Competition and you aren't on it, even though you are the best math problem solver in your class. Your teacher said that you weren't picked because she said you didn't have all of your homework turned in, even though you are positive you did. You…

   a. Argue about it being unfair.

   b. Make your parents come to school and explain.

   c. Complain that your teacher can't keep track of the assignments.

   d. Politely ask if she would mind checking again because you are certain that you are caught up.

3. The guinea pig got out of his cage and is missing somewhere in your house. Your brother accuses you of leaving the top off the cage even though you weren't even home. Now your parents are mad at you. You…

   a. Refuse to look for the guinea pig.

   b. Tell your brother it was somebody else's fault.

   c. Try to help find the guinea pig.

   d. Insist that you were not even at the house and get witnesses.

4. Your father changes his mind about letting you go on a weekend camp-out with some friends. Now he says you can't go because he's too tired to drive you there. You have been looking forward to this for a long time and you are very upset. You…

   a. Ask your dad calmly if you can talk about it.

   b. Tell your dad how much you need to go on this camp-out.

   c. Don't speak to him for a week.

   d. Try to talk him into changing his mind.

5. You find out that your best friend has been saying untrue mean things about you. You…

   a. Say means things about him (or her).

   b. Ask what is wrong.

   c. Stop speaking to your former friend.

   d. Demand that he (or she) stop talking about you immediately.

# II-10A. Mean, Unpleasant, Unfair

**Review**

Forgiving means l_____ b_____ feelings for someone

g_____.

**Directions:** Below are some examples of bad feelings that someone has for another person. Are these bad feelings from situations that are mean, unpleasant, or unfair? Write your answers next to each item.

1. Why can't you get these answers right? You are just plain lazy! _____

2. Mom! My socks came out pink!! _____

3. Mary said that you are always trying to show off and that's why people don't like you. _____

4. We lost the soccer game, but the other team was cheating and that's why they got so many more points than we did. _____

5. Someone was touching my model car while it was on display and now the roof is broken. _____

6. My aunt said I probably won't be so fat when I'm older. _____

7. Dad yelled at me for letting the dog get into the garbage, but it was my sister's turn to take the dog out in the morning. _____

8. You will probably get an F on your report because it's really stupid. _____

9. We were supposed to have until Friday to turn in our art projects for the contest, but the judges changed the deadline to Wednesday and now I won't be done on time. _____

10. I am invited to Jamie's birthday party at the circus, but it's the same day as my cousin's wedding and my parents say I have to go to the wedding. _____

Name _____  Date _____

# II-10B. Holding a Grudge

**Review**

Forgiving means l_____ b_____ feelings for

s_____ go.

**Directions:** If people have not let bad feelings go, they are "holding a grudge." Read each example and circle the person who is not forgiving by holding a grudge.

1. This is my son Bob. But we call him "Bobb-o." It's a little nickname we gave him when he was little. Cute, isn't it?

I hate it when he calls me that. I'll get him back.

Ha, oh come on, Dad! I'll tell them the crazy names for you!

2. Rick, you really could have done a better job on that report. It wasn't your best effort.

I was in a hurry. I'll try harder next time.

She makes me so mad! I'll do a terrible job on purpose.

3. Sorry I'm late with your water. We were very busy with a large group.

I'll just forget your tip.

Yes, it is busy today. Don't worry about it.

4. Here's an invitation to my birthday party. Can you come?

No way. You didn't come to mine.

Thanks. I'll try to come.

5. I am so sorry I spilled paint on your shirt and ruined it.

Accidents happen.

You better pay me for a new one.

# For the Teacher
## (Script for Worksheet II-10C, The Softball Game)

Follow along with the pictures as I read a story about a softball game that involves bad feelings between two girls. I will stop once in awhile to ask you questions about forgiving.

**(Picture 1)** Heather and Angela are in the same grade at school, but they are on different softball teams. They don't like each other because several years ago they got into a fight and they still have bad feelings toward each other. Whenever they see each other in school, they give each other dirty looks.

**STOP.** How long have these girls been carrying a grudge against each other? *(several years)* How do you know they haven't forgiven each other? *(still give dirty looks)*

**(Picture 2)** The two girls' teams are going to play each other in the championship. The coaches tell both girls that they both want to win, but the teams are going to play by the rules and they don't want any dirty tricks going on. The girls on each team talk to Angela and Heather about it. They ask them to try to be nice to each other. The girls agree.

**STOP.** How does their attitude affect others? *(the coaches and other players are aware of the problem)*

**(Picture 3)** Angela is up first and hits a ground ball. A girl gets it and tosses it to Heather, who plays first base. "You're out," Heather tells Angela. Angela stares at Heather. "Well, duh," she says. "What a genius you are." Heather is beginning to get mad. "I am just telling you that you are out; I'm not making fun of you." Angela sticks her tongue out at Heather.

**STOP.** Do you see problems brewing? *(tempers are beginning to flare)*

**(Picture 4)** After three outs, Heather's team is up. Heather hits a fly ball to center field and it hits Angela on the head. At first it is funny, but when Angela doesn't get up right away, Heather begins to worry. "You did that on purpose!" yells someone from Angela's team. Heather says, "I just hit the ball! I didn't aim for her! You think I can aim that accurately that I aimed for her?" She is amazed that people think she did it on purpose.

**STOP.** How do you think Heather feels about hitting Angela with the ball? *(at first not caring, but now concerned that people think she did it on purpose)*

**(Picture 5)** Angela has a huge bruise appearing on her head, and several players help to carry her off the field. Heather runs to get an ice pack for her. "It really was an accident, Angela," Heather tells her, putting the ice pack on her head, "and I really am sorry. I would never intentionally hurt anyone like that." Angela just stares at her. Heather doesn't know what Angela is thinking.

**STOP.** What do you think about Heather getting the ice pack for Angela? *(seems like a nice thing to do)* How do you think Angela is going to respond? *(angry?)*

**(Picture 6)** Angela sits up a little bit. "You mean you really didn't try to hit me with the ball?" she asks. Heather sits next to her. "Angela, I know we have not been any kind of friend to each other in years, and to tell you the truth, I can't even remember what got it all started. Can you?" Angela shakes her head and says, "It just seems like I've always been angry at you! You have new equipment, you have brothers who play softball, you have rich parents... you have everything!" Heather's mouth flies open.

**STOP.** Why do you think Angela was angry at Heather for all these years? *(jealous of what she had)*

**(Picture 7)** Heather tries not to laugh. "My stuff isn't new, I can't stand my brothers, and I don't think my parents are rich," she says. "I was always jealous of *you* because you could play so much better than I could and I wished I could be as good as you." Now it is Angela's turn to open her mouth. "Are you kidding? I never could go to the sports camps like you did. I thought you were so good because your parents paid for everything and you had brothers to teach you."

**STOP.** Why was Heather jealous of Angela? *(better player)*

**(Picture 8)** Heather laughs. "Well, I think it's time we started over with each other. You are more than welcome to come over and play softball with my creepy brothers if you think it will make you a better player. But I'd sure like for you to show me how you pitch." Angela laughs. "It's a deal. But I want to tell you something… that was quite an impressive hit you made, even if it did connect with my head. Sometime we'll have to play on the same team and make it to the finals together!"

**STOP.** What agreement do the girls come to? *(share their skills)*

Name _____ Date _____

# II-10C. The Softball Game

1.

2.

3.

4.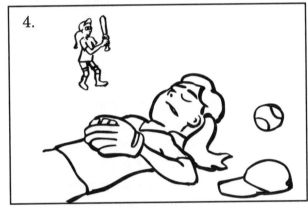

5.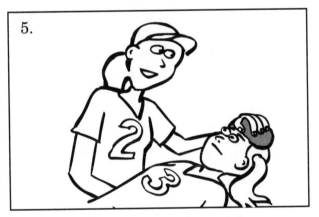

6.

7.

8.

# Lesson II-11: Recognizing Forgiving

**The contents of Lesson II-11 include:**
- Worksheet II-11A, Does This Show Forgiving?
- Worksheet II-11B, Making Things Right or Keeping it Going?
- Worksheet II-11C, You're Not Always Right!

## Worksheet II-11A, Does This Show Forgiving?

1. Pass out the worksheet to students and have them complete the review section at the top.
2. Directions for the rest of the worksheet ask students to circle yes or no to indicate whether the example shows someone forgiving.

### Answers

1. no; 2. yes; 3. yes; 4. no; 5. no; 6. no; 7. yes

### Discuss

1. In situation 1, why do you think your friend didn't pick you for the team? Would this make you have bad feelings for your friend?
2. In situation 2, would arguing with the neighbor (because you are right) help anything? Would you have bad feelings for this neighbor?
3. In situation 3, why would your friend be short-tempered? Why would you forgive your friend for treating you this way?
4. In situation 4, is your dad being unfair? Why or why not?
5. In situation 5, did your mother break a promise? Why would this be hard to forgive?
6. In situation 6, how are you holding a grudge for something that happened a year ago?
7. In situation 7, why would it be easy to still have bad feelings for this neighbor?

## Worksheet II-11B, Making Things Right or Keeping It Going?

1. Pass out the worksheet to students and have them complete the review section at the top.
2. Directions for the rest of the worksheet ask students to circle the answer that shows forgiving by making the situation right.

### Answers

1. a; 2. a; 3. b; 4. b; 5. a; 6. a

### Discuss

1. Which answer in each shows someone making things right?
2. Which answer in each shows someone keeping the bad situation going?
3. Do you think the people in each example are trying to be mean, unpleasant, or unfair on purpose?

## Worksheet II-11C, You're Not Always Right!

1. Pass out the worksheet to students and have them complete the review section at the top.
2. Directions for the rest of the worksheet ask students to discuss the situations in which someone has bad feelings for someone else, but is wrong for having these feelings. In other words, they are the ones who need to be forgiven! Questions to consider are on the worksheet.

# II-11A. Does This Show Forgiving?

**Review**

Forgiving means _____ bad

_____ for someone

_____ .

**Directions:** Read each situation and decide whether or not someone is forgiving someone else by letting the bad feelings go. Circle **yes** or **no** to show your answer.

1. When choosing sides for a team, your best friend doesn't pick you. You tell him later that you are no longer friends.  **YES**  **NO**

2. Your neighbor accuses you of trampling on her flowers. You were not even in her yard, but you do not argue with her; in fact, you offer to help her replant some new ones.  **YES**  **NO**

3. Your friend's mother has to go into the hospital for tests and now your friend has a lot of extra things to do at home. You ask him if you could borrow his bike and he snaps at you and says he doesn't have time to get it for you. It hurts your feelings, but you don't talk about it with other people and don't bother him since you realize he has a lot on his mind.  **YES**  **NO**

4. Your father is upset with you because you didn't clean out the garage. You have a paper route on the weekends and you told him that you would do it later, but he still is mad at you because you had promised you would finish it earlier. You clean out the garage, but complain loudly the whole time about how unfair he is.  **YES**  **NO**

5. Your mother had to go on a business trip for three days and she missed your very important game that she had promised she would come to. When she gets back, you remind her of the broken promise.  **YES**  **NO**

6. The principal calls your parents into the office to talk about your bad behavior on the playground and you are really mad about it. The next year when you are in a different grade, you still talk about how mean the principal was to you.  **YES**  **NO**

7. You accidentally broke a neighbor's window while playing ball and she made you pay for it. You gave her the money and an apology. Now when you see her, you tell her that you are still being careful about where you play and try to be nice to her because you understand that it could have been a dangerous situation.  **YES**  **NO**

# II-11B. Making Things Right or Keeping It Going?

**Review**

Forgiving means _____

_____ feelings for

_____ go.

**Directions:** You can show that you forgive someone by making things right with the other person. By keeping the bad feelings going, you are not going to stop the bad feelings; in fact, they will continue to grow. Circle the answer that shows forgiving by making things right.

1. Your sister teases you about getting an F on your spelling test.
   a. Stop talking about it.
   b. Remind her that she got an F on her math test.

2. The teacher tells you that your desk is messy and embarrasses you in front of the whole class.
   a. Clean up your desk.
   b. Argue with her about it.

3. A friend takes your great idea for a play and says it was his idea all along.
   a. Make sure everyone knows it was your idea.
   b. Talk to your friend privately about what happened.

4. The coach says you stepped out of bounds while playing tennis, but you didn't.
   a. Quit the team rather than play for someone so blind and unfair.
   b. Keep playing and drop the subject since it was only one time.

5. Your grandmother keeps telling you that you would look so much better if you would only cut your hair. Whenever you see her now, it seems like that's all she talks about and you are sick and tired of it.
   a. Laugh and tell her that you are trying to be stylish.
   b. Tell her to leave you and your business alone.

6. A year ago, someone in your class called you a name and it has bothered you ever since.
   a. Talk to the person privately and explain that this still bothers you.
   b. Go out of your way to find something mean to say about this person.

# II-11C. You're Not Always Right!

**Review**

Forgiving means _____ bad

_____ for _____

_____.

**Directions:** Discuss the following situations in which someone has bad feelings for someone else, but in these situations the person may be in the wrong!

1. Tony's mother asks him to clean his room and he just doesn't get around to it because he is busy doing other things. His mother finally comes into the room and throws out a lot of his stuff. Tony is very angry when he finds out that his stuff is gone. He throws a tantrum and says very mean things to his mother.
   - Why isn't this entirely his mother's fault?
   - Is Tony right or wrong for being angry?

2. Paula's teacher hands back a language paper with red marks and corrections all over it. She tells Paula that she has to recopy the assignment during recess. Paula goes home and tells her father that the teacher is being unfair to her. Paula's father goes to the school and complains about the teacher. He says the teacher did the same thing to his other daughter two years ago and it didn't help her either.
   - What are some of the problems here?
   - Is the father holding a grudge?

3. Miguel asks Antonio if he could borrow his bike, and Antonio says yes. The bike comes back with a dent, a scratch, and a flat tire, so Antonio is very upset with Miguel. Miguel insists that he did not do it, but Antonio calls him a liar and a careless person. Later Antonio finds out that his sister took his bike after Miguel brought it back and did the damage.
   - Who was wrong in this situation?
   - Who needs to be forgiving?

4. Laura really likes Ryan, but she has seen him with another girl several times. Ryan says they are just friends, but Laura doesn't believe him and starts to call them both traitors. Later Laura finds out that he was planning a surprise party for her (Laura) and the other girl's father owns a skating rink—which is where he wanted to have the party.
   - Who is wrong in this situation?
   - What could have changed things?

5. A list is posted for everyone who can go on the YMCA field trip to the zoo on Saturday, but David's name is not on the list. He asks about it and finds out that since his parents didn't sign the permission slip, he can't go. He knows for a fact, however, that he brought in a signed slip two days ago and argues with the organizers of the trip. They still don't let him go and he goes home to find out that his parents changed their minds, called the YMCA, and have different plans for David for Saturday.
   - What happened because of this change in plans?
   - What could have prevented this?

# Lesson II-12: Applying Forgiving

**The contents of Lesson II-12 include:**
- Worksheet II-12A, Forgive…
- Worksheet II-12B, …and Forget
- Quiz on Part 10: Forgiving
- Game: Holding the Grudge

## Worksheet II-12A, Forgive…

1. Pass out the worksheet to students and have them complete the review section at the top. Remind them that the opposite of forgiving is holding a grudge.
2. Directions for the rest of the worksheet ask students to complete sentences that involve hurt feelings and forgiving others.

### Discuss

1. What are some things that are hard for everyone to forgive?
2. When has someone forgiven you?
3. When have you hurt someone else's feelings?

## Worksheet II-12B, …and Forget

1. Pass out the worksheet to students and have them complete the review section at the top.
2. Directions for the rest of the worksheet ask students to come up with specific ways they can "forget" about something that has been forgiven. It might be easier if they think of a specific incident or problem that they got over and forgave.

### Discuss

1. How does it help to mark the "end" of your anger by an action, such as destroying a piece of paper?
2. If you say you have forgiven someone for something, why shouldn't you keep talking about it or bringing it back up again?
3. Are there some things that are too important to just be forgotten? What are some examples of things that you might need to take action on before you forget about it? *(abuse, cruelty, personal problems, etc.)*

## Quiz on Part 10: Forgiving

This quiz can be used as a follow-up for the lessons in Part 10.

### Answers

1. *(definition)* Forgiving means letting bad feelings for someone go.
2. *(example)* a, d
3. *(applying)* Answers will vary.

## Game: Holding the Grudge

Directions and sample cards for this game are at the end of this lesson.

# II-12A. Forgive...

**Review**

Forgiving means _____

_____.

The opposite of forgiving is _____.

**Directions:** Complete the following sentences as they apply to you. Be as honest as you can!

1. I find it hard to forgive when someone _____

_____

2. When I am angry at someone, I _____

_____

3. When someone has wronged me, it makes me _____

_____

4. One time I hurt someone's feelings was when I _____

_____

5. Someone forgave me one time when I _____

_____

6. I carry a grudge when _____

_____

7. When things are not right between me and a friend or family member, I _____

_____

8. The hardest thing for me to forgive is _____

_____

9. It is easy for me to forgive _____

_____

10. It is hard for me to forgive _____

_____

# II-12B. ...and Forget

**Review**

Forgiving means _____

_____.

The opposite of forgiving is _____.

**Directions:** Once you have decided to forgive someone, what are some ways you can "forget" about it? Write as many ways as you can. Three are given to help you get started.

1. _Write down what you are mad about on a piece of paper, then burn it._
2. _Stop talking about it with all of your friends._
3. _Don't embarrass the person by bringing up the situation again._
4. _____

   _____
5. _____

   _____
6. _____

   _____
7. _____

   _____
8. _____

   _____
9. _____

   _____
10. _____

   _____

# Quiz on Part 10: Forgiving

1. What is forgiving?_____

_____

2. Which examples show forgiving?

3. A good friend of yours thinks you took something of hers/his when you were over to visit and has told a lot of people that you are a thief. Later, the missing item turns up in the basement of her/his house. You are very angry at your friend for lying about you and it is embarrassing when people look at you as though you are dishonest. What will you do?

_____

_____

_____

_____

_____

# Game for Forgiving: Holding the Grudge

**Materials:**
    You need 22 cards (10 pairs, 1 Grudge card, 1 Forgive and Forget card). Sample cards are provided.

**Players:** 3–6

**Objective:** To get rid of all your cards and not be the last one holding the "Grudge" card

**How to Play:**

1. Shuffle all of the cards and deal 5 to each player.

2. The remaining cards stay in a pile in the middle.

3. Players check to see if they are holding a matched pair in their hand. (*Hint*: Check for the symbols.) If they have a pair, they should lay both cards down as a set and select enough cards so that they still have 5 in their hand.

4. Dealer goes first. Hold up a card and read it (for example: "Someone stepped on your foot and said 'sorry' as they went by.") Then say: "Who has my match?"

5. The person with the matching card (*hint*: check the symbol) reads his/her card: "You say, 'No problem.'" Give it to the dealer.

6. The dealer sets both cards down in front, earning 1 point. Since the dealer got a match, he or she takes a new card from the center but his or her play has ended until it is his or her turn again.

7. Play goes to the person on the dealer's left and continues until it gets back to the dealer again.

8. When play reaches the dealer again, the dealer instructs everyone to take a card they don't want and pass it quickly to the person on their right. This is the opportunity for whoever is holding the "Grudge" card to slip it to the next person. Of course, it will be impossible to keep a straight face if you are the giver or the receiver of the "Grudge" card, but that's part of the fun.

9. If a player is holding the "Forgive and Forget" card, he or she should hang on to it because it is worth an extra point.

10. When a player is out of cards, he or she can select one from the middle until all of the cards in the middle are gone. Then that player is finished.

11. Play continues until all of the cards in the middle are gone and all matches have been made. There should be two cards left that are unmatched: the "Grudge" card and the "Forgive and Forget" card.

12. Players total up their points—one point for each matched set, one point for the "Forgive and Forget" card, and one lost point for having the "Grudge" card.

© 2002 by The Center for Applied Research in Education

You are mad because your mother overslept and everyone is late for school or work.
● 1

You forgive your mother by saying, "We will help each other get ready this morning."
● 2

You are upset because your friend called you "chubby."
■ 1

You talk to your friend about how it feels to be called names, and he says he is sorry.
■ 2

Someone pushes you in a crowded store and steps on your foot, then says "excuse me."
▲ 1

You say, "No problem, I know it is crowded in here."
▲ 2

Your sister spills ink all over your math book and is worried that you will hit her.
♥ 1

You tell your sister that she can help you clean it up and you won't be mad.
♥ 2

A long time ago, your neighbor yelled at you for making too much noise outside.
♣ 1

You try hard to be friendly to the crabby neighbor.
♣ 2

Your friend took your homework and copied it without telling you.
★ 1

You tell your friend that you will be happy to help him if he doesn't know how to do his work.
★ 2

You are mad because you aren't picked for the spelling bee.

◆ 1

You cheer for your friends who were picked for the spelling bee.

◆ 2

Your teacher loses your homework and gives you a D on the assignment.

▶ 1

You calmly talk to your teacher and don't get upset while she looks for your assignment on her messy desk.

▶ 2

Your mother says she will eat lunch with you at school, but she doesn't make it to school.

✖ 1

You plan to eat together on a different day.

✖ 2

Your best friend says she can't come over because she is going to a different friend's house.

➤ 1

You realize that people can have other friends, so you don't get upset about it.

➤ 2

THE GRUDGE

FORGIVE and FORGET

# Lesson II-13: Defining Understanding Others

**The contents of Lesson II-13 include:**

- Journal Ideas
- Pre-/posttest on understanding others
- Worksheet II-13A, Same and Different
- Worksheet II-13B, Life Experiences
- Worksheet II-13C, My Way

## Journal Ideas

Have students select the ideas they would like to write about. Be sure to have them share their entries with each other and with the class.

## Pre-/Posttest

Pass out the pre-/posttest to students and explain that they are to read the situations and circle the response that best shows understanding of others.

### Answers

1. b; 2. d; 3. a; 4. d; 5. c

## Worksheet II-13A Same and Different

1. Write the definition of *understanding others* on the board or other place where students can easily see it. "Understanding others means knowing how someone else would feel or act."

2. Briefly discuss what it means to know how someone else would feel or act. Basically this is putting yourself in their place and seeing a situation through another person's eyes and experience. For this lesson, emphasize the idea of feeling and taking action that might be different from your own.

3. Pass out the worksheet to students and have them complete the review section at the top. For the rest of the worksheet, they are to read the examples and write how the two people in each are the same and how they are different.

### Answers

1. *same:* both like sports, both like to read; *different:* from different places, read different types of material

2. *same:* both have collections, both are interested in cars; *different:* their interests are different

3. *same:* both are African-Americans, live with one parent; *different:* live in different types of housing, one is in a wheelchair

### Discuss

1. If you took any two people and compared them, would you find things in common?

2. Do people have to be exactly alike or interested in exactly the same things to get along or be friends?

3. What are some ways that two people can be interested in the same thing, but show their interest in different ways? *(for example, collecting cars vs. building cars; reading about horses vs. riding horses)*

# Worksheet II-13B, Life Experiences

1. Review the definition of understanding others.

2. Pass out the worksheet to students and have them complete the review section at the top.

3. Read and discuss the seven examples of life experiences that are the choices to match on the rest of the worksheet. Each is an example of something that can and does deeply affect how a person views things.

4. On the rest of the worksheet, students are to match the life experience with the example of how it might affect someone.

### Answers

1. d (his attitude is probably because he feels insecure and shy about moving); 2. h (this person has to deal with asthma and its restrictions); 3. b (this girl is dealing with separated parents and it is a sensitive issue for her); 4. e (Mark is beginning to get interested in girls rather than in playing on a playground); 5. f (the kids are making Zelda feel left out); 6. a (the death of her father has caused many changes for her); 7. g (surgery has made Alfred lose his status on the team); 8. c (Debbie has some catching up to do because of her illness)

### Discuss

1. Have you ever had to deal with any of these problems or situations? How did it affect the way you felt about something?

2. Did passing of time help heal some of these issues for you? Did things get better because you and people around you got used to how things became?

3. Do you think someone who has experienced something like the examples given would be understanding of someone else going through the same problem?

4. Have you run into people who feel terribly sorry for themselves? Have you found people who have dealt with issues like these and have overcome them?

# Worksheet II-13C, My Way

1. Review the definition of understanding others.

2. Pass out the cartoon section of the worksheet.

3. Explain that you are going to read a story about a girl who sees things from only her point of view. As you read, you will stop and ask questions about seeing these events from another person's point of view.

### Answers

See the teacher's script.

# Journal Ideas: Understanding Others

1. How understanding of other people are you? *Rate yourself:* 0 (not understanding at all of another's point of view) to 5 (very understanding).

   0   1   2   3   4   5

2. Who would you like to switch places with for a month? Think about that person's lifestyle, friends, job, possessions, and so on. Why would you like to be that person? Do you think that person would like some things about your life? What?

3. Who would you least like to switch lives with for a month? What would you dislike about that person's life?

4. What movies or books have you read where the people or characters switch places or lives? What did they conclude at the end?

5. List 5 friends or people you know well. For each one, write ways you are like that person and then ways you are different from that person. Do you have common interests? Common relatives? Do you have different interests? Different abilities?

6. Sometimes having a very good or a very bad experience can help you understand someone else who also goes through a similar experience. What are some unpleasant or bad life experiences you have had? These might include: death of a relative or pet; extended illness; moving; a bad experience at school.

7. On the other hand, what are really good experiences you have had in your life? These might include: winning something; taking a trip; owning something expensive or important to you.

8. Do you know of anyone in your close family who is physically or mentally challenged? How do you see that affecting his or her life and the life of the family?

9. Have you ever visited a foreign country? What was it like? If you could go to a different country to live for a year, what country would you pick and why?

10. When you are with another person you know very well (friend, relative), how much time do you think you spend listening to that person, not talking? How about when you are with someone you don't know very well? Are you a talker or a listener?

Name _____ Date _____

# Understanding Others: Pretest/Posttest

Read each situation. Choose the response that best shows understanding others.

1. Grandma has come to visit for a week and she always turns the TV up very loud.
   a. Grandma is very annoying and only thinks about herself.
   b. Grandma is hard of hearing and can't hear the TV.
   c. Grandma is trying to drown out the noise of others around her.
   d. Grandma likes loud TV.

2. Whenever Tommy is asked to read out loud in school, he misses a lot of really easy words, repeats the words, and stops and gives up.
   a. Tommy is stupid because he can't read.
   b. Tommy doesn't pay attention to what he is doing.
   c. Tommy can't see the words in the book.
   d. Tommy does not know how to read very well and is embarrassed.

3. Mary spends weekends with her father and the rest of the week with her mother. She has two sets of keys and two sets of clothes, depending on where she is.
   a. Mary's parents are separated and she spends time with both of them.
   b. Mary hates her father.
   c. Mary's family is very rich and they have two houses.
   d. Mary has lots of keys.

4. You are anxiously awaiting a package in the mail for your birthday from your aunt. She said she would send it to you this week. It's past your birthday, and the package still hasn't arrived.
   a. Your aunt didn't care enough to send it on time.
   b. Your aunt forgot your birthday.
   c. Your aunt didn't have enough money to mail the package.
   d. Your aunt probably was busy and didn't get it to the post office right away.

5. Your little brother is supposed to go to the doctor for a check-up. He is crying and screaming, saying that he doesn't want to go. You tell him that you have been to the doctor many times and there is nothing to be afraid of.
   a. Your little brother wants to play instead.
   b. The doctor looks like a mean man.
   c. Your little brother is afraid he might get a shot.
   d. Your little brother is just being silly.

# II-13A. Same and Different

**Review**

Understanding others means knowing how s_____ else would

f_____ or a_____.

**Directions:** How are the people in each example the same? How are they different?

## Example 1

- Tomás is from Mexico, loves to play baseball, and likes to read all kinds of books.
- Sandy is from California, is really good at volleyball, and reads only books about horses.

Same: _____

_____

Different: _____

_____

## Example 2

- Jeff skates, likes rock music, and has a collection of model cars.
- Pete is interested in gathering rocks from all over the country, and is helping his father restore an old car.

Same: _____

_____

Different: _____

_____

## Example 3

- Annalee is an African-American who is very tall, loves the computer, and lives with her mother in a big house at the beach.
- Charmane is an African-American who is in a wheelchair and lives in an apartment in Chicago with her father.

Same: _____

_____

Different: _____

_____

# II-13B. Life Experiences

**Review**

Understanding others means k_____ how someone e_____

would f_____ or a_____.

**Directions:** Match the life experience that might explain how someone feels in the situations below. Write the appropriate letter on the line in front of each experience.

| | | | |
|---|---|---|---|
| **a. death** | **b. divorce** | **c. illness** | **d. moving** |
| **e. growing up** | **f. handicap** | **g. surgery** | **h. asthma** |

_____ 1. Tommy is new in your school and always talks about how good things were in the place where he used to live. Everything was bigger and better there.

_____ 2. Alisha can't run so fast or so hard as the other kids because she will get out of breath and will have to use her inhaler. When the kids ask her to run with them, she says no.

_____ 3. Darla doesn't want to have anything to do with the mother-and-daughter tea at church. She acts as though it is really silly and it would be boring to go to. You know that she lives with her father most of the time.

_____ 4. Timmy wants his older cousin Mark to play on the swingset with him, but Mark says he would rather go to the mall with some girls in his class. Timmy thinks Mark is crazy.

_____ 5. The class is going on a field trip to the zoo. Zelda is in a wheelchair and has to make sure she can get around. Some of the kids act as though they don't want Zelda to come because it would be harder for them to get around.

_____ 6. Janelle and her sisters used to live in a big house, but after her father died, they had to move to a smaller house. Janelle never wants anyone else to come see her house because she thinks it's not very nice.

_____ 7. Alfred used to be the best runner on the track team, but he injured his knee and had to have an operation. While it was healing, someone else became the top runner. Now Alfred seems to have a really bad attitude about the coach and the team.

_____ 8. Debbie is far behind the rest of the class in reading because she was sick for several weeks at the beginning of the year and didn't get to school very much. She doesn't like to read in the class and always acts up if the teacher wants her to read.

# For the Teacher (Script for Worksheet II-13C, My Way)

Take a look at the pictures on your worksheet while I read a story about a girl named Jamie who goes through a day seeing things only her way, from her perspective. I will stop after each picture to ask you some questions.

**(Picture 1)** Jamie is getting ready for school when she realizes that she has forgotten to collect some leaves that she needs for a school science project. She notices that her older sister, Carla, has some leaves on her desk, so she takes them and puts them in her backpack. "Where are you going with my leaves?" Carla asks her. "I need those for decorations for our party at school." Jamie waves goodbye from the door. "It's easy to get leaves, Carla—just look outside. They are all over."

**STOP.** What is Jamie's point of view about the leaves? *(anyone can use them; there are plenty outside)* What is Carla's point of view? *(she needs them)* Is Jamie seeing things from Carla's perspective? *(no)*

**(Picture 2)** Jamie gets to school and is talking to a friend while the teacher asks for a show of hands for students to choose what they want for lunch. When it is lunch time, the count doesn't come out right and the cafeteria lady is upset with Jamie's teacher. Jamie smiles at her teacher as she goes out for recess.

**STOP.** What is Jamie's view on the lunch count? *(it's not important)* How about her teacher's view? *(it is important)*

**(Picture 3)** On the playground, a stray black-and-white dog comes up to the kids and tries to chase after the ball. "Don't go near that dog!" yells the playground supervisor. Jamie goes up to the dog anyway. "This dog is friendly. He won't hurt anybody." She bends down and tries to pet him.

**STOP.** Why do you think the playground supervisor doesn't want anyone touching the dog? *(it might bite someone)*

**(Picture 4)** After school, Jamie and her friends go to the park to play kickball. One of her friends, Sammie, brings along her cousin who is handicapped. Jamie tries to be nice to the girl, so she goes up to her and says, "It's too bad you can't play, but we really need somebody to hold our books. Would you like to do that?" The girl says, "No, thank you. I always play on our team at home, and I would like to play."

**STOP.** What opinion does Jamie have about the handicapped girl? *(the girl cannot play)* What does the handicapped girl intend to do? *(play kickball)*

**(Picture 5)** When Jamie gets home, she sits by the phone waiting for her friend Mona to call. She waits and waits but the phone does not ring. Jamie calls her other friend Lindsay to tell her that Mona is really a fickle friend and does not keep her promises. Lindsay says she has just seen Mona and she was complaining that they were having phone problems and she couldn't make her calls.

**STOP.** What does Jamie think is going on with Mona? *(she's not a true friend, and doesn't keep promises)* What is the truth? *(Mona's phone is out of order)*

**(Picture 6)** Finally, it is evening and time to watch TV. Jamie turns on the cartoons that she always likes to watch, but then her dad comes into the room and changes the channel to the news without even asking her! "Hey!" Jamie says, "I was watching that program!" Her dad says, "Well, maybe you don't want to see your dad on TV, but I was interviewed in town today and there I am!" He points to the TV.

**STOP.** What is Jamie's feeling about watching TV? *(she wants to watch cartoons)* What is her dad's interest in watching the TV? *(he's being interviewed on the news)*

**(Picture 7)** Bedtime. It is Friday night, so the family stays up later than usual and plays some card games at the table. Her mom looks at the clock. "It's nearly midnight!" she says. "It's really late." Jamie laughs. "Mom," she says, "it's early! There's no school tomorrow. I want to stay up until 2 A.M. to watch monster movies!"

**STOP.** Is it early or late? *(depends)*

# II-13C. My Way

**1.**

**2.**

**3.**

**4.**

**5.**

**6.**

**7.**

# Lesson II-14: Recognizing Understanding Others

**The contents of Lesson II-14 include:**
- Worksheet II-14A, Which One Is Understanding?
- Worksheet II-14B, This Is NOT Understanding
- Worksheet II-14C, What Will Happen?

## Worksheet II-14A, Which One Is Understanding?

1. Pass out the worksheet to students and have them complete the review section at the top.
2. Directions for the rest of the worksheet ask students to circle the person in each example who is showing understanding of others.

**Answers**

1. second; 2. first; 3. second; 4. first; 5. first

**Discuss**

1. What is the mother's point of view about the clothes in situation 1? *(she thinks it's fine; it's a good color)* Why might the boy not want to wear it? *(it's very unusual)*
2. In situation 2, how is the second person not showing understanding? *(giving no help)*
3. In situation 3, what do you think of the first person's comments? Have you heard people say that to other people?
4. In situation 4, what is the second person really telling the boy? *(that they are both lousy painters)*
5. In situation 5, how did the first person show understanding? *(he noticed the good things the girl did in the game)*

## Worksheet II-14B, This Is NOT Understanding

1. Pass out the worksheet to students and have them complete the review section at the top.
2. Directions for the rest of the worksheet ask students to read about the people who are not understanding another person and to write the thoughts of the person who is misunderstood.

**Answers**

(Will vary) 1. I don't have any money. How can I go with them?; 2. It's hard for me to do math. If I use my fingers I can get the right answer.; 3. There are too many steps for me.; 4. I miss my mother and it's not the same making a card for my aunt.; 5. Now, where am I going to sit? I'm left out.

**Discuss**

1. These are examples of people who are not demonstrating understanding how another person thinks, feels, or acts. How could you rewrite what each person is saying to show that they are understanding of the other person?
2. Have you been in situations or seen others in similar situations to these? What happened?

# Worksheet II-14C, What Will Happen?

1. Pass out the worksheet to students and have them complete the review section at the top.

2. Directions for the rest of the worksheet ask students to draw a picture to show what the people in the examples might do next in these situations. Each situation shows a person who is under some kind of pressure or has had an experience that would affect what he or she does next.

**Answers**

(May vary) 1. arguing with mom; 2. feeling sad, crying; 3. getting angry; 4. sad, crying

**Discuss**

1. In situation 1, even if David's mother is understanding, can she change her situation? What are ways that this could be worked out? *(Mom could make sure he is not babysitting the next week; friends could come over to David's house instead)*

2. In situation 2, what is a kinder response that someone could have had to Barbara? *(sorry you were sick, we'll do it next month)*

3. In situation 3, would you expect Jeff's friends to skip the roller coaster ride and stay with him? *(no)* How does Jeff feel? *(left out, embarrassed)* What could the friends say to Jeff? *(we'll find other rides we can all go on)*

4. In situation 4, is it wrong for Karin to feel sad about her dog dying? *(no, very normal)* Do you think her friends are showing understanding for Karin's feelings? *(no)* What do you think should happen? *(maybe the friends could say they are sorry for Karin, then try to distract her)*

# II-14A. Which One Is Understanding?

**Review**

Understanding others means _____ how someone _____

would _____ or _____.

**Directions:** Which person is showing that he or she is trying to understand how someone else would feel or act? Circle your answer.

1.
*What? I can't wear that!*
*Why not? It's a good color.*
*Maybe it's not the best choice and you should try to find something else.*

2.
*I'm lost— I can't find North Avenue.*
*Just go that way for two blocks. You'll find it.*
*Boy, are you lost!*

3.
*I really don't feel like going to the party tonight. My mom is pretty sick.*
*Oh, cheer up! A party will make you feel better. Be happy!*
*I would be happy to do something else with you instead if you want to skip it.*

4.
*Is that your painting? It looks like a kindergartener did it! Ha, Ha!*
*Don't let her bother you. I think your painting is just fine.*
*I am a lousy painter, too.*

5.
*Thanks to you, we lost the game.*
*You had some good shots and made a lot of points for our team.*
*BUMMER. Now our season is over.*

# II-14B. This Is NOT Understanding

**Review**

Understanding others means _____ how someone else would

_____ or _____.

**Directions:** These people are not showing understanding of how others would feel or act. Write what you think each person is thinking. You may use another sheet of paper for your answers if you prefer.

1. Hey, we're going to the movies and out to eat. Get $20 and come with us. Hurry, we're all going.

2. Why are you using your fingers to do math? Don't you have those facts memorized yet?

3. Hurry, Grandpa, we want to get to the top before the zoo closes.

4. We're making cards for Mother's Day for our moms. You can make one for your aunt, I guess, since your mom died.

5. Oh, there aren't enough seats for everybody. Can you find somewhere else to sit?

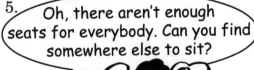

Name _____ Date _____

# II-14C. What Will Happen?

**Review**

Understanding others means _____ how someone else would

_____ or _____.

**Directions:** Once you understand someone else, you might be able to predict how he or she would act in a certain situation. On another sheet of paper, draw a picture that shows what these people might do next in each situation.

1. David has been babysitting for his crabby little sister all morning while his mother went to work. He can't wait for her to come home so he can go out with his friends to the movies. The phone rings and his mother tells him that she has to work overtime so she won't be home for another three hours.

2. Barbara was the only one in her class who didn't get a special award for reading 10 books last month. She had been sick with the flu and her parents were away so she didn't make it to the library to get the books she wanted to read. One of the other kids in the class comes up to her and says, "You are the only one who didn't read ten books. Now we can't have a class pizza party."

3. Jeff wants to ride the roller coaster at the amusement park but he isn't tall enough. Even though he is the same age as his friends, the ride operator won't let him go on the ride because it is a rule. Jeff's friends wave goodbye and say they will meet him after the ride is over.

4. Karin's dog, that her family has had for her whole life, finally had to be euthanized. She loved her dog and can't even remember a day when they didn't have Fluffy. She went out with her friends who said, "Oh, just get another dog."

# Lesson II-15: Applying Understanding Others

**The contents of Lesson II-15 include:**

- Worksheet II-15A, Getting to Know You
- Worksheet II-15B, Tell Me About Yourself
- Quiz on Part 11: Understanding Others
- Game: Walk in My Shoes

## Worksheet II-15A, Getting to Know You

1. Pass out the worksheet to students and have them complete the review section at the top. Remind them that the opposite of understanding others is being self-centered. Discuss what this means, how it places yourself first instead of trying to understand the point of view of someone else.

2. Directions for the rest of the worksheet ask students to complete an interview project in which they select five people who fit the descriptions given. They will ask the interviewees several questions after making predictions as to what they think the answers will be. Then they will compare their predictions with the actual answers.

### Discuss

1. How closely did your predicted answers and actual answers match?

2. Do you think it is harder or easier to understand people who are about your own age?

3. What are some ways that you can learn to understand other people? What types of questions might help you with this?

## Worksheet II-15B, Tell Me About Yourself

1. Pass out the worksheet to students and have them complete the review section at the top.

2. Directions for the rest of the worksheet involve having students pair up and listen to each other talk for 3 minutes, then try to remember as much as they can of what the person said.

### Discuss

1. Did you find out some interesting things about the person you listened to? What?

2. Did it seem like the 3 minutes were long or short?

3. Was it difficult to keep yourself from interrupting the other person?

## Quiz on Part 11: Understanding Others

This quiz can be used as a follow-up activity for the lessons in Part 11.

### Answers

1. *(definition)* Understanding others means knowing how someone else would feel or act.

2. *(examples)* a, b, c

3. *(applying)* Answers will vary.

## Game: Walk in My Shoes

Directions, game pieces, and gameboard are given at the end of this lesson.

# II-15A. Getting to Know You

**Review**

Understanding others means _____

_____ .

The opposite of understanding others is being _____ .

**Directions:** Choose 5 people who fit the descriptions below. Think about what you already know about them, then predict what you think their answers will be to the questions. Then interview each of them to find out what they think, how they feel, and what they would do in each situation. How well do you really know and understand them?

*Person 1:* Choose a person (a boy if you are a boy; a girl if you are a girl) who is about your own age.

_____

*Person 2:* Choose an adult who lives in your house.

_____

*Person 3:* Choose an older adult, such as a grandparent.

_____

*Person 4:* Choose a young child, someone under the age of 5.

_____

*Person 5:* Choose a person you know very little about.

_____

**Questions** (First predict, then interview.)

1. What is your favorite game?
2. What is your favorite food?
3. What is something that frightens you?
4. What is something that you really like to do?
5. What makes you laugh?
6. What is something that is hard for you to do?
7. What is something that you are proud of?
8. What would you really like to accomplish?
9. What hurts your feelings?
10. What is the nicest thing someone else said about you?

Name _____ Date _____

# II-15B. Tell Me About Yourself

**Review**

Understanding others means _____

_____.

The opposite of understanding others is being _____.

**Directions:** Pair students with a partner (this could be someone in the class or someone from another class so that participants don't know each other). Each person in the pair talks for 3 minutes about herself or himself while the other listens without interrupting. Then they switch. When finished, have students take turns telling the class things that they learned about their partners.

**Did you find out:**

- What kind of clothes he/she likes to wears?
- What is the last book he/she read?
- What subject in class is hard/easy/fun/dull?
- Who is his/her best friend?
- What is his/her favorite game?
- If he/she is right- or left-handed?
- What he/she had for breakfast?
- What is his/her favorite food?
- When his/her birthday is and how old he/she is?
- How many people are in his/her family?
- What his/her favorite music groups are?

# Quiz on Part 11: Understanding Others

1. What is meant by understanding others?

_____

_____

2. Circle each person below who is showing that he or she understands someone else.

3. There is a new kid in your neighborhood, and no one really knows anything about him. You ask him to come and play baseball several times, but he says he can't. What do you think is going on? What could you do to find out? Would you keep trying to make friends with him? How?

_____

_____

_____

_____

_____

_____

# Game for Understanding Others: Walk in My Shoes

**Objective:** To lay down the most cards (having the least left at the end of the game) when a certain characteristic is described

**Players:** 2–6

**Materials:**

- 1 die
- shoe markers (see samples)
- gameboard (see sample)
- 10 sets of Category Cards (see samples)
  Category 1 (Who You Are) 6 cards     Category 6 (Skills) 6 cards
  Category 2 (What You Look Like) 12 cards     Category 7 (Family) 6 cards
  Category 3 (Physical Abilities) 6 cards     Category 8 (Money) 6 cards
  Category 4 (School Abilities) 6 cards     Category 9 (Personality) 6 cards
  Category 5 (Hobbies) 6 cards     Category 10 (Career) 10 cards
- 10 Description Cards (see samples)
  These cards describe the outcomes of each category as determined by the roll of the die:
  If a 1 is rolled, follow option A.
  If a 2 is rolled, follow option B.
  If a 3 is rolled, follow option C.
  If a 4 is rolled, follow option D.
  If a 5 is rolled, follow option E.
  If a 6 is rolled, the player chooses whichever option he/she wants.

**How to Play:**

1. The description cards are put in order upside down (they follow the categories 1–10 in order).
2. Each player randomly takes one characteristic card from each of the 10 categories. These characteristics now define him or her (e.g., I am a young boy with red hair, a good runner, a C student, I like skateboarding, can drive a car, have one sister, have $100, am generous, and am a fashion designer.). Players can make or find small "shoes" to use as their markers as play continues along the gameboard. They can also draw shoes to put in front of them with their characteristic cards. (Players will enjoy designing shoes to use for this game.)
3. Play begins with Category 1 and continues through the 10 areas. Players take turns rolling the die and reading the corresponding directions. All players lay down appropriate cards.
4. The game ends when Category 10 is completed. Players count their cards. The player who holds the least cards is the winner.

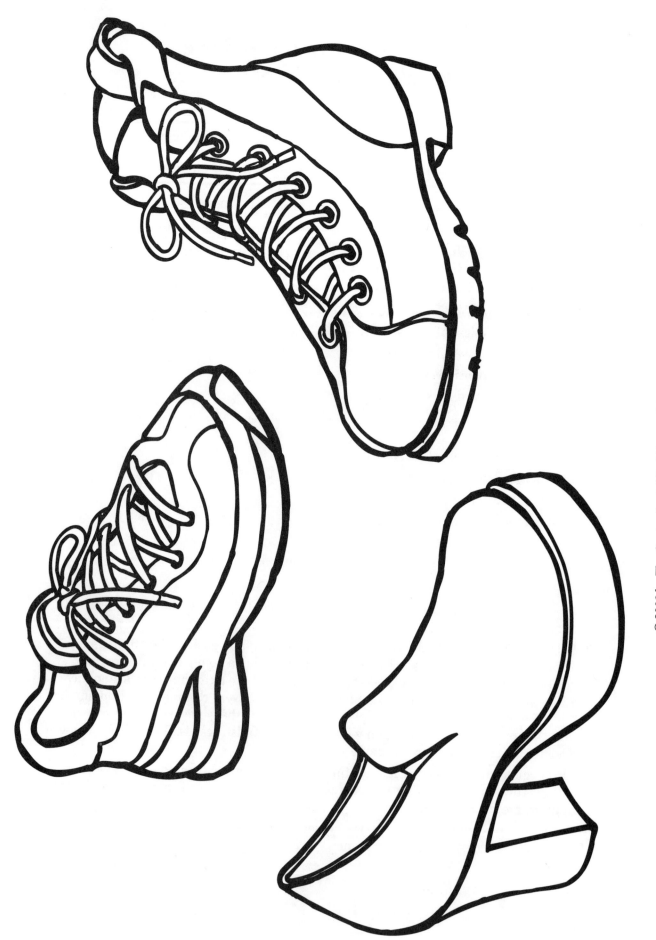

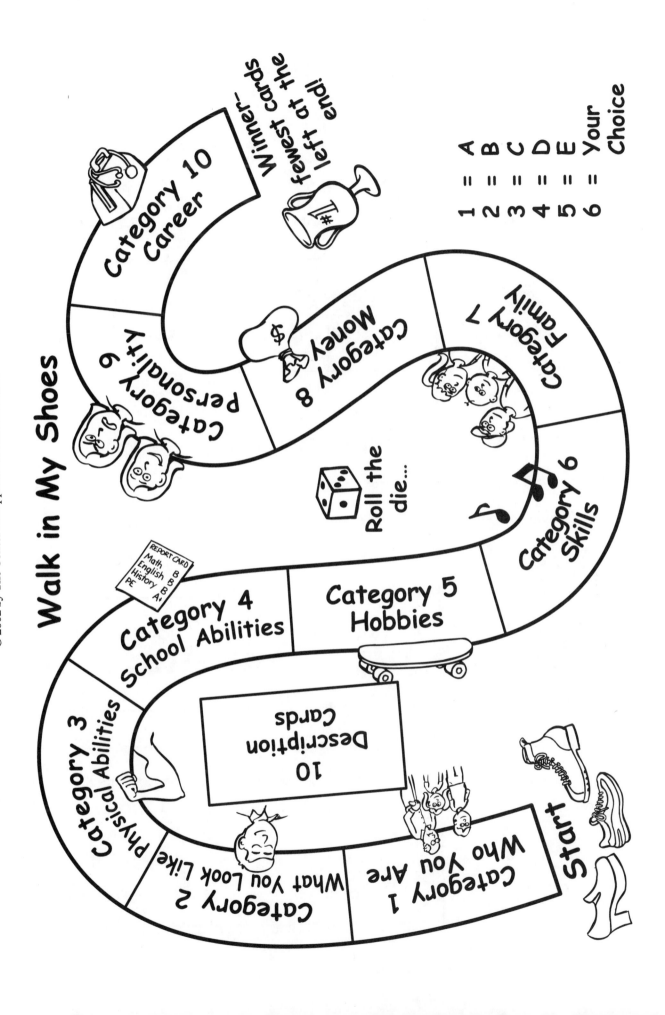

© 2002 by The Center for Applied Research in Education

Walk in My Shoes

| (Category 1) YOUNG BOY | (Category 1) YOUNG GIRL | (Category 1) ADULT MAN |
|---|---|---|
| (Category 1) ADULT WOMAN | (Category 1) OLD MAN | (Category 1) OLD WOMAN |
| (Category 2) RED HAIR | (Category 2) TALL | (Category 2) DARK CURLY HAIR |
| (Category 2) STRAIGHT BROWN HAIR | (Category 2) STRAIGHT RED HAIR | (Category 2) SHORT |
| (Category 2) FAT | (Category 2) MEDIUM BUILD | (Category 2) THIN |
| (Category 2) FRECKLES | (Category 2) A SCAR | (Category 2) BRACES |
| (Category 3) GOOD RUNNER | (Category 3) SLOW RUNNER | (Category 3) GOOD AT TENNIS |
| (Category 3) BLIND | (Category 3) DEAF | (Category 3) IN A WHEELCHAIR |

| (Category 4) | (Category 4) | (Category 4) |
|---|---|---|
| STRAIGHT A's | A's AND B's | C's |
| (Category 4) | (Category 4) | (Category 4) |
| SOMETIMES AN F | C's AND D's | A's, B's, C's |
| (Category 5) | (Category 5) | (Category 5) |
| SKATEBOARDING | SWIMMING | SKIING |
| (Category 5) | (Category 5) | (Category 5) |
| COLLECTING STAMPS | COLLECTING DOLLS | BASEBALL |
| (Category 6) | (Category 6) | (Category 6) |
| CAN DRIVE A CAR | GOOD READER | CAN BUILD THINGS |
| (Category 6) | (Category 6) | (Category 6) |
| CAN COOK | GOOD ATHLETE | CAN SING |
| (Category 7) | (Category 7) | (Category 7) |
| NO BROTHERS OR SISTERS | 1 SISTER | 3 SISTERS |
| (Category 7) | (Category 7) | (Category 7) |
| 1 OLDER BROTHER | A BABY BROTHER | 10 SIBLINGS |

| (Category 8) | (Category 8) | (Category 8) |
|---|---|---|
| **HAVE $1** | **HAVE $10** | **HAVE $100** |
| (Category 8) | (Category 8) | (Category 8) |
| **HAVE $1,000** | **HAVE $10,000** | **HAVE $1,000,000** |
| (Category 9) | (Category 9) | (Category 9) |
| **GENEROUS** | **RESPONSIBLE** | **FORGIVING** |
| (Category 9) | (Category 9) | (Category 9) |
| **SHOWS EFFORT** | **HONEST** | **HUMBLE** |
| (Category 10) | (Category 10) | (Category 10) |
| **A COMPUTER PROGRAMMER** | **A FIREFIGHTER** | **A GREETER AT A STORE** |
| (Category 10) | (Category 10) | (Category 10) |
| **VICE PRESIDENT** | **HOMEMAKER** | **TEACHER** |
| (Category 10) | (Category 10) | (Category 10) |
| **FASHION DESIGNER** | **WINDOW WASHER** | **RACE CAR DRIVER** |
| (Category 10) | | |
| **VETERINARIAN** | | |

**Moving Along the Board:**

The question reader moves a small pair of shoes to the first stop (Who you are). He/she selects a describing card that matches that color and reads the instructions.

## Category 1 Description Cards:

A. If you are male, put down your card.

B. If you are not young, but down your card.

C. If you are an adult or old woman, put down your card.

D. If you are an adult, put down your card.

E. Put down your card unless you are a young boy.

## Category 2 Description Cards:

A. If you have red hair, put down your card.

B. If you have braces or freckles, put down your card.

C. If you are short or thin, put down your card.

D. If you have straight hair, put down your card.

E. Put down your card unless you have braces.

## Category 3 Description Cards:

A. If you are a runner, put down your card.

B. If you are blind or deaf, put down your card.

C. If you are in a wheelchair, put down your card.

D. If you run or play tennis, put down your card.

E. Put down your card unless you are a slow runner.

## Category 4 Description Cards:

A. If you get straight A's, put down your card.

B. If you get C's or above, put down your card.

C. If you sometimes get an F, put down your card.

D. If you get lower than C's, put down your card.

E. Put down your card unless you get straight A's.

## Category 5 Description Cards:

A. If your hobby is a sport, put down your card.

B. If your hobby is collecting something, put down your card.

C. If your hobby is collecting dolls, put down your card.

D. If your hobby is baseball, put down your card.

E. Put down your card unless you collect stamps.

## Category 6 Description Cards:

A. If you can drive, read, or cook, put down your card.

B. If you can build or sing, put down your card.

C. If you are a good athlete, put down your card.

D. If you can read or sing, put down your card.

E. Put down your card unless you are a good athlete.

## Category 7 Description Cards:

A. If you have any sisters, put down your card.
B. If you have any brothers, put down your card.
C. If you have more than one sibling, put down your card.
D. If you have only sisters, put down your card.
E. Put down your card unless you have a baby brother.

## Category 8 Description Cards:

A. If you have more than $100, put down your card.
B. If you have $100 or less, put down your card.
C. If you have $1,000,000, put down your card.
D. If you have $1, put down your card.
E. Put down your card unless you have $10,000.

## Category 9 Description Cards:

A. If you are honest or humble, put down your card.
B. If you are generous or forgiving, put down your card.
C. If you are responsible or show effort, put down your card.
D. If you are humble or generous, put down your card.
E. Put down your card unless you are humble.

## Category 10 Description Cards:

A. If you work indoors, put down your card.
B. If you work outdoors, put down your card.
C. If you work with animals or children, put down your card.
D. If you are a firefighter or a window washer, put down your card.
E. Put down your card unless you are a race car driver.

# Lesson II-16: Defining Loyalty

**The contents of Lesson II-16 include:**

- Journal Ideas
- Pre-/Posttest on loyalty
- Worksheet II-16A, Being a Friend
- Worksheet II-16B, All of the Time
- Worksheet II-16C, Making a Choice

## Journal Ideas

Have students select the ideas they would like to write about and include them in their journal entries. Allow time periodically for students to share and compare their ideas.

## Pre-/Posttest

Pass out the pre-/posttest to students and explain that they are to read the situations and circle the answer that best shows loyalty.

**Answers**

1. c (defending your brother to the clerk); 2. b (sticking up for your friend even though he isn't there); 3. a (being supportive of your team); 4. b (it is reasonable to wait a short time, then go on); 5. a (be loyal to your new partner)

## Worksheet II-16A, Being a Friend

1. Write the definition of *loyalty* on the board or other place where students can easily see it. *"Loyalty means being a friend to someone all of the time."*

2. Briefly inform students that you are going to break this definition into two parts and spend some time understanding what it means and how it applies to many situations. The first part of the definition refers to "being a friend."

3. Pass out the worksheet to students and have them complete the review section at the top. Explain that on the rest of the sheet, they should write yes or no to indicate if it shows someone being a friend.

**Answers**

1. yes (buying from sister); 2. yes (deciding to spend time with Mother); 3. no (didn't save the seat); 4. yes (if his intention was really to be loyal to Alan, rather than just avoiding the boy who asked to be his partner); 5. no (if Sam is expecting him to wait for him); 6. no (the girl is not sticking up for her friend)

**Discuss**

1. In situation 1, who is the boy being loyal to? *(his sister who is selling cookies)* If he bought cookies from both people, would that be OK? *(yes)*

2. In situation 2, who is the girl being loyal to? *(her mother)* Do you think it is important to the girl's mother that everyone is there for her party? *(apparently so)*

3. In situation 3, what don't you know about this situation? *(how long she was saving the seat)* Is it possible that Alicia might not be upset if someone else takes her seat? *(yes, we don't know the whole situation)*

4. In situation 4, it seems as though the boy is being loyal to Alan. Do you think he could be using it as an excuse, though, to avoid being partners with the boy who asked? *(possibly)*

5. In situation 5, what makes you think the boy is not being loyal to his friend? *(he said "who cares")*

6. In situation 6, how could the girl have been loyal to her friend Jill? *(she could stick up for her friend by saying nice things about Jill)* What if she really does feel that Jill is annoying? *(maybe she should think before she actually says it to the other girl)*

## Worksheet II-16B, All of the Time

1. Review the definition of loyalty.

2. Pass out the worksheet to students and have them complete the review section at the top.

3. Briefly discuss what being a friend "all of the time" might mean. Explain that loyalty involves being true to your friend even when other people turn against your friend. It also involves giving your friend time and space to make mistakes, but yet still be considered a loyal friend. For example, if you and a friend have an argument, there may be an uncomfortable time until you get things settled, but loyal friends will work it out. A loyal friend is a friend when times are good, when times are bad, when other people are involved, and when mistakes happen. A "fair weather" friend is a term used to categorize people who are friends only when it is convenient for them. This is not a loyal friend.

4. On the rest of the worksheet, have students read the examples and circle the character in each who is a "fair weather" friend.

### Answers

1. second (gave up on team); 2. first boy (agrees with bad comments about brother); 3. second girl (mean comments); 4. first boy (admits that he's going to "ditch" his friend); 5. first girl (she is expecting to drop her old friends)

### Discuss

1. In each example, what would a loyal friend do differently from the "fair weather" friend?

2. What does "blood is thicker than water" mean? Why do people assume that you will stick with your family just because they are family? *(family bonds can last a lifetime because you are related to the individuals)*

3. In situation 4, how did the third boy come up with a way to be loyal to his friend and still go to the party? *(invite Tony to come with them)*

## Worksheet II-16C, Making a Choice

1. Review the definition of loyalty.

2. Pass out the cartoon section of the worksheet.

3. Explain that you are going to read a story about a girl who has to make some choices about to whom she will be loyal. As you read, you will stop after the pictures and ask questions about loyalty.

### Answers

See the teacher's script.

# Journal Ideas: Loyalty

1. How loyal are you to other people? *Rate yourself* 0 (not loyal at all ) to 5 (completely always loyal to others).

   0   1   2   3   4   5

2. People often say that dogs are very loyal animals. What do you think they mean by this? What do dogs do that makes them loyal?

3. What is a time when you were very loyal to a friend? Did the friend ever find out about it? How did he or she react?

4. Has a friend ever done something to betray you? What happened? How did you feel about the friend after that? What do you think the friend should have done instead?

5. What would you do if a friend asked you to wait for him or her, and then didn't show up? How long would you wait?

6. Have you ever been friends with someone who was unpopular? What was hard about having this person as a friend? What made you stay friends with him or her?

7. Who is the number-one person you would trust as being loyal to you? Why did you pick this person?

8. What would you do if someone was picking on a member of your family? Would you go out of your way to defend your relative or stick up for him or her? How important is "family pride" to you?

9. Think about a winning sports team. What are some ways you can pick out a very loyal fan of this team?

10. Can you think of examples from books, stories, or movies in which a friend was very loyal to another friend?

# Loyalty: Pretest/Posttest

Read each situation and circle the answer that best shows loyalty.

1. You are with your mother and little brother in the grocery store. Your little brother accidentally knocks over a stand of cereal boxes and the boxes spill into the aisle. An older boy who was stocking the shelves comes over and starts to yell at your little brother. You…

   a. Apologize to the boy.

   b. Say nothing, but help pick up the boxes.

   c. Tell the older boy that it was just an accident, your brother didn't mean to do it.

   d. Call for your mother.

2. At school, you overhear someone saying that your best friend was cheating on a spelling test, but you know that isn't true. You…

   a. Tell your friend that people are telling lies about him.

   b. Tell the people that your friend did not cheat.

   c. Tell the teacher that kids are trying to get your friend in trouble.

   d. Tell the people that they are crazy.

3. Your school's basketball team is playing a really tough team. It looks as though they are going to lose by a lot of points. The cheerleaders come out and try to get the audience to cheer for the team. You…

   a. Cheer as loudly as you can.

   b. Tell the cheerleaders to go home.

   c. Cheer for the other team.

   d. Say nothing.

4. You told your friend Terry that you would wait for her so that you could walk to the library together. She is late and you are afraid the library will close. You wait for 15 minutes. It seems as though she isn't going to show up. You…

   a. Wait an hour longer.

   b. Wait 5 more minutes, then go to the library before it closes.

   c. Just go home and try to call her when you get there.

   d. Go to the library, then call her that night to let her know how angry you are.

5. Your coach assigns everyone on the tennis team to work in pairs to practice drills. Your partner is a person you don't really like. You are assigned to play together against another pair. You…

   a. Try your hardest to work with your partner to play well.

   b. Get annoyed when your partner misses some easy shots.

   c. Let your partner get the difficult shots.

   d. Don't put forth a lot of effort to win.

Name _____ Date _____

# II-16A. Being a Friend

**Review**

Loyalty means b_____ a f_____ to someone

a _____ of the t_____.

**Directions:** Read each example. Write YES if you think it shows someone being a friend. Write NO if it does not.

1. Would you like to buy some cookies from me? It's for a good cause.

   Oh, I'm sorry, my sister is selling them, too. I better buy them from her.

   _____

2. Would you like to come over on Saturday for a sleepover?

   It's my mom's birthday and I think she would like it if I stayed home for her party.

   _____

3. May I sit in that seat?

   I'm supposed to be saving it for Alicia, but go ahead.

   _____

4. Choose a partner for tennis.

   Want to be partners?

   I promised Alan.

   _____

5. Hey, there's an earlier bus leaving for the game. Should we catch it?

   I usually ride the late bus so I can ride with Sam, but who cares?

   _____

6. I know you are good friends with Jill, but she drives me crazy!

   I know what you mean. She can blab all night long and be so annoying!

   _____

# II-16B. All of the Time

**Review**

Loyalty means b_____ a f_____ to someone

a_____ of the t_____.

**Directions:** Which character in each example is a "fair-weather friend"? Circle that person.

1.

Go Packers!! Go team!

Bunch of losers, they can't win anything.

2.

Your little brother is a real pest and a dork!

Yes, I know. I have to live with him.

Hey! He's my brother! Don't talk about him like that!

3.

Nobody likes me.

Oh, Stacy, you are just in a bad mood because you didn't get invited to the party. You have lots of friends!

That's because you are so crabby to people.

4.

Want to come over to my house for a party this weekend?

I'm supposed to do something with Tony, but I can ditch him!

May Tony come too?

5.

I'm leaving for the whole summer, so I'll probably make new friends at camp.

I know I'll be gone for a long time, but I'll send postcards and call you! We'll stay in touch!

# For the Teacher
## (Script for Worksheet II-16C, Making a Choice)

Follow along with the pictures as I read the story about a girl who has some experiences with loyalty. I will stop after each picture to ask you some questions.

**(Picture 1)** Early one summer, Carmella is interested in the new family that is moving into the house next door. She soon discovers that one member of the family is a handicapped girl named Mary. Mary is in a wheelchair, but she can get around pretty well and she has full use of her arms. Since the two girls are about the same age, Carmella goes to Mary's house to get to know her. She finds out that Mary is interested in painting and that she is quite a good artist. Carmella also likes to draw, and has made some comic books.

**STOP.** What do the two girls have in common? *(same age; interested in drawing, painting)*

**(Picture 2)** When it is time to go to school in the fall, Carmella and Mary are in the same class. They have become good friends over the summer and Carmella is anxious to introduce Mary to her friends. She is sad to discover, however, that her friends are not so interested in Mary as she has hoped they would be. Instead, her friends are busy organizing roller-skating parties and going places where Mary would not easily be able to go. Carmella likes Mary, but she also wants to spend time with her old friends. She tells Mary that she will come over on Saturday afternoons so they can draw together and make a comic book.

**STOP.** What problem is Carmella facing now? *(choosing between friends)* To whom is Carmella feeling loyalty right now? *(both old friends and Mary)*

**(Picture 3)** Mary knows that Carmella has other friends and she tells Carmella not to feel badly about leaving her to go out with them. She says they will still be able to do things together. Carmella is relieved, because she really wants to go to the swimming party that Annie is having that weekend. Still, she feels badly about Mary, but she decides to go to the party.

**STOP.** Should Carmella feel badly about leaving Mary? *(no, it seems that Mary is OK with Carmella having other friends)* Is Carmella being disloyal to Mary? *(no)*

**(Picture 4)** At the swimming party, Annie says to Carmella, "You should really spend more time with us like you used to. We are all going out for cheerleading. Why don't you join us? We practice every Saturday." Carmella says that she would like to, but she usually spends Saturdays with Mary. Annie sighs. "Carmella, you don't have to feel sorry for Mary and spend all that time with her. Spend time with us! You would make a great cheerleader!"

**STOP.** What problem is Carmella in the middle of? *(deciding what to do with her Saturdays)* What do you think Carmella should do?

**(Picture 5)** "But I like Mary," Carmella tells Annie and the others. "I really enjoy spending time with her and we have fun drawing together." The girls say, "Well, you will have to decide what you want to do. All of the cheerleaders hang out together and have parties and get to go to all of the games. It's really fun and you would definitely be good enough to make the squad." One of the girls adds: "Besides, you were our friend first. You should be loyal to us." Another girl says: "Mary will understand! It doesn't matter to her if you show up on Saturday or not. Didn't she say that to you?"

**STOP.** What kind of pressure are the girls putting on Carmella? *(tempting her with the fun that cheerleading will be; arguing that they were friends first and that Mary will understand)*

**(Picture 6)** After the party, Carmella goes home and thinks for a long time. She decides that she will give up the cheerleading and spend Saturdays with Mary, because she had told Mary that she would and, besides, she really enjoys drawing with Mary. So she goes over to Mary's house, but finds that she isn't home. "She's not here right now," says Mary's mother. "She went out bowling with some friends." "Bowling?" asks Carmella. "How?" Mary's mother laughs. "She's going to start bowling every Saturday. She's in a league of wheelchair bowlers. She's actually pretty good!"

**STOP.** What surprises did Carmella find out about Mary? *(she bowls and has other friends)*

**(Picture 7)** Carmella feels sad. "Well, I had hoped that she and I would be able to draw together on Saturdays," she says. "I guess she has other things to do." Carmella leaves to go home, feeling left out and let down. She was ready to give up cheerleading to spend time with Mary, but Mary wasn't ready to give up bowling for her. Carmella wonders if it is too late to join the cheerleaders, but now she isn't sure they would want her to. She just feels awful.

**STOP.** What do you think about Mary now? *(seems disloyal)* What feelings is Carmella having? *(sad, betrayed, uncertain about whether or not her cheerleader friends will take her back)*

**(Picture 8)** The phone rings. "It's for you, Carmella," calls her mom from downstairs. "It's Mary." Carmella picks up the phone and says, "Oh, so you have time for me now? I thought you were too busy with your other friends." There is silence for a few seconds on the line. Carmella begins to feel badly about her mean words. "Carmella," Mary says, "I signed up for a bowling league that meets on Saturday mornings, not afternoons. I was hoping that you and I would still get together to draw in the afternoons like we did all summer, so I didn't sign up for the afternoon games." Carmella feels even worse than she did before! "I'm so sorry," she says to Mary. "I didn't realize that you could do both things in the same day. Of course I'm hoping we'll keep doing our drawings together!" Mary laughs. "You could come bowling with us if you want," she says. "But I'll have to warn you: I'm pretty good!"

**STOP.** Was Mary being disloyal to Carmella? *(no)* How does Mary help Carmella feel as though they are still good friends? *(invited her to go bowling with them)*

# II-16C. Making a Choice

1.

2.

3.

4.

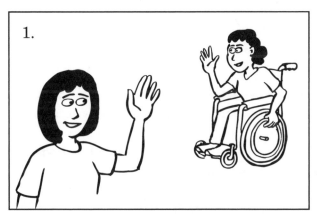

5.

6.

7.

8.

# Lesson II-17: Recognizing Loyalty

**The contents of Lesson II-17 include:**
- Worksheet II-17A, Does This Show Loyalty?
- Worksheet II-17B, What Next?
- Worksheet II-17C, Loyalty with Common Sense

## Worksheet II-17A, Does This Show Loyalty?

1. Pass out the worksheet to students and have them complete the review section at the top.
2. Directions for the rest of the worksheet have students read the examples of people who are or are not showing loyalty. They should complete the questions for each example.

**Answers**

- *Example 1:* 1. no, Fred chose to do something else rather than help Michael; 2. Michael might not have had a problem with changing the time, but Fred did not check with him; 3. it would be fine for Fred to go and then reschedule with Michael
- *Example 2:* 1. yes, she didn't forget about her when her plans changed; 2. instead of walking, she got a ride to school; 3. Darla would have waited or at least wondered what happened to her
- *Example 3:* 1. Todd is upset with Ricardo, but not to the point of ending their friendship; 2. he wanted to stay on Ricardo's team; 3. yes, because their friendship is still intact; 4. yes, friends have disagreements but friends work through them and keep them in perspective

## Worksheet II-17B, What Next?

1. Pass out the worksheet to students and have them complete the review section at the top.
2. On the rest of the worksheet, students are to draw a picture that shows the person in each example doing something that shows loyalty.

**Answers**

(May vary). 1. person voting; 2. person saying "He's my friend and I'll hang out with him if I want to."; 3. Josh showing his sister how to skateboard; 4. person going to Grandpa's party

**Discuss**

1. In situation 1, what if the person had not made a promise to vote for the person running for president? Do you have to vote for someone just because he or she is a friend? What if you disagree with what they are running for? *(if you have promised to vote, you should; if you disagree with the position, tell the person that you cannot vote for him or her and why)*
2. In situation 2, what if the person doesn't like Mark anyway? *(then there is no disloyalty; however, if there is a friendship between Mark and the person, he should stick up for Mark)*

3. In situation 3, why is Josh obligated to spend time with his sister? *(because family members should do things to help each other)*

4. In situation 4, why is it important to go to Grandpa's birthday party? *(if it means a lot to Grandpa, it goes along with loyalty to family; in this case, if Grandpa doesn't really care, it still is important to the mother asking him to go to the party)*

# Worksheet II-17C, Loyalty with Common Sense

1. Pass out the worksheet to students and have them complete the review section at the top.

2. On the rest of the worksheet, students are to read the situations that involve loyalty pushed to the extreme, which do not take common sense into account. For example, it is important to wait for someone if you give your word, but waiting for hours is ridiculous. Students should answer the questions that follow the examples.

### Answers

1. Maria is waiting far too long for Beth, who is obviously not going to show up. She could leave a note, call Beth at home, call home to see if Beth is there, or ask people if they have seen Beth.

2. The problem is that Tommy did not do well on his spelling test, but Steve is blaming it on the teacher, not Tommy. Common sense would say that he deserves a bad grade if he didn't pass the test, and that Tommy was not studying properly and that accounts for the poor grade. Steve could ask the teacher for ways to help study with Tommy. Steve thinks he is defending Tommy's honor, but the grade was fair based on the performance on the test.

3. Ellen is embarrassed. Jenny was trying not to be impolite, but it really was a funny situation and giggling is probably appropriate. Ellen and Jenny could just laugh about it and go on. Jenny is still Ellen's friend. She must suggest that Ellen just laugh about it and not take it so seriously.

### Discuss

1. In situation 1, the loyalty issue was how long you wait for a friend. How long should you keep your promise to someone? Do you have to keep it if the situation has obviously changed?

2. In situation 2, Steve thinks he is sticking up for his little brother, but that is not the problem. Should you stick up for a family member even if he or she is wrong? What about finding out that a family member was getting in trouble?

3. In situation 3, Ellen accused Jenny of being disloyal for laughing at her. What is Ellen's perspective? What is Jenny's perspective? Who needs to change?

# II-17A. Does This Show Loyalty?

**Review**

Loyalty means _____ a

_____ to someone

_____ of the

_____.

**Directions:** Which of these are examples of loyalty to someone else? Discuss how they show or do not show loyalty. Answer the questions on another sheet of paper.

## Example 1

Fred says he will help Michael with his 4-H project on Saturday afternoon. Earlier in the afternoon, some of Fred's friends come over and want him to go canoeing with them. It is a beautiful day, and Fred thinks he can help Michael on a different day, so he goes with his friends.

1. Is Fred being loyal to Michael?

2. Do you think Michael will mind if Fred changes the time?

3. If Fred calls Michael and asks him if he would mind if they change the date, how will that change things?

## Example 2

Karen and Darla usually walk to school together each morning. One morning it is raining, so Karen's dad offers to give her a ride to school. Karen asks if he would mind stopping by to pick up Darla, too.

1. Is Karen being loyal to Darla?

2. How has the normal plans changed?

3. What do you think might have happened if Karen did not call Darla?

## Example 3

Todd and Ricardo, who are usually good friends, get into an argument during a football game. They cannot agree about the rules, so they both decide to quit and leave. Later Todd runs into Alex, who tells Todd that he should leave Ricardo's football team and join his team. Todd says no, that he and Ricardo just had an argument but it isn't worth quitting over.

1. How does Todd feel about Ricardo now?

2. Why doesn't Todd join Alex's team?

3. Is Todd still being loyal to Ricardo, even though they had an argument?

4. Do you think they will still be friends after this settles down?

# Worksheet II-17B. What Next?

**Review**

Loyalty means being a _____ to _____ all of the

_____.

**Directions:** These people are in situations where they must choose how to be loyal to someone. Draw a picture that shows what the person could do next to be loyal.

1. Will you vote for me for class president? I will meet with the principal every week and let her know about our concerns!

2. Don't hang around with Mark. He is really boring and nobody thinks he's neat.

3. Josh, please teach your sister how to skateboard. She really wants to learn how and it will only take a little while.

4. It's Grandpa's 80th birthday on Sunday. I know you want to go out with your friends, but it would mean a lot to him if you came over.

# II-17C. Loyalty with Common Sense

**Review**

Loyalty means _____ a _____ to someone

_____ of the _____.

**Directions:** These people want to be loyal to someone all of the time, but what is wrong in each case? How are they forgetting to use common sense? Write a better solution for each problem.

1. Maria said she would wait for her friend Beth after school. She waited for an hour. No Beth. She waited another hour. No Beth. It was getting dark outside and the custodian wanted to lock the school. Maria said she couldn't leave because she was supposed to wait for her friend Beth.

   How isn't Maria using common sense? _____

   _____

   What could Maria do? _____

   _____

2. Steve helps his little brother Tommy study for his spelling test, but Tommy really isn't paying attention to him. When Tommy takes the test, he spells a lot of words wrong and gets a D on the test. Steve marches into the classroom and tells the teacher that she has got to quit picking on his little brother or she'll hear about it from him!

   What is the real problem here? _____

   _____

   How isn't Steve using common sense to explain the poor grade? _____

   _____

   What could Steve do? _____

   _____

3. Ellen and Jenny are in line in the cafeteria getting their lunch, when Ellen slips and spills beans all over her hair. She isn't hurt, but she is embarrassed. Jenny starts to giggle as she pulls beans out of Ellen's hair. One bean falls on her glasses and Jenny really starts to laugh. Ellen gets mad and says, "You are supposed to be my friend! Stop laughing!"

   How does Ellen feel about this situation? _____

   _____

   Was Jenny wrong to laugh about it? _____

   What could Ellen and Jenny do? _____

   _____

   Is Jenny really being disloyal to Ellen? _____

   _____

# Lesson II-18: Applying Loyalty

**The contents of Lesson II-18 include:**

- Worksheet II-18A, Being Loyal to Others
- Worksheet II-18B, Ways I Can Show Loyalty
- Quiz on Part 12: Loyalty
- Activity: Role-Playing

## Worksheet II-18A, Being Loyal to Others

1. Pass out the worksheet to students and have them complete the review section at the top. Remind them that the opposite of loyalty is disloyalty, or betraying (turning your back on) someone.

2. Directions for the rest of the worksheet ask students to read a situation and decide how they would handle it, keeping loyalty and common sense in mind. They should write their responses.

### Answers

Will vary.

1. Have an understanding with your friend that you will pick him eventually, but later in the choices. Or decide that having your friend on the team with you is more important than choosing by simple ability.

2. Hopefully your friend will understand the importance of this event to you.

3. Check with the friend to make sure everything is OK between you.

4. Talk to your friend and find other things to do together instead.

5. Realize that your dad had a bad day and don't hold it against him.

6. If you trust your friend, talk about it with him and give him more time. Or maybe your friend is being disloyal to you and has forgotten about the loan or doesn't think he needs to pay it back on time.

### Discuss

1. Are you being disloyal to someone if you expect that person to understand that a great or unusual opportunity has come your way and you would like to take advantage of it? How is it showing good friendship skills if you allow a friend to enjoy an opportunity without making him or her feel disloyal to you?

2. Why is it important to have an honest talk with a friend if you aren't sure about the truth of what you are hearing?

3. Sometimes interests change, and friendships change because of that. Is it being disloyal to someone if you are no longer interested in doing things together that you used to do, i.e., playing with dolls, playing games, going to camp, etc.?

4. When you lend things to friends (a bike, money, etc.) and they don't seem to take care of them or intend to pay you back, do you need to remain loyal to them? Does this show that they don't care about you?

## Worksheet II-18B, Ways I Can Show Loyalty

1. Pass out the worksheet to students and have them complete the review section at the top.
2. Directions for the rest of the worksheet ask students to think of specific individuals (family member, school friend, teammate, relative, etc.) and list ways that they can demonstrate loyalty to these people in situations that are likely to come up.

### Discuss

1. Is it easier to show loyalty to people you like, rather than people to whom you are related?
2. Why is it important to show loyalty to family members?
3. Why is it important to have connections with relatives, even if they are not close family members?

## Quiz on Part 12: Loyalty

This quiz can be used as a follow-up activity for these lessons.

### Answers

1. *(definition)* Loyalty is being a friend to someone all of the time.
2. *(examples)* a. no (fair-weather friend); b. no (giving up on team); c. yes (waiting for friend); d. no (leaves friend after he just said they were best friends)
3. *(applying)* Answers will vary. Could talk to David and ask him if he told anyone.

## Activity: Role-Playing

This activity involves students in acting-out situations in which loyalty or disloyalty is shown to others. Specific instructions are given on the activity page.

# II-18A. Being Loyal to Others

**Review**

Loyalty means _____

_____.

The opposite of loyalty is _____.

**Directions:** What would YOU do in the following situations? Does it show loyalty or disloyalty to someone?

1. You are the captain of one of the two kickball teams. You know that your good friend expects you to pick him, but he's not a very good player. What will you do?

_____

_____

2. You tell your friend that you will come over, but you get an unexpected offer of free tickets to a concert that you had been wanting to see for months! What will you do?

_____

_____

3. Someone tells you that your good friend is spreading bad rumors about you. What will you do?

_____

_____

4. You and a friend have always gone to camp together each summer for a week. This summer, however, you are not so interested in going anymore and would like to do something different. You think your friend still wants to go, though. What will you do?

_____

_____

5. Your dad has a really bad day at work and comes home in a bad mood. He forgets that he promised to play catch with you when he got home. You are really counting on him spending time with you, but he seems really irritated. What will you do?

_____

_____

6. Your friend borrowed a lot of money from you to buy a bike and he promised that he would pay you back. A lot of time has passed and you haven't gotten any money from your friend. In fact, he doesn't even mention it at all. Your parents are telling you that you made a big mistake trusting this friend. What will you do?

_____

_____

# II-18B. Ways I Can Show Loyalty

**Review**

Loyalty means _____

_____.

The opposite of loyalty is _____.

**Directions:** Think of people who fit the descriptions below. List 3 ways you can show loyalty to these people in situations that might come up.

1. A member of your family

_____

_____

_____

2. Your best friend

_____

_____

_____

3. A good friend at school

_____

_____

_____

4. A teammate or club member

_____

_____

_____

5. A relative who does not live with you

_____

_____

_____

6. Someone in your class with whom you work on projects

_____

_____

_____

Name _____  Date _____

# Quiz on Part 12: Loyalty

1. What is meant by loyalty?

_____

_____

2. Which of these is an example of loyalty?

3. Your friend David has always been a good listener whenever you have had a problem. He never repeats to others what you say is private. You tell him that you think your parents are getting a divorce and it really worries you. The next day at school, several people seem to know what is going on. Did David tell your secrets? What will you do?

_____

_____

_____

_____

# Activity for Loyalty: Role-Playing

Players form small groups to perform these role-plays. Players randomly select the following situations and decide whether or not they will show loyalty or disloyalty in each. Members of the audience should decide whether or not the role-play was clear. If disloyalty was selected, the role-play should be performed a second time to show loyalty. Can students think of other situations to role-play?

## Helping a Sibling

*Players:* Mother, Father, Siblings

*Idea:* A brother or sister needs help or attention, but something else comes up that is much more fun or interesting.

## Family Reunion

*Players:* Adults, Children

*Idea:* One person does not really want to attend a family reunion because of the strange relatives in the family.

## Spreading Gossip

*Players:* Friends

*Idea:* Someone starts a rumor about someone else and the rumor gets bigger and more wild.

## Trouble with the Teacher

*Players:* Teacher, Principal, Students

*Idea:* A student is misunderstood by a teacher and talks back, getting in trouble. Does the friend defend him (or her)? How?

## Pick Me!

*Players:* Students

*Idea:* Students are choosing sides for a game and there is one student who is always the last to be picked—someone's sister!

## Friends Forever

*Players:* Friends

*Idea:* One friend is extremely possessive, demands time and attention, and won't let other people be your friend.

# Section III

# Having a Positive Outlook

The third and final section of this book deals with having a positive outlook. It is possible to change one's nature, to become a better, more social, more thoughtful person? Is fairness, for example, a characteristic that someone can learn to become or cultivate? The idea that we can change ourselves to become "better" is what gives us hope. Even if a person does not feel like being in a good mood or want to consider someone else's opinion, it is possible to learn to behave in such a way that one can develop these characteristics. Some of the characteristics that can help shape us into more positive people are:

- **sense of humor**—looking for the lighter side of things
- **fairness**—following the rules of a situation
- **open-minded**—accepting new information
- **initiative**—knowing what needs to be done and doing it
- **optimistic**—finding good or hopeful things about something
- **risk-taking**—trying something new or difficult

# Lesson III-1: Defining Sense of Humor

**The contents of Lesson III-1 include:**

- Journal Ideas
- Pre-/Posttest on sense of humor
- Worksheet III-1A, The Lighter Side
- Worksheet III-1B, Being Funny?
- Worksheet III-1C, Twins

## Journal Ideas

Have students select ideas they would like to write about in a personal journal. Give them time to share their entries with each other.

## Pre-/Posttest

Pass out the pre-/posttest to students and explain that they should read the situations and circle the response that best shows using a sense of humor appropriately.

### Answers

(There are other appropriate answers, but these attempt to show humor.) 1. c (lighthearted, not blaming him); 2. d (teasing); 3. b (not making her feel badly); 4. a (teasing Grandmother but not embarrassing her); 5. b (using humor)

## Worksheet III-1A, The Lighter Side

1. Write the definition of *sense of humor* on the board or other place where students can easily see it. *"Sense of humor means looking for the lighter side of things."*

2. Discuss that a healthy outlook on life includes being able to see humor in situations that might otherwise be negative or just neutral. Having a sense of humor involves being able to see the "lighter side," or an aspect of something that is amusing. While some people naturally are optimistic and funny, everyone can cultivate this skill to some degree.

3. Pass out the worksheet and explain that this worksheet focuses on understanding what the "lighter side" of a situation means.

4. Have students complete the review section at the top. The rest of the worksheet asks students to circle the character who demonstrates seeing the lighter side of a situation.

### Answers

1. second; 2. first; 3. first; 4. second; 5. first; 6. first

### Discuss

1. In situation 1, how does the second character use a sense of humor to deal with a rainy day? *(made it sound as though her wish caused the weather)*

2. In situation 2, how does the first character use a sense of humor to deal with being late? *(he makes it sound as though they planned to arrive at that exact moment to miss the previews)*

3. In situation 3, how does the first character show humor? *(laughing at himself, as though he is a funny-looking character)*

4. In situation 4, how does the second character laugh at himself? *(teasing himself as though he was doing it on purpose)*

5. In situation 5, how is the first character laughing at himself? *(comments that he fell so hard that it felt like an earthquake)*

6. In situation 6, how does the first character use humor? *(kind of sarcastic, but implies that her Fridays are now going to be spent studying)*

## Worksheet III-1B, Being Funny?

1. Review the definition of sense of humor.

2. Pass out the worksheet to students and have them complete the review section at the top.

3. Briefly discuss that having a sense of humor does not mean that you laugh at everything or make light of serious situations. The definition should imply that a sense of humor is used appropriately (using common sense).

4. Students should complete the rest of the worksheet by writing an answer to explain why using humor is not appropriate in each situation.

### Answers

1. she named a specific person, which might be mean; 2. death of a pet can be very sad; 3. Mr. Taylor would not think it was funny; 4. the girl is shy and does not want attention for her grade; 5. some people might not think making a joke about cancer is funny

### Discuss

1. What are some other occasions that should not be made fun of? *(divorce, race, religion)*

2. If something hurts someone's feelings, should you make a joke about it?

3. If someone makes fun of himself or herself, is it then OK for another person to make jokes? What if you are sure that it doesn't hurt that person's feelings? *(be careful about this—sometimes people who make jokes about themselves are really sensitive)*

## Worksheet III-1C, Twins

1. Review the definition of sense of humor.

2. Pass out the cartoon section of the worksheet.

3. Explain that you are going to read a story about twins, one with a good sense of humor and the other who starts out with not having a very good sense of humor. As you read, students should be listening for examples of an appropriate sense of humor. As you read, you will stop after the pictures to ask questions.

### Answers

See the teacher's script.

# Journal Ideas: Sense of Humor

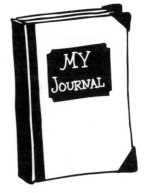

1. How is your sense of humor? Rate yourself:

   0— I don't think anything is very funny.

   1— I don't have a good sense of humor very often.

   2— Sometimes I have a good sense of humor.

   3— I have a pretty good sense of humor.

   4— I usually have a good sense of humor.

   5— I always have a good sense of humor.

2. What do people tease you about? Do you enjoy being teased? When you tease other people, do they seem to like it? What do you tease other people about?

3. What are your favorite TV shows that make you laugh? Which characters do you like and why?

4. What's a good joke or riddle you have heard?

5. Have you ever played a practical joke or trick on someone else? How did it go? Did the person you trick think it was funny?

6. What is an embarrassing moment you have had? How did you feel? Did anyone laugh at you? Did a sense of humor help you?

7. Who is someone you know personally who has a good sense of humor? How does this person show a good sense of humor?

8. Have you ever had an experience in which someone hurt your feelings and then laughed about it? How did it make you feel and what did you do? Would a sense of humor have helped you?

9. What's the best way to get you out of a bad mood and into a good mood?

10. List 10 things that make you laugh. Which one(s) make you laugh out loud? Tell about them.

# Sense of Humor: Pretest/Posttest

Read each situation and circle the response that shows using a sense of humor appropriately.

1. Terry waits and waits for his friend Mike to show up outside the theater so they can go to the movies. Finally, it is almost time for the movie to begin, so Terry starts to go into the theater. There is Mike—already sitting in his seat, waiting for the movie. "What took you so long?" Mike asks, popping popcorn in his mouth. What could Mike do?
    a. Take the popcorn and dump it on Mike's head.
    b. Say, "Well, I'm glad you get to see the movie. I nearly missed it waiting for you!"
    c. Say, "Earth to Mike! Weren't we supposed to meet outside the theater?"
    d. Point to his watch and keep tapping it.

2. Ellen misses a free throw in the last minute of the basketball game and her team loses. She feels terrible about it. What could her coach say?
    a. "You need to practice those free throws."
    b. "Your position was wonderful at the free-throw line. Too bad you didn't get it in."
    c. "If they awarded points for the most determination, Ellen, you would have won it! Nice try."
    d. "That was very suspenseful, Ellen. See this gray hair? That's from you. See all these other gray hairs? Those are from all of your teammates. At least I'm not bald!"

3. Jackie and her family are eating at a fancy restaurant when she accidentally tips over her water glass, spilling water all over the table. What could the waitress say or do?
    a. "Help me mop it up!"
    b. "If you wanted more water, all you had to do was raise your hand!"
    c. "There are so many clumsy people here today!"
    d. "Don't worry. At least water won't ruin the tablecloth."

4. Richard is at the mall with his grandmother and suddenly sees a cute girl he likes. His grandmother is embarrassing him, talking very loudly and trying to hold his hand as if he is a little boy. What could Richard say to the girl?
    a. "Hi. This is my grandmother. She does all those great grandmotherly things like pinch my cheeks and talk about how cute I am, right, Grandma?"
    b. "Hi! This is my grandmother. I'm stuck with her this afternoon."
    c. "This is just some woman who keeps following me around. I don't know where she came from."
    d. "Grandma, this is my friend. Don't say anything to embarrass me or I'll die."

5. Ted is giving a speech in front of the class, but he cannot read his handwriting on the note cards, so he stops and freezes for a second. What could he say or do next?
    a. "Hmmmm. I can't read that next word."
    b. "Oh dear, my personal secretary didn't type that word right! I'll have to fire her!"
    c. "Whoopsie."
    d. "Oops, sorry, hang on… I'll figure it out."

# III-1A. The Lighter Side

**Review**

Sense of humor means l_____ for the l_____

s_____ of things.

**Directions:** Looking at the "lighter side" means finding something good or happy about a situation. Which character in each example below shows a lighter side of an unpleasant situation?

---

1. **a rainy day**

Oh great. A day of staying indoors.

I got my wish! It's a good day to read!

---

2. **being late to the movies**

We have great timing! We only missed the previews!

We have to walk into the theater in the dark.

---

3. **a missing tooth**

Just call me Mr. Pumpkin!

I'm not going out of the house!

---

4. **spilling food**

It takes talent to do that!

I'm such a klutzy dope!

---

5. **falling**

Did you feel that earthquake?

Did anyone see me?

---

6. **getting a poor grade**

I don't have to worry about what I'll be doing every Friday night from now on...

It wasn't fair! The test was too hard!

---

Name _____  Date _____

# III-1B. Being Funny?

**Review**

Sense of humor means l_____ for the l_____

s_____ of th_____.

**Directions:** A sense of humor means that you use humor appropriately. Why aren't these people showing a good sense of humor? Write your answers on the lines.

1. **bad hair day**

   _____

   _____

   _____

My hair looks awful! I look like Jennifer Smith!

2. **a dead pet**

   _____

   _____

   _____

Sorry your little puppy died. Can we stuff him and use him for a pillow?

3. **appearance**

   Let's all wear fake mustaches to class so we'll look like Mr. Taylor.

   No, he's really sensitive about that. He wouldn't think it was funny.

   _____

   _____

   _____

4. **teasing**

   Oh come on, Alice, show us your A-plus paper! Come on!!

   No...I don't want to.

   _____

   _____

   _____

5. **sickness**

   _____

   _____

   _____

cough cough cough Wow, I sound like my dad who is sick from lung cancer!

# For the Teacher (Script for Worksheet III-1C, Twins)

Follow along with the pictures that show how Molly and Polly (twins, of course) go through their day. The two girls have a very different sense of humor. I will stop after each picture to ask some questions.

**(Picture 1)** The day begins with a lot of snow! There is at least a foot of new snow on the ground and more on the way. The twins run to the window to watch it fall. Molly says, "Oh, we'll have indoor recess for sure today. Bummer." Polly says, "Let's have a snowball fight! Come on, it'll be fun!"

**STOP.** Do you think Molly could possibly have fun with indoor recess? *(yes)* Do you think Molly thinks she can? *(no)* What does Polly think about the snow? *(new opportunity for fun)*

**(Picture 2)** At school, the teacher asks Molly to pass back the math tests that they had taken the day before. Molly has gotten a B on the test. She says, "Well, a B is pretty good." Polly looks at her test—also a B. She says, "I think this 'B' stands for Beautiful, right, Mrs. Taylor?" Mrs. Taylor laughs and says, "No, it means 'B—Be sure to study harder!'"

**STOP.** What examples of sense of humor do you see in this situation? *(Polly and Mrs. Taylor joking about the grade)*

**(Picture 3)** At dinner, Molly is trying to get the ketchup out of the bottle by shaking it, and suddenly it spurts all over the table and her sweater. "Oh no, my sweater is a mess!" she cries, trying to clean off the ketchup. "Hey, wait," says Polly. "Leave it just as it is— can I turn it in for my modern art project? It's perfect!" Molly stops and looks at it. "No way, sis. I'm going to turn it in! It was my creation!"

**STOP.** What is the unpleasant situation? *(spilled ketchup on sweater)* How does Molly react to it the first time? *(thought it was a mess)* How does she react to it after Polly says something? *(saw that it could be funny)*

**(Picture 4)** The phone rings. "Hello? This is the Taylor Madhouse. How may I help you?" says Polly, picking it up. "What? My father won a million dollars? No, I don't think he would be interested. Thanks anyway." She puts the phone down. "Well, who was that, Polly?" asks her dad from behind the newspaper. "Did I win a million dollars?" Polly laughs. "No, it was just a recorded call from the dentist reminding you that you have an appointment tomorrow." Molly says, "Why can't you just answer the phone like a normal person? When my friends call here, you always say something weird!" Polly laughs. "That's because I AM weird! And you're my twin sister so that makes you weird, too!!!! Hee hee ha ha ha!"

**STOP.** How does Polly show a sense of humor? *(answered the phone funny, joked with her father about the call)* Does Molly find Polly funny or irritating? *(irritating this time)*

**(Picture 5)** Their parents have some company stop over that evening and end up pulling out the baby books and showing very embarrassing pictures of the girls when they were little. "Mom, this is so embarrassing," complains Molly. "Do you really have to do this?" "I love this one," says Mrs. Taylor. "Look at Molly riding the pony! We thought she was going to grow up to be a cowgirl!" Polly holds up a picture. "Look at this one, Mom. I'm sitting in the litterbox with the kitten. What did you think I would grow up to be? And were you worried?"

© 2002 by The Center for Applied Research in Education

**STOP.** How does Polly use sense of humor to cover the embarrassment of the pictures? *(laughed about herself)*

**(Picture 6)** Finally it is bedtime, and Molly and Polly have to sleep on the couch in the basement because their company is using their beds and their bedroom. "Good night, everyone," calls Molly from the basement. "I hope you don't find anything icky in the bedroom." "Good night, everybody," calls Polly, "and if you do find something icky…" Everyone waits to hear what she will say. "…put it in Molly's bed. Good night!" Everyone laughs. "Well, if we do find something icky, we will certainly take a picture of it so we can embarrass you on our next visit."

**STOP.** What examples of sense of humor do you find in this scene? *(Molly and Polly talking about finding icky things; the visitors' comment)*

# III-1C. Twins

1.

2.

3.

4.

5.

6.

# Lesson III-2: Recognizing Sense of Humor

**The contents of Lesson III-2 include:**
- Worksheet III-2A, Laughing at Yourself
- Worksheet III-2B, Sense of Humor with Others
- Worksheet III-2C, Sense of Humor with Common Sense

## Worksheet III-2A, Laughing at Yourself

1. Pass out the worksheet to students and have them complete the review section at the top.
2. Directions for the rest of the worksheet have students read the situations and decide whether or not the character is showing a sense of humor by laughing at herself or himself. They are to write yes or no on the lines.

### Answers

1. yes (not upset about it); 2. no (bad sport); 3. no (nothing humorous here); 4. no (angry response); 5. yes (comparing self to a great scientist); 6. yes (embarrassing moment turned into humor); 7. no (nothing humorous, just polite); 8. yes (poking fun at his burned skin)

### Discuss

1. Is it important to turn every embarrassing moment into something humorous? *(no, only when appropriate)*
2. If someone else had made fun of the girl in situation 1 with the mismatched socks or the boy in situation 8 with burned skin, would that have been funny? *(not if the person didn't think it was funny; these people were laughing at themselves)*
3. Do you think some people find it hard to laugh at themselves, especially their own mistakes or embarrassing moments? Why? *(it still turns the attention to them and to the mistake)*

## Worksheet III-2B, Sense of Humor with Others

1. Pass out the worksheet to students and have them complete the review section at the top.
2. Students should circle the character who is showing a sense of humor with others on the remainder of the worksheet.

### Answers

1. second person; 2. first person; 3. first person; 4. second person; 5. first person

### Discuss

1. In situation 1, what do you think of the response by the first person? *(just laughing at the girl's mistake)*
2. In situation 2, the boy knocked over the glass and it landed in a bucket. How is the first response showing humor? *(it was unlikely that it would land in the bucket; the first person was comparing it to making a basket)*
3. In situation 3, what do you think of the second person's response? *(it is sympathetic, but not really showing humor)*

4. In situation 4, how does the girl with the perm feel? *(embarrassed)* What would happen if the girl didn't think the second character's response was funny? *(probably would hurt her feelings)*

5. In situation 5, how did the first girl use humor? *(made a comment about her name mistake, but still said she was glad to meet her)*

6. In each of the six examples, how could the person who did something embarrassing have used a sense of humor to laugh at himself or herself?

# Worksheet III-2C, Sense of Humor with Common Sense

1. Pass out the worksheet to students and have them complete the review section at the top.

2. On the rest of the worksheet, students should read the examples of people trying to show a sense of humor but at inappropriate times. Students should discuss why the use of humor is not really appropriate under these situations.

**Discuss**

1. In situation 1, the girl is making jokes about the spot, but what would have happened if she didn't call attention to it at all? *(probably no one would have noticed)*

2. In situation 2, why isn't it OK for him to lighten things up by telling jokes? *(no one wants to listen to 200 of them)* What would have been more appropriate? *(telling one or two, finding a more interested audience, telling the jokes at a different time, etc.)*

3. In situation 3, why shouldn't the boy bring firecrackers to a wedding? *(no doubt it will be disruptive, the bridal party may not appreciate it, might be dangerous, etc.)*

4. In situation 4, the father is unhappy with the boy's grade and the boy is trying to be funny, but what isn't working about this? *(it is a serious situation and the father probably is not in a good mood; the boy is being a smart alec and not taking it seriously)*

Name _____ Date _____

# Worksheet III-2A. Laughing at Yourself

**Review**

Sense of humor means _____ for the

_____ side of _____.

**Directions:** Read each situation and decide whether or not the character is showing a sense of humor by laughing at himself or herself. Write YES or NO on the lines.

1. Beth notices that she has on two different colored socks. She says, "Oh, my! You can tell that I got dressed in the dark this morning."   _____

2. Randy doesn't make the football team at school. He tells his friends that he doesn't really want to play with those kids anyhow.   _____

3. Martha is supposed to turn in a book report, but her dog has walked all over it with paw prints. She tells the teacher that she was in a hurry and left it where the dog could get to it.   _____

4. Pete drops his lunch box in the cafeteria and several kids stop to laugh at him. He says, "If you want something to laugh about, just wait until I hit you over the head with it!"   _____

5. Amy's science experiment spills all over the science table. She says, "I wonder if Albert Einstein got started this way?"   _____

6. Carl is standing in front of the magazine rack looking through some magazines and he thinks his friend is standing behind him. He says, "Why don't you buy me that truck?" Then he turns around to see a complete stranger. He says, "Oh, I thought you were my friend! But you can still buy me the truck if you want to."   _____

7. Alison dials the wrong number on the phone. She apologizes to the people, and then dials the same number—getting the same people again! She says, "I am so sorry!"   _____

8. Frank gets sunburned over the weekend and comes to school on Monday with a bright red face. He tells everyone he is practicing to be a lobster.

_____

# III-2B. Sense of Humor with Others

**Review**

Sense of humor means _____ for the _____ side of

_____.

**Directions:** Which of these characters is using a sense of humor to show the lighter side of something with others? Circle the character.

# III-2C. Sense of Humor with Common Sense

**Review**

Sense of humor means _____ for the _____

_____ of things.

**Directions:** These characters are trying to show a sense of humor, but they are not using common sense. Why not? Read each situation and discuss your answers.

1.

Oh, I have a spot on my shirt! Everybody, see this spot? Well, I'm going to get a marker and make it into a smiley face! Won't that be cute?

2.

I know a great knock-knock joke! In fact, I know about 200 of them and I'll be happy to cheer you up by telling you all of them! Where are you going? Wait up!!!

3.

Hurry up! Get ready to go to the wedding.

This will be so funny!

FIRECRACKERS

4.

I am not happy about this poor grade, young man!

Yeah? Well, that makes two of us!

# Lesson III-3: Applying Sense of Humor

**The contents of Lesson III-3 include:**

- Worksheet III-3A, What Could You Do?
- Worksheet III-3B, Looking for Humor
- Quiz on Part 13: Sense of Humor
- Game: The Good Humor Game

## Worksheet III-3A, What Could You Do?

1. Pass out the worksheet to students and have them complete the review section at the top. Remind them that the opposite of a sense of humor is being very serious, perhaps grouchy or sensitive. Be sure to point out that using humor must be done appropriately, and that there are situations and occasions in which humor is not appropriate. Just because someone is not laughing about something does not mean that person doesn't have a good sense of humor; it might be that the situation is not appropriate for humor. Common sense must dictate what is appropriate. Sense of humor under *normal* conditions is desirable.

2. Students are to write what they might do in each situation that shows using a sense of humor.

**Answers**

(Will vary.) 1. "Wow, he had good aim!"; 2. "You never know when you might need an extra sock."; 3. "Just call me 'Grace'!"; 4. "We've got to quit meeting like this!"; 5. "My little brother takes this very seriously and wants to be an artist now."; 6. "I'm last again! This really makes me m-a-d-e!" (spelling the word *mad* incorrectly); 7. "Hey, guys! We got second!"; 8. Take Grandma into a video arcade where there is lots of noise anyhow.

**Discuss**

1. What situations have you encountered when you showed a sense of humor?
2. Which of the situations on this worksheet would be the easiest or hardest for you to deal with?

## Worksheet III-3B, Looking for Humor

1. Pass out the worksheet to students and have them complete the review section at the top. Discuss again the appropriateness of humor and being careful not to be critical of those who are not finding humor because of serious situations.

2. On the remainder of the worksheet, students are to think of ways that they can find and enjoy humor, particularly for the purpose of developing their own sense of humor.

**Answers**

(Will vary.) Encourage students to be creative!

**Discuss**

1. Do people credit you with a good sense of humor? If so, how does that make you feel?
2. Do you find that watching comedies on TV makes you feel happier? Do you believe laughing is actually good for you?
3. When you are in a tense or serious situation, what are some ways you help yourself remember to use a good sense of humor?

## Quiz on Part 13: Sense of Humor

This quiz can be used as a follow-up activity for this lesson.

**Answers**

1. *(definition)* Sense of humor means looking for the lighter side of things.

2. *(examples)* a. yes (the person is laughing at his own hat); b. no (Richard might be embarrassed and not know he is in the wrong line); c. no (the person is trying to make a joke at the wrong time); d. yes (the girl got all wet and is laughing at herself)

3. *(applying)* Answers will vary. Perhaps you might say, "She's for sale! Best offer!"

## Game: The Good Humor Game

Directions and gameboard are at the end of this lesson.

# III-3A. What Could You Do?

**Review**

Sense of humor means _____

_____.

The opposite of a sense of humor is being _____.

**Directions:** What could you do in each situation to show a good sense of humor?

1. You are walking to school and bird droppings land on your head.

   _____

   _____

2. You have a sock stuck on the back of your sweater.

   _____

   _____

3. You slip off the sidewalk and land in a mud puddle.

   _____

   _____

4. You and your best friend knock into each other and both fall down.

   _____

   _____

5. Your little brother scribbles all over your report on famous artists.

   _____

   _____

6. You are the last one picked for the spelling bee challenge.

   _____

   _____

7. Your soccer team loses by one point.

   _____

   _____

8. You are shopping with your grandmother who talks very loud.

   _____

   _____

# III-3B. Looking for Humor

**Review**

Sense of humor means _____

_____.

The opposite of a sense of humor is being _____.

**Directions:** What are some ways you can learn to develop a good sense of humor? Add to this list…

1. _Read the comics._____
2. Watch comedies on TV._____
3. Collect jokes and riddles._____
4. _Observe people who have a good sense of humor._____
5. _____
   _____
6. _____
   _____
7. _____
   _____
8. _____
   _____
9. _____
   _____
10. _____
    _____

Name _____ Date _____

# Quiz on Part 13: Sense of Humor

1. What is meant by sense of humor?

_____

_____

2. Which of these people are showing a sense of humor appropriately?

3. You are walking through the toy store with your little sister, who keeps pointing to all of the toys and wanting to touch all of them. You tell her "No," so she starts screaming and crying and fussing. People are looking at you! What will you do?

_____

_____

_____

_____

# Game for Sense of Humor: The Good Humor Game

**Materials:**

a gameboard

die or spinner

identity cards (6 available: Mr. Crabb, Miss Good-Humor, Mrs. Serious, Dr. Laffalot, Ms. Gloom, Professor Sillyface)

marker to move along gameboard for each player (6 available)

**Players:** 2–6

**Objective:** To be the first player to the finish line

**How to Play:**

1. Players each select an identity. This is how they should then refer to each other. *Note:* There are spaces on the gameboard in which students change identities.

2. Players put their markers on the start space and take turns rolling the die (or spinning) to move along the gameboard.

3. Each player must give a reaction that shows a sense of humor to each situation that he/she lands on as players move along the board.

4. Play continues until all players pass the finish line.

5. The winner is the player who finishes first.

**The Gameboard:**

Place the following situations in the spaces on the board. (Feel free to think of others.)

You have a black eye.

You have on one red sock and one black sock.

You knock over a glass of water.

You dial a wrong number on the phone.

CHANGE IDENTITIES WITH ANYONE YOU WANT.

You call the teacher "Mom" by mistake.

You have peanut butter in your hair.

You trip over someone's feet and fall down.

Your hair turns purple.

You rip your pants.

CHANGE IDENTITIES WITH THE PERSON ON YOUR RIGHT.

You burn the hamburgers on the grill.

You are very sunburned.

You have a sock hanging from the back of your shirt.

Your dog eats your homework.

EVERYONE CHANGE IDENTITIES—PASS TO THE LEFT.

You fall on a banana peel.

You make an "out" in softball.

You have bird droppings on your head.

You get all wet from being in the rain.

You drop your lunch tray on the floor.

EVERYONE CHANGE IDENTITIES—PASS TO THE PERSON ACROSS FROM YOU.

You are singing and really get off key.

You are hit in the head by a volleyball.

You misspell a very easy word on a test.

You have a big black bruise on your leg.

You can't stop hiccupping.

You are afraid of a noise that turns out to be a little mouse.

CHANGE IDENTITIES WITH ANYONE YOU WANT.

You sneeze while eating and food comes out of your mouth.

You have to square dance with your teacher.

The Good Humor Game

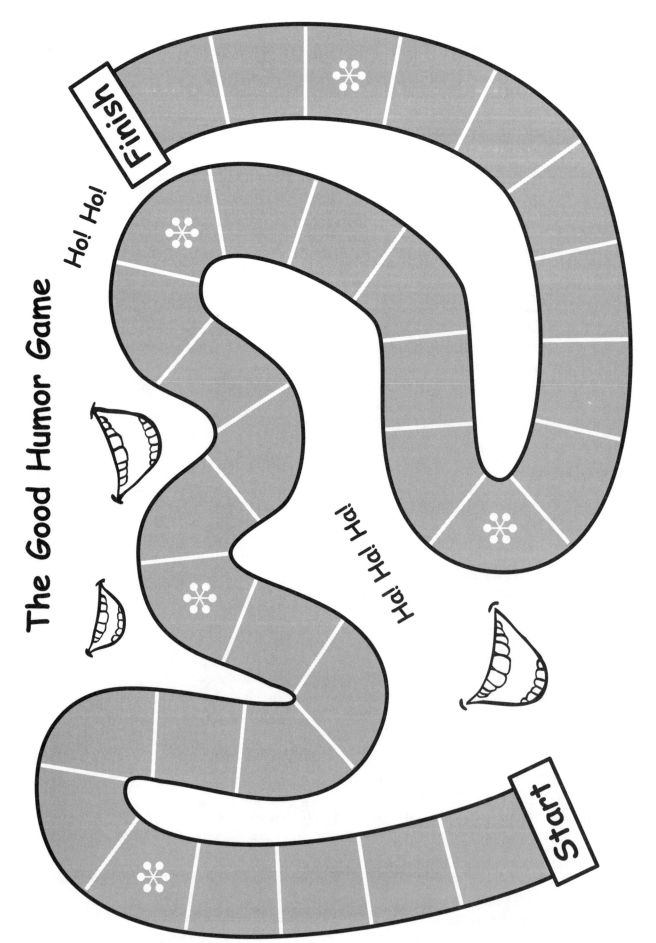

Ho! Ho!

Finish

Ha! Ha! Ha!

Start

# Lesson III-4: Defining Fairness

**The contents of Lesson III-4 include:**

- Journal ideas
- Pre-/Posttest on sense of humor
- Worksheet III-4A, Understanding the Rules
- Worksheet III-4B, "Unwritten" Rules
- Worksheet III-4C, Not Fair!

## Journal Ideas

Students can select ideas from the list to write about in their personal journals. Be sure to allow students time to share their ideas with others.

## Pre-/Posttest

Pass out the pre-/posttest to students and explain that they should read each situation listed and write "fair" or "not fair" on the line.

### Answers

1. fair (this is a weather-related situation with no rule that says it has to be sunny; it is "unfortunate"); 2. fair (it sounds as though there are specific rules about who has chores on certain days); 3. fair (these people probably are happy with the arrangement); 4. unfair (the students were tested on material they were not informed about); 5. unfair (standing in line implies there is an order that should be followed, especially if it inconveniences others); 6. unfair (these two boys are unequally matched for this event); 7. fair (students should have been prepared to take the test on Friday; they had extra time so should be ready to take it on Monday); 8. fair (if it is true that Yvonne missed a lot of leaves; there may be a difference of opinion here and the original agreement would have to be reviewed)

## Worksheet III-4A, Understanding the Rules

1. Write the definition of fairness on the board or other place where students can easily see it. *"Fairness means following the rules of a situation."*

2. Discuss that the first part of following rules implies that you know what the rules are. On this worksheet, students are going to have some practice in determining whether people apparently understand the rules they are to follow.

3. Pass out the worksheet to students and have them complete the review section at the top.

4. Explain that for the rest of the worksheet, they are to read each situation and determine whether or not the characters understand the rules for the situation in which they find themselves.

### Answers

1. second person; 2. first person; 3. first person; 4. second person

### Discuss

1. In situation 1, why is the first girl protesting that something isn't fair? *(she didn't understand the rule about touching the base)*

2. In situation 2, why is it fair for the first boy to take a small piece when everyone else might get a bigger piece? *(he doesn't really want a big piece; a small one is fine with him and he considers it fair to him)*

3. In situation 3, what is the rule that should be followed? *(highest number goes first)* Why is the second girl protesting? *(she thinks the rule is that everyone takes a turn)*

4. In situation 4, both characters are laughing, so what is the problem with the first person? *(he's laughing, but too loudly; inappropriate because it's bothering other people)*

# Worksheet III-4B, "Unwritten" Rules

1. Review the definition of fairness.

2. Pass out the worksheet and have students complete the review section at the top.

3. Briefly discuss the idea that situations may have rules (such as playing baseball, dividing up pizza, knowing who goes first, etc.) "Unwritten" rules are "understood" among people; they are not written rules that everyone would follow. Some examples are when you are with friends and you have an agreement among yourselves of how you will do things. There may be classroom procedures that are "understood" among class members; these rules may differ from class to class.

4. Directions for the rest of the worksheet ask students to identify the "unwritten" rule for each situation.

## Answers

1. Bobby might be smaller or younger, so it is fair for him to have an advantage by getting an extra kick; 2. people in this family share chores; 3. four wrong on a spelling test is a "B"; 4. in their community, people are expected to clean up after their dogs; 5. kids get their choice of TV at that time; Dad gets his choice at 7; 6. the Webster family does not want people riding on their property; 7. it is OK for a person to get up and borrow a pencil during a test if necessary; 8. in this class, on this day, girls line up first before lunch

## Discuss

1. Why do rules change from one situation to another; for example, one classroom to another, among different groups of people, etc.? *(different people have different rules, different needs, different expectations)*

2. In situation 3, how did Sandy know four wrong was a "B"? *(the grading scale must be the same all of the time, perhaps it is posted)*

3. In situation 7, do you think it would be OK in any class for a student to get up and get a new pencil in the middle of a test? *(probably not—have to follow the rules of the class you are in)*

4. In situation 8, do you think the girls always line up first every day? *(probably not; it would not be completely fair for one group to always be first)*

# Worksheet III-4C, Not Fair!

1. Review the definition of fairness.

2. Pass out the cartoon section of the worksheet.

3. Explain that you are going to read a story about a boy named Freddie who has to deal with some situations in his day that he doesn't always think are fair. As you read the story, students should listen and evaluate the episodes of fairness/unfairness that Freddie encounters.

## Answers

See the teacher's script.

# Journal Ideas: Fairness

1. How fair are you in situations? *Rate yourself:*

    0—I never take fairness into account when I make decisions.

    1—I'm usually not very fair.

    2—Sometimes I am fair.

    3—I'm usually pretty fair about things.

    4—I am fair most of the time.

    5—I make sure I am being fair about things.

2. Would you rather play a game in which everyone has a turn and goes in order OR would you enjoy a game that involves chance, such as rolling dice or using a spinner, even if it means you may not get a turn every time?

3. What do you think about people who never study and get a really good grade on a test, compared to people who work really hard at studying and then don't get a good grade? Do you think this is fair? Why or why not?

4. What would you do if you were waiting a long time to go on a roller coaster at an amusement park and a group of people cut in right ahead of you? Would you say anything to them? What would you do?

5. Is it ever fair to give someone else a head start when running a race or playing a game? When is it fair? When is it not fair?

6. What jobs or careers require a great degree of fairness? Why is it important in those jobs?

7. If there were three people who each wanted to eat a cream-filled cupcake that came in packages of two, how could you split it fairly? What if five people wanted to split a pizza that was cut into four pieces? How could four people divide up nine cookies? What creative ways can you think of to be fair to an odd number of people?

8. When was a time you were treated unfairly? Why did you feel this way? What did you do about it?

9. Have you ever been to a sporting event (or participated in one) and heard someone say, "That isn't fair!" What was the situation? What was the person's complaint? Did you agree or disagree?

10. How would you feel if someone kept changing the rules? For example, let's say that on Monday, you have to have 100% on a paper to get an A. On Tuesday, 50% correct is enough to get an A. On Wednesday, it's 89%—but only if you are a girl. If you are a boy, you have to have 98%. On Thursday, anyone with red hair gets an A, no matter what their grade is. On Friday, people with green pencils get an A. How could you make sure you always got an A? Would that even be possible? Would it be fair?

Name _____ Date _____

# Fairness Pretest/Posttest

Read each situation and decide if it shows a situation that is FAIR or NOT FAIR. Write your answers on the lines.

1. Jamie wants to go swimming at the beach on Saturday, but it rains and she can't go. _____

2. In the Miller family, Sasha washes the dishes after meals on Monday, Wednesday, and Friday; Brienna washes the dishes after meals on Tuesday, Thursday, and Saturday. On Sunday, the family goes out to eat. _____

3. There are five candy bars in a bag. Joel and Terry each take two and give one to their sister, Alison, who says that it's fine with her to just get one. _____

4. The science teacher gives a really hard test and includes information on the test that isn't in the book, so students don't have a chance to study for it. _____

5. It is a really hot day and students are standing in line to get a drink from the water fountain. One of the kids in front lets other kids cut in line to get drinks. _____

6. Peter and Tony are playing tug-of-war. Peter is 12 years old and really strong; Tony is in kindergarten and is small. _____

7. The teacher says there will be a test on Friday. But on Friday, school is cancelled due to bad weather so the teacher decides to give the test on Monday instead. _____

8. Yvonne says that she will rake the neighbor's lawn for $10. When she finishes, the neighbor says she missed a lot of leaves and will only pay $7. _____

# III-4A. Understanding the Rules

**Review**

Fairness means f_____ the r_____ of a

s_____.

**Directions:** Which person in each situation below shows that he or she understands the rules?

---

1. **playing baseball—the runner must touch each base while running**

 What do you mean I'm OUT? I went past you a long time ago!

Oops, I went so fast I didn't touch the base with my foot.

---

2. **dividing up pizza—one person may not care how much he or she gets**

I'm not very hungry. I'll just take a small piece.

Everyone gets one big slice and one little slice.

---

3. **game rules—the highest number goes first**

 I rolled a 6—I get to go first!

Hey, no fair! You went first last time. It's someone else's turn to go first.

---

4. **movie rules—be quiet in the theater**

Ha ha HA HA! This is so funny!!

Shhh...

Ha ha ha!

# III-4B. "Unwritten" Rules

**Review**

Fairness means f_____ the

r_____ of a

s_____.

**Directions:** Some rules are decided by the group you are with. What do you think are the "unwritten" rules in each situation below?

1. When playing kickball, Bobby always gets two tries to kick the ball.

   _____

2. Jackie takes out the garbage every week; her sister Kathryn washes the dishes; their brother Jason washes the cars.

   _____

3. Sandy got four wrong on her spelling test, so she wrote "B" at the top of her paper.

   _____

4. Alex takes his dog for a walk in the park. He brings along a little bag and shovel to clean up after the dog.

   _____

5. At 6 o'clock, the kids watch cartoons on TV. At 7 o'clock, their father switches the channel to watch the news.

   _____

6. The neighborhood kids all ride their bikes on the trails behind the Johnsons' house, but they don't go on the Websters' property.

   _____

7. Beth's pencil breaks during a spelling test, so she goes to the teacher's desk to get another pencil to use.

   _____

8. Before going to lunch, the girls line up at the door first and go to the restroom to wash their hands; then the boys line up and go.

   _____

# For the Teacher (Script for Worksheet III-4C, Not Fair!)

Follow along with the pictures about Freddie and his "not fair" day. I will stop to ask you some questions after each picture.

**(Picture 1)** First thing in the morning, Freddie's mom asks him to take out the dog. "Why do I have to?" Freddie asks. "I always have to take out the dog! Why doesn't Teresa ever have to take out the dog? It's not fair!" Freddie's mom hands him the leash. "You know that Teresa leaves before you do," she says. "She doesn't have time, and you do. OUT!"

**STOP.** Is this an unfair chore for Freddie to have to do? *(no)*

**(Picture 2)** Freddie lines up at the bus stop. The bus driver always wants the little kids to line up first and the bigger kids to line up at the back. "Why should those little kids get the best seats?" he asks his friend. "Sometimes I would like to get on first and get the good seats in the back of the bus."

**STOP.** Is this unfair to the bigger kids? *(answers will vary)*

**(Picture 3)** At school, Freddie looks at his math test and sees a big black C at the top. The teacher tells him that he didn't put his name on the paper, so that cost him 2 points, and then he used ink instead of pencil, so he lost points for that. "If you had followed my instructions, you would have had enough points for a B," she tells him. Freddie looks at the paper. "My answers were mostly right," he says. "This grade is not fair."

**STOP.** Is this grade unfair to Freddie if he got the answers right? *(no because he did not follow instructions)*

**(Picture 4)** In P.E., the kids are divided into two teams for soccer. The big kids get the ball all the time and the little kids hardly ever get to play. Freddie is one of the big kids. When one of the little kids complains about not being able to play very much, Freddie says, "You'll get your chance to play when you're bigger. It's our turn right now."

**STOP.** Does Freddie feel that this is a fair arrangement? *(yes)* Is it fair to the little kids? *(no)*

**(Picture 5)** That night Freddie and his friends want to go out for ice cream. "Wait just a minute, young man," he hears his father say. "You're not going out until your homework is done." Freddie protests, "But Dad… I'll do it later! You can't make me stay in while my friends go out without me!" Dad shakes his head. "Sorry, son," he says. "It will only take you about a half hour to finish if you get busy."

**STOP.** Is Dad being fair to Freddie? *(answers will vary)*

**(Picture 6)** While Freddie finishes his homework, his friends decide to go to the drugstore and get some magazines. They want to buy some car magazines and some sports magazines, but don't have enough money. When Freddie catches up with them, they ask if he could give them some money so they could buy the magazines. "I don't know," says Freddie. "How are we going to share the magazines? There are four of us. You want me to buy both magazines?" The boys nod. "Yes. Remember when Jack bought magazines last month? Then you ended up keeping them. It's your turn to buy. We'll all look at them, pass them around, and then you can keep them."

**STOP.** Is this a fair arrangement? *(answers will vary)*

**(Picture 7)** Finally, it is time to head home. Freddie doesn't want to turn out the lights and go to bed right away; he wants to look at his car magazine. His mother thinks he should go to bed. "How about if I look at it for just one hour, and then I'll go right to bed?" he asks his mother. "How about 30 minutes?" she says. "Deal," says Freddie. They shake hands on it, and Mom says goodnight.

**STOP.** Is this a fair arrangement? *(yes)* How do they both benefit? *(Freddie gets to read his magazine and his mother knows he'll be in bed in 30 minutes)*

# III-4C. Not Fair

1.

2.

3.

4.

5.

6.

7.

# Lesson III-5: Recognizing Fairness

**The contents of Lesson III-5 include:**

- Worksheet III-5A, Does This Show Fairness?
- Worksheet III-5B, Unfair or Bad Luck?
- Worksheet III-5C, Fairness with Common Sense

## Worksheet III-5A, Does This Show Fairness?

1. Pass out the worksheet to students and have them complete the review section at the top.

2. On the rest of the worksheet, inform students that they should circle *yes* if it shows fairness or *no* if it does not. They should keep in mind that fairness means following the rules, so they should be on the lookout for the rules of each situation.

### Answers

1. yes (work equals money); 2. yes (bad behavior costs privilege); 3. no (why should one group always go first, unless there is a particular reason, which should then be explained); 4. yes (as long as the homerun was within the rules, no cheating); 5. probably yes (Tony may have adaptations that are necessary for success in school); 6. no (the agreement was for weeding only); 7. no (there is no apparent reason why the boy can't stand in line and wait his turn); 8. no (both agreed to pay); 9. no (this punishment does not fit the problem); 10. no (both should have worked)

### Discuss

1. In some of the examples, the issue of fairness is simply that if you work or do something, you will get something in return. What are some examples of this type of fairness? *(getting an allowance for chores, paying for something or a service)*

2. In other examples, the rule for fairness is taking turns. What are some examples of this type of fairness? *(waiting in line for something, going in order and not switching places)*

3. Yet another type of fairness rule is that of privileges. What are some examples of this type of fairness? *(being allowed to use a calculator, line up first, get something for free)*

## Worksheet III-5B, Unfair or Bad Luck?

1. Pass out the worksheet to students and have them complete the review section at the top.

2. Discuss briefly the concept of "life isn't fair" and how it applies to rules. Basically, there are rules that people make and try to follow in order to be fair; however, nature and accidents and coincidences are not obligated to follow people's rules. Therefore, we sometimes have to deal with things that are not the way we think they should be, but there is little or nothing that can be done about them.

3. On the remainder of the worksheet, have students select the items that show unfairness due to bad luck, etc., rather than breaking of a rule made by people.

## Answers

1. bad luck (unless you were careless with it); 2. bad luck (can't control the weather); 3. no (poor choice); 4. bad luck (sometimes they run out); 5. bad luck (broken machine); 6. no (poor choice); 7. bad luck (no skill involved, just the way the dice fall); 8. no (weren't fast enough to win); 9. bad luck (accident); 10. bad luck (someone wasn't careful about packing it); 11. bad luck (accident); 12. bad luck (accident); 13. bad luck (accident); 14. bad luck (unless there was a specific reason why you were late; it would be no if it was a choice to do something else first to make you late); 15. bad luck (can't control who is on the other team)

## Discuss

1. What are some other examples of weather- or nature-related episodes of unfairness?

2. What are some other examples of episodes of bad luck that you can't control but are unfair?

# Worksheet III-5C, Fairness with Common Sense

1. Pass out the worksheet to students and have them complete the review section at the top.

2. Directions for the rest of the worksheet require students to read the examples and discuss how the characters are trying to be fair but not using common sense.

## Answers

1. the situation has now changed; it is not possible to honor the original promise to get a dog since they can't keep one in the apartment; 2. under normal conditions, it seems as though the boys take turns (which is fair), but one boy had an unusual situation in that there was a party so it isn't really fair to require the other do the extra work; 3. this person demands fairness but is being very picky over who owes what; 4. in this situation, a small child is getting extra "privileges" but the child doesn't even realize what is happening

## Discuss

1. Why isn't it possible to be 100% fair to everyone all the time? (*too many unusual circumstances*)

2. In situation 1, is the mother really being unfair to the boy? Do you think that, under other circumstances, she would get Jason a puppy?

3. In situation 3, the person calculating the bill is very picky. Do you think most people require that degree of "fairness" when dealing with a group decision?

4. In situation 4, there is a very young child playing a game. Do the rules have to apply equally to all players or is this a fair "head start" for the boy?

# III-5A. Does This Show Fairness?

**Review**

Fairness means _____ the _____ of a _____.

**Directions:** Read each example. Circle YES if it shows fairness or NO if it doesn't. Be ready to discuss your answers.

1. Charlie has to do yard work every week to get an allowance from his parents.                                    **YES  NO**

2. The kids are misbehaving at recess, so they lose 5 minutes off their time.                                    **YES  NO**

3. The girls go first to lunch every day.                                    **YES  NO**

4. The baseball team you are playing against gets a homerun in the last inning and wins the game.                                    **YES  NO**

5. Tony is allowed to use a calculator to help him do his math.                                    **YES  NO**

6. Amanda's neighbor says that he will pay her for weeding the garden, but while she is there he asks her to mow the lawn and does not pay her any extra.                                    **YES  NO**

7. Zach is standing in line for a video game at the arcade when an older boy cuts in front of him.                                    **YES  NO**

8. Frank says he will split the cost of a pizza with Ray, but when the pizza comes he finds something else to do and never pays anyone for the pizza.                                    **YES  NO**

9. The kids in a class are very noisy, so the teacher gives them a surprise math test and says it will count for their grade.                                    **YES  NO**

10. Sharon and Michelle agree that they will work together on a science project, but Michelle always seems to have something else to do and Sharon ends up doing most of the project.                                    **YES  NO**

Name _____ Date _____

# III-5B. Unfair or Bad Luck?

**Review**

Fairness means _____ the _____ of a _____.

**Directions:** Sometimes "life isn't fair" and things happen that are no one's fault; they are just bad luck, coincidence, or an accident. Which of the items on the list below are unfair because of bad luck?

1. losing your homework _____

2. having it rain on the day of your field trip _____

3. skipping an assignment because you don't want to do it _____

4. trying to use a pen on a test but it doesn't work _____

5. losing money for a candy bar in a vending machine _____

6. not having enough money to buy a book because you bought candy instead _____

7. losing a game because you didn't get enough points from the dice _____

8. losing a race because you weren't fast enough _____

9. dropping a model car and breaking it _____

10. buying a new board game and finding out that some pieces are missing _____

11. falling off a new bike because you lost your balance _____

12. falling off a board because it was broken _____

13. buying a new sweater and spilling ink all over it _____

14. getting in line too late to get tickets for a concert _____

15. having to play soccer against an older team _____

Name _____ Date _____

# III-5C. Fairness with Common Sense

**Review**

Fairness means _____ the _____ of a _____.

**Directions:** What is wrong with each situation below in which the person is trying to be fair but not using common sense? Discuss your answers.

1.

Mom! You said you would let me have a puppy if I got all A's. Well, I did, so where's my puppy?

Jason, we moved into an apartment when your dad lost his job. We can't keep a puppy here.

2.

We are supposed to take turns washing the dishes. Well, it's your turn. Get busy.

But you had the party and there were 25 people here. It's not really a normal situation!

3.

We agreed we would split the bill. Your share is $13.75. You also drank 1/3 of the extra liter of soda, so you should pay for that as well. And Tommy gave you one of his garlic breadsticks, so that should be added, too. Where is my calculator?

4.

Every time we play this game and I land on your property, you make me pay! But you don't make Billy pay!

Billy is 2 years old.

© 2002 by The Center for Applied Research in Education

# Lesson III-6: Applying Fairness

**The contents of Lesson III-6 include:**
- Worksheet III-6A, Playing Fair, Working Fair, Being Fair
- Worksheet III-6B, Looking for Fairness
- Quiz on Part 14: Fairness
- Game: Follow My Rules

## Worksheet III-6A, Playing Fair, Working Fair, Being Fair

1. Pass out the worksheet to students and have them complete the review section at the top. Remind them that the opposite of being fair is being unfair.
2. Directions for the rest of the worksheet ask students to explain how they could show fairness in various situations.

**Answers**

(Examples) 1. people taking turns; 2. show you are a good sport by shaking hands with the other team, no complaining; 3. cut in pieces; 4. taking turns; 5. taking turns; 6. no cutting in line; 7. asking people to be quiet; 8. starting together

**Discuss**

1. What are ways you can show fairness when playing with others, for example, organized sports, leisure activities, games, etc.?
2. What are ways you can show fairness when you have completed a job or worked on something for someone else?
3. What are ways you can show fairness involving interacting with other people in general?

## Worksheet III-6B, Looking for Fairness

1. Pass out the worksheet to students and have them complete the review section at the top.
2. Explain that their assignment (which may take a few days to complete) is to observe other people in all types of situations, looking for examples of fairness and unfairness. They are to record their findings and impressions (without using real names) on the worksheet.
3. You may want to use a practice sheet as a recording sheet (listing the event, people involved, etc.) and then transfer their information to the actual worksheet, paying attention to filling in the information requested.
4. Have students share their observations with the class.

**Discuss**

1. Was it easy or hard to pick out examples of fairness and unfairness?
2. Do you think your observations were affected by whether or not you knew the people you were observing?
3. Have you been in similar situations? What did you do?

## Quiz on Part 14: Fairness

This quiz can be used as a follow-up activity for this lesson.

**Answers**

1. *(definition)* Fairness means following the rules of a situation.

2. *(examples)* yes (the mother has been doing an unpleasant chore while the child is lying in bed—it seems like they could share this); b. no (it's the child's responsibility to do her homework); c. yes (the person is old, an unwritten rule involved of letting someone older have a break); d. no (he doesn't want to pay for the public pool, but there are expenses involved in maintaining a pool)

3. *(applying)* You may talk to your friends and see if they could possibly share the book; see if one is a fast reader and could read it first, then pass it to the other; see if all three of you can go in together and just buy a copy of the book, etc. Look for creative solutions!

## Game: Follow My Rules

Directions, gameboard, and cards are at the end of this lesson.

# III-6A. Playing Fair, Working Fair, Being Fair

**Review**

Fairness means _____

_____.

The opposite of being fair is being _____.

**Directions:** Draw a picture to show or explain how you could show fairness in these situations:

1. doing chores at home _____

_____

_____

2. losing a close game _____

_____

_____

3. splitting a candy bar with friends_____

_____

_____

4. sharing equipment on the playground _____

_____

_____

5. taking turns using a skateboard_____

_____

_____

6. lining up to get free ice cream _____

_____

_____

7. sitting behind loud people in a movie theater _____

_____

_____

8. running a race _____

_____

_____

# III-6B. Looking for Fairness

**Review**

Fairness means _____

_____.

The opposite of being fair is being _____.

**Directions:** Look for examples of people showing fairness or unfairness all around you. Observe others and record what you see happening. Why do you think it is fair/unfair? What would YOU have done differently?

> **Event/situation:** *(Example: in the park)* **People involved:** *(Example: big kids and little kids)* **What I saw:** *(Example: kids fighting over the swings)* **Fair/unfair:** *(Example: unfair—the big kids were taking them away from the little kids)* **If it were me:** *(Example: I would have let the little kids use the swings)*

**Event/situation:** _____

_____

_____

**People involved:** _____

_____

_____

**What I saw:** _____

_____

_____

**Fair/Unfair:** _____

_____

_____

**If it were me:** _____

_____

_____

# Quiz on Part 14: Fairness

1. What is meant by fairness? _____

_____

_____

2. Which of these people are showing fairness?

3. How could you show fairness in this situation?

Everyone in your class wants to read the new Harry Potter book, so there is a sign-up list in the library. Both of your friends want you to sign them up, and you want to sign up, too. The librarian says there is only room for two more people on the list. What will you do?

_____

_____

_____

_____

# Game for Fairness: Follow My Rules

**Materials:**

- 4 different colored markers (red, blue, green, yellow)
- gameboard (see sample)
- 21 instruction cards (10 are "FAIR" cards with instructions that apply to everyone; 10 are "UNFAIR" cards in which the person who draws the card makes up the rule for movement; 1 COMPLETELY WILD card allows the player to make up an especially generous move)

**Players:** 4

**Objective:** To be the first player to get to the "You Win" square by moving his/her marker according to the rules

**How to Play:**

1. Shuffle all of the FAIR/UNFAIR cards and place them on the table.
2. All players place their markers on the "start" square of the board.
3. Players take turns taking the top FAIR/UNFAIR card, reading it (if it is a FAIR card) and following the instructions. If it is an UNFAIR card, the player who picked up the card gets to make the rules. For example, "If you are red or blue, move ahead one square." Or "If you are green, move backward one square."
4. General rules for the UNFAIR cards:
   a. Movement can only be one square at a time (either forward or backward).
   b. You can choose only one or two colors to move (probably you would choose your own to move forward, but it may be to your advantage to move the opponents backward).
5. Rules for the COMPLETELY WILD card:
   a. You can make your rule apply to any or all of the markers.
   b. You can make your movement rule (forward or backward) up to 5 squares.
6. Play continues by selecting and reading the cards until one player has reached the "YOU WIN" square.
7. FAIR/UNFAIR cards are shuffled and continue to be used until there is a winner.

© 2002 by The Center for Applied Research in Education

| FAIR<br>Everyone moves<br>ahead 1 | FAIR<br>Everyone moves<br>ahead 2 | FAIR<br>Everyone moves<br>ahead 3 |
|---|---|---|
| FAIR<br>Everyone moves<br>ahead 1 | FAIR<br>Everyone moves<br>back 1 | FAIR<br>Everyone moves<br>back 2 |
| FAIR<br>Everyone moves<br>back 3 | FAIR<br>Everyone moves<br>back 1 | FAIR<br>Everyone moves<br>ahead 2 |
| FAIR<br>Everyone moves<br>back 2 | UNFAIR<br>(You choose who moves<br>forward/back 1 space.)<br>(1 or 2 players) | UNFAIR<br>(You choose who moves<br>forward/back 1 space.)<br>(1 or 2 players) |
| UNFAIR<br>(You choose who moves<br>forward/back 1 space.)<br>(1 or 2 players) | UNFAIR<br>(You choose who moves<br>forward/back 1 space.)<br>(1 or 2 players) | UNFAIR<br>(You choose who moves<br>forward/back 1 space.)<br>(1 or 2 players) |
| UNFAIR<br>(You choose who moves<br>forward/back 1 space.)<br>(1 or 2 players) | UNFAIR<br>(You choose who moves<br>forward/back 1 space.)<br>(1 or 2 players) | UNFAIR<br>(You choose who moves<br>forward/back 1 space.)<br>(1 or 2 players) |
| UNFAIR<br>(You choose who moves<br>forward/back 1 space.)<br>(1 or 2 players) | UNFAIR<br>(You choose who moves<br>forward/back 1 space.)<br>(1 or 2 players) | COMPLETELY WILD<br>(You choose 1, 2, 3, or<br>4 players to move<br>forward/back 1, 2, 3, 4,<br>or 5 spaces!) |

# Follow My Rules

| You Lose | You Lose | You Lose | You Lose |
|:---:|:---:|:---:|:---:|
| 10 | 10 | 10 | 10 |
| 9 | 9 | 9 | 9 |
| 8 | 8 | 8 | 8 |
| 7 | 7 | 7 | 7 |
| 6 | 6 | 6 | 6 |
| 5 | 5 | 5 | 5 |
| 4 | 4 | 4 | 4 |
| 3 | 3 | 3 | 3 |
| 2 | 2 | 2 | 2 |
| 1 | 1 | 1 | 1 |
| **Start** | **Start** | **Start** | **Start** |
| 1 | 1 | 1 | 1 |
| 2 | 2 | 2 | 2 |
| 3 | 3 | 3 | 3 |
| 4 | 4 | 4 | 4 |
| 5 | 5 | 5 | 5 |
| 6 | 6 | 6 | 6 |
| 7 | 7 | 7 | 7 |
| 8 | 8 | 8 | 8 |
| 9 | 9 | 9 | 9 |
| 10 | 10 | 10 | 10 |
| You Win | You Win | You Win | You Win |

# Lesson III-7: Defining Open-Minded

**The contents of Lesson III-7 include:**

- Journal ideas
- Pre-/Posttest on open-minded
- Worksheet III-7A, Accepting New Information
- Worksheet III-7B, New Information
- Worksheet III-7C, Class Election

## Journal Ideas

Students can select these or other topics to write about in their personal journals.

## Pre-/Posttest

Pass out the pre-/posttest to students and have the students select the response that shows being open-minded.

**Answers**

1. b (maybe if she tried it she would like it); 2. d (women are quite competitive in sports these days!); 3. a (meeting them will help the person get to know them); 4. d (by getting to know the family, Mom can better decide if she wants Nick to go or not); 5. b (she will probably soon make friends)

## Worksheet III-7A, Accepting New Information

1. Write the definition of *open-minded* on the board or other place where students can easily see it. *"Open-minded means accepting new information."*

2. Discuss that people are always learning new things and part of growing up is learning to make decisions about things based on good information. This lesson is all about being open to new information which might cause you to change your mind to make a better, informed decision.

3. Pass out the worksheet to students and have them complete the review section at the top.

4. Directions for the rest of the worksheet ask students to read the situations and identify the people who are showing that they are accepting new information.

**Answers**

1. first response; 2. second response; 3. second response; 4. first response

**Discuss**

1. What was the new information that the mother got in situation 1? *(her son got an A in reading)*

2. What was the new information in situation 2? *(the neighbor is hard of hearing)*

3. What was the new information in situation 3? *(the team they are going to play has improved a lot)*

4. What was the new information in situation 4? *(there is a wonderful zoo in Chicago)*

5. How could the new information have changed minds in all of these cases? *(the mother could encourage her son to read; the girl might be more understanding of her neighbor; the boy might try harder at practice; the boy might have a better attitude about the trip)*

## Worksheet III-7B, New Information

1. Review the definition of open-minded.

2. Pass out the worksheet and have students complete the review section at the top.

3. Explain that having new information can directly affect what someone does. On the rest of the worksheet, students should read each situation and think about how the new information might change the opinion and actions of the first person. Students should write a brief new ending (with illustrations if desired).

**Answers** (examples)

1. "Cheerleaders really are good athletes and work hard." 2. "I think Donna should be allowed to babysit for the kids." 3. "Sally probably feels pretty sad today." 4. "Maybe Mrs. Jones isn't too tough on kids as a teacher." 5. "I think I'll read the adventure story."

**Discuss**

1. New information is important, but even more important is whether or not the new information is true—from a reliable source. In each situation, what might be a different outcome if the information was wrong? *(would change the outcome—you would have to look for other reasons to explain the situation)*

2. Do you think new information that comes from friends and family is trustworthy? *(could be—as these people might know a situation very closely)*

3. In situation 5, the person is making a personal decision about which book to read. The new information is based on opinions, not fact. Do you think this would affect which book you would pick? *(answers will vary)*

## Worksheet III-7C, Class Election

1. Review the definition of open-minded.

2. Pass out the cartoon section of the worksheet.

3. Explain that you are going to read a story about a class having an election to decide on which student will be the class representative. As you read, students should follow along with the pictures. There are questions to answer after each picture.

**Answers**

See the teacher's script.

# Journal Ideas: Open-Minded

1. How open-minded are you? *Rate yourself* 0 (very close-minded) to 5 (very open-minded)

   0  1  2  3  4  5

2. What is something that you have a very strong opinion about? Why do you feel so strongly about this?

3. If someone wanted to convince you to change your mind, how should he or she go about it? What type of reasoning or arguments appeal to you?

4. When is a time you realized that you had made a big mistake about something? What made you realize that it was a mistake? What changed your mind?

5. What do you do when you want to convince your parents to do something for you or get you something? Write down a possible conversation that you have with your parents. Does it usually work?

6. When you meet someone for the first time, what things help you decide your "first impression" of him or her? The way a person looks? What he or she says? Are you usually right about someone after you get to know him or her?

7. What is a rumor that was going around that turned out to be completely false? How do you think it got started?

8. What do you think older people, perhaps your grandparent's age, think about some of the fads or things that kids your age do? Are they accepting of kids or do you think they have some "old-fashioned" ideas that should change?

9. What are some things that your parents did when they were young that now seem silly or strange? Why do you think they did them?

10. Would you rather know exactly what is going to happen during a day or would you rather be surprised?

# Open-Minded: Pretest/Posttest

Read each situation and choose the response that shows someone being open-minded.

1. Sharon is having dinner at a friend's house. She doesn't like vegetables, but finds several of them on her plate. She could…
   a. Put them on the side of her plate and not eat them.
   b. Try a little bite of each one.
   c. Tell her friend that she is allergic to all vegetables.
   d. Tell her friend that she might throw up if she eats them.

2. Your dad says that girls can't play basketball very well. You sit down with him and have him watch professional women's basketball on television. He could…
   a. Say that men still play better.
   b. Say that the women are pretty.
   c. Say that it's just for fun.
   d. Say that the women do play well.

3. A new neighbor has moved in next door to you. You see a lot of kids and animals running around and are afraid that you are going to have noisy neighbors. You could…
   a. Go over to meet them to find out who your neighbors are.
   b. Spy on them to see how many are going to stay there.
   c. Leave a note that they better be quiet and keep the dogs tied up.
   d. Turn up your music really loud so they don't disturb you.

4. Nick wants to go on a week-long vacation with one of his new friends, but his mom doesn't know the people and doesn't want him to go. She could…
   a. Let Nick go on a trip with his relatives.
   b. Take a family vacation.
   c. Have Nick stay home and do things around the house.
   d. Get to know Nick's friend and his family.

5. Stephanie doesn't want to go to a new school, but her father has been transferred to a new job in a new state. She could…
   a. Live with a friend so she can go to her old school.
   b. Give the new school a try.
   c. Ask her father to get a different job.
   d. Go to the new school, but don't talk to anyone.

Name _____ Date _____

# III-7A. Accepting New Information

**Review**

Open-minded means a_____ n_____ i_____.

**Directions:** Which situations below show someone accepting new information?

1. That book is really hard. You won't be able to read it.

Mom, I got an A in reading. I have really improved.

OK, go ahead and get it.

You are wasting your time and my money. It's too hard.

2. The neighbor is so rude! She never says hi when I talk to her.

Did you know that she is very hard of hearing?

Well, she could still wave!

Oh, I'll have to make sure I speak loudly enough to her.

3. That team is lousy. We won't have any trouble beating them!

They beat last year's champions last week. I think they have improved.

They still are a lousy team.

Maybe they will be tougher than I thought. We better have an extra practice.

4. I don't want to take a vacation to Chicago. There's nothing for kids to do there.

We went to Brookfield Zoo when we were there last summer, and we all had a good time.

Zoos are boring.

I didn't know there was a zoo. We'll go!

Name _____ Date _____

# III-7B. New Information

**Review**

Open-minded means a_____ n_____ i_____.

**Directions:** Write a possible ending for each situation given the new information.

| Situation | New information | Ending |
|---|---|---|

1.
Cheerleaders don't do anything but wave their arms and jump around.

Our cheer-leaders all went to a gymnastics camp last summer and got first place in the competition.

_____
_____
_____
_____

2.
I don't think Donna is responsible enough to be a babysitter for young kids.

Donna babysat all last summer for a family with two small children and they were very happy with her.

_____
_____
_____
_____

3.
Sally is really grouchy.

Her old family dog had to be put to sleep this morning.

_____
_____
_____
_____

4.
Mrs. Jones makes all of the kids in her class write 20-page reports.

Those were the enrichment projects, not for all of the kids, and it was voluntary.

_____
_____
_____
_____

5.
Which book should I read— the adventure story or the biography?

Five kids in the class read the adventure story and really liked it.

_____
_____
_____
_____

# For the Teacher
## (Script for Worksheet III-7C, Class Election)

Follow along with the pictures about a class having an election while I read the story. I will stop to ask questions after each picture.

**(Picture 1)** Mrs. Mack's class is having an election to vote for the Student Council representative. The person who is elected will be the one to meet with the principal to help decide things about the school. There are three students running for election. The first student is a boy named Ramon. Most kids like Ramon because he is a good athlete and friendly to others. Ramon puts signs up all over the school that say: "VOTE FOR RAMON—HE CARES!"

**STOP.** What do you think about Ramon so far? Do you think he might be someone you would consider voting for? *(he's popular, gets along with others)*

**(Picture 2)** The next candidate is a girl named Elizabeth. Elizabeth is a straight-A student and gets along well with her teachers. She was on the Student Council last year, so she already knows what it's like.

**STOP.** Do you think Elizabeth might be a good candidate? Why or why not? *(the experience would probably be helpful)*

**(Picture 3)** The third candidate is Angela. Angela is very artistic and makes beautiful signs that she displays all over the school walls. Everyone knows that Angela is a hard worker and loves to draw.

**STOP.** Would Angela make a good candidate? Do you need more information? *(we don't really know much about her qualifications for Student Council)*

**(Picture 4)** Joey is new to the school, so before he votes for someone for Student Council, he decides to talk to people around school about the candidates. First he talks to Ramon's brother. "Do you think Ramon would make a good Student Council member?" he asks. The brother laughs. "Ramon wants to be on the council because they take a field trip at the end of the year. That's the only reason he wants to get elected."

**STOP.** How do you feel about Ramon now? *(might question how committed he would be)*

**(Picture 5)** Then Joey talks to last year's teacher about Elizabeth, since he knows that the teachers like her. Mrs. Brown sighs and says, "Elizabeth is a hard worker and she is very smart, but her family is moving to Florida so I don't think she'll even be here for the full year."

**STOP.** Will this affect whether you vote for Elizabeth or not? *(probably—why vote for someone who isn't even going to be there?)*

**(Picture 6)** Finally, Joey tries to find out about Angela. He talks to her neighbor. "Angela is always drawing," he says. "She draws on the sidewalk, she draws on the garage, she even draws on the walls of her house. She's pretty good though!"

*(Script for Worksheet III-7C, continued)*

**STOP.** Does this information help you decide whether or not to vote for Angela? *(not really, it doesn't tell anything about her experience or leadership or how she gets along with others)*

**(Picture 7)** The day before the election, all three candidates get up before the class and answer questions.

**STOP.** What questions would you like to ask of the candidates? *(What plans do you have to improve the school? What are your experiences in leadership? Why are you running for this office?)*

**(Picture 8)** Who will you vote for?

Name _____  Date _____

# III-7C. Class Election

1.

2.

3.

4.

5.

6.

7.

8.

# Lesson III-8: Recognizing Open-Minded

**The contents of Lesson III-8 include:**
- Worksheet III-8A, Is This an Open-Minded Person?
- Worksheet III-8B, An Open-Minded Reaction
- Worksheet III-8C, How New Information Can Help You

## Worksheet III-8A, Is This an Open-Minded Person?

1. Pass out the worksheet to students and have them complete the review section at the top.
2. On the rest of the worksheet, students should write YES or NO on the line to indicate whether or not each example shows an open-minded person.

**Answers**

1. no; 2. yes; 3. no; 4. no; 5. yes

**Discuss**

1. In situation 1, why is this person resisting being open-minded? *(does not want to eat the beets)* Do you think he should have to try them? *(maybe, if it is important to a parent or to be polite)*
2. In situation 2, how did the girl change her opinion about the snake? *(she touched it and realized it was not slimy)*
3. In situation 3, the boy did not change his mind about the other boy, even knowing that he is from another country. What do you think might cause the boy to change his mind? *(maybe getting to know him, learning about his culture, learning his language)*
4. In situation 4, the girl does not want to wear the funny dress, even though the other parents are buying it for their daughters. Why doesn't this information cause her to change her mind? *(she just doesn't like the dress and the other daughters are very young and probably don't care so much about the clothes)*
5. In situation 5, why did the boy change his mind about Coach Mike? *(a friend of his had a brother who liked Coach Mike a lot)*

## Worksheet III-8B, An Open-Minded Reaction

1. Pass out the worksheet to students and have them complete the review section at the top.
2. On the rest of the worksheet, students are to select the response that shows how an open-minded person might react to new information.

**Answers**

1. b; 2. a; 3. b; 4. a

**Discuss**

1. In situation 1, why shouldn't Mom be upset with Charles about not doing the dishes? *(it was not his fault that the bus was late)*
2. In situation 2, do you think Alec could have fun on a cruise even if it isn't his first choice for a vacation? *(yes, there are many fun and interesting places to go to, even if they aren't warm)*

3. In situation 3, how would knowing that Rachel didn't have on her glasses make a difference to Darla? *(she would realize that Rachel was not ignoring her on purpose, she just couldn't see her)*

4. In situation 4, why shouldn't Beth feel upset about Julia not inviting her to the party? *(it was a situation in which it was family only, so would not include Beth)*

# Worksheet III-8C, How New Information Can Help You

1. Pass out the worksheet to students and have them complete the review section at the top.

2. Discuss the various ways that new information can be helpful to someone who wants to be open-minded. There are three examples given on the top of the sheet:

A—New information can help you change an opinion that you are wrong about. For example, if you have false beliefs about someone or something, new information can help you realize that you are making a mistake and should change your mind.

B—New information can help you make up your mind. If you are not sure what to choose in a situation, seek out more information which will help you make the best decision.

C—New information can help you confirm what you think; it can reassure you that you are "on the right track." For example, if you believe that someone is your friend and find out that he or she stood up for you when you weren't there, this would help you believe even more strongly that this person is your friend.

3. Have students complete the rest of the worksheet by matching the situations to the three examples (A, B, C) at the top.

### Answers

1. A *(change opinion about the intelligence of poodles)*; 2. B *(helps him decide to ride with a safer driver)*; 3. B *(helps her decide to order something that will be good)*; 4. C *(David thought the game would be difficult and this is confirmed by another person)*; 5. C *(the newspaper confirmed that this will be a tough team to play)*; 6. A *(Sharon will probably change her mind about dying her hair purple)*

### Discuss

1. What are some other examples of having information that will help you change your mind? How do television commercials try to do this?

2. What are some other examples of having information that helps you make choices? Why is it important to make sure you have a good source?

3. What are some other examples of having information that confirms what you think? Have you had personal experience with someone reassuring you that you are doing the right thing?

Name _____ Date _____

# III-8A. Is This an Open-Minded Person?

**Review**

Open-minded means _____ _____ _____.

**Directions:** Read each situation below and decide if it shows an open-minded person. Write YES or NO on the line.

1. I will not eat beets. They are gross.

   Have you ever tried them?

   No, but I know I don't like them.

   _____

2. Snakes are so disgusting! They are ugly!

   Look at the beautiful coloring on my pet snake, Fluffy. He's tame and he won't bite.

   Oh, he's not slimy. Maybe this is a nice one.

   _____

3. That new kid is weird. He looks different.

   He's from Germany. I don't think he understands our language very well.

   He still looks different.

   _____

4. Mom, nobody wears clothes like that!

   That's not true, sweetie. Mrs. Smith and Mrs. Jones both got these cute outfits for their daughters.

   Their kids are 6 years old. I'm not wearing it!

   _____

5. I don't want to sign up for Coach Mike's soccer team. I heard he is really mean.

   My brother was on his team last year and Coach Mike really helped him a lot.

   Your brother played really well last year. Maybe I should sign up for his team.

   _____

Name _____ Date _____

# III-8B. An Open-Minded Reaction

**Review**

Open-minded means _____ _____ _____.

**Directions:** How might someone react to this new information if he or she were open minded? Choose your answer.

1. Charles's mom comes home from work and finds out that Charles has not washed the dishes like he was supposed to. There is a sink full of dirty breakfast dishes! She thinks he is lazy or has forgotten to do them. Then she gets a phone call from the school that says the bus he rides had some engine trouble and is running late.

   a. Mom could be upset with Charles for not washing the dishes before school.

   b. Mom could understand that it wasn't Charles's fault.

2. Alec's family is going to take a trip over spring break, and Alec wants to go somewhere warm. His dad brings home a travel brochure about a cruise to Alaska. He says it might not be warm up there, but there are some really neat things to see.

   a. Alec could decide that a cruise might be fun.

   b. Alec could demand to go somewhere warm.

3. Darla is upset because her friend Rachel seems to be ignoring her at school. Rachel walked right past her and didn't say anything to her. A friend tells her that Rachel has lost her glasses and doesn't see very well without them.

   a. Darla could continue to be mad at Rachel for ignoring her.

   b. Darla could pay attention to whether or not Rachel is wearing her glasses.

4. Beth decides not to invite Julia to her slumber party because Julia did not invite her to the big birthday party she had last weekend. Then Beth finds out that Julia's party was for family only and no friends were invited.

   a. Beth could invite Julia to her slumber party.

   b. Beth could be mad because she wasn't invited.

# III-8C. How New Information Can Help You

**Review**

Open-minded means _____ _____ _____.

**Directions:** Here are three ways that new information can help you:

> A = helps you change an opinion that you are wrong about
> B = helps you make up your mind
> C = helps you confirm what you think

Match each example below to the way (A, B, C) the new information can help you.

| Situation | New Information | How it helps |
|---|---|---|
| 1. Jane thinks that poodles are dumb dogs. | Poodles are quick to learn and are often used in circuses to do tricks. | _____ |
| 2. Pete doesn't know whether to get a ride with Tim or James. | Tim drives very fast. | _____ |
| 3. Carol doesn't know what to order at a restaurant. | The waitress says that pizza is a specialty of the restaurant. | _____ |
| 4. David thinks the video game his dad just bought is very complicated. | David's friend spent about an hour trying to figure out the directions, and he is really good at computers. | _____ |
| 5. Jerry thinks their softball team is going to lose when they play the Eagles. | The newspaper announced that the Eagles are the #1 team in the state right now. | _____ |
| 6. Sharon wants to dye her hair purple. | The dye that Sharon wants to use made other people's hair fall out. | _____ |

# Lesson III-9: Applying Open-Minded

**The contents of Lesson III-9 include:**
- Worksheet III-9A, How I Feel About…
- Worksheet III-9B, Ways to Become More Open-Minded
- Quiz on Part 15: Open-Minded
- Game: Consider the Source

## Worksheet III-9A, How I Feel About…

1. Pass out the worksheet to students and have them complete the review section at the top. Remind them that the opposite of being open-minded is being close-minded.

2. Directions for the rest of the worksheet ask students to think about various ideas in terms of how they feel about them: whether they are open-minded, not sure, or haven't even thought about them at all. They are to list ideas for each of the three areas.

**Discuss**

1. What are some things you are absolutely sure about?

2. Do you think it is important to NOT be open-minded about some things?

3. Do you think it is important to BE open-minded about many things?

4. What are some topics or ideas important in your school or community that you have not given any thought to? Why do you think this is?

5. Do you think you are becoming more open-minded as you learn more about things that are important to your school and the community?

## Worksheet III-9B, Ways to Become More Open-Minded

1. Pass out the worksheet to students and have them complete the review section at the top.

2. On the rest of the worksheet, students should refer to worksheet III-9A when they complete the questions and comments on this worksheet. At the end, they will share some of their ideas with a partner.

**Discuss**

1. What are some sources that can provide information? *(people, books, news)*

2. How can you tell if a source is reliable or not? *(Are they truthful? Are they informed? Do they have a history of being reliable?)*

3. Do you think some people just do not want to be open-minded or change their opinions about something, no matter how much information they are given? Why do you think this is?

4. Why is it important to be open-minded? *(so you are available to make better decisions)*

## Quiz on Part 15: Open-Minded

This quiz can be used as a follow-up activity for this lesson.

**Answers**

1. *(definition)* Open-minded means accepting new information.

2. *(examples)* a. yes (considering the possibility of a mistake); b. no (has already decided that rats are stupid); c. yes (just realized that Tom was embarrassed by the fall); d. no (the team has not won a game in the last seven and it is unlikely they will win the championship)

3. *(applying)* a. Might talk to some of the other neighbors to see what they want to do about this; b. You might think about sticking up for your mother and not planting any flowers; c. This might change your mother's mind since there is no work involved; d. You might ask your mother to reconsider starting up another all-neighbor rule since she found it difficult at first to want to conform to the first one.

## Game: Consider the Source

Directions, sample gameboard, and cards are at the end of this lesson.

Name _____  Date _____

# III-9A. How I Feel About...

**Review**

Open-minded means _____
_____.

The opposite of being open-minded is _____.

**Directions:** Think about what things you are open-minded about, what things you have made up your mind about (and why), and some things you have never even given any thought to! There are some examples given, but add your own ideas to the list.

## I have made up my mind about...

I believe my father is wonderful.

I believe we are put on the Earth for a reason.

I am sure that having my own bedroom is really necessary.

**My ideas:**

_____

_____

_____

## I am open-minded about...

what kinds of pets are interesting.

the best basketball team.

what to do this weekend.

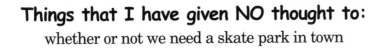

**My ideas:**

_____

_____

_____

## Things that I have given NO thought to:

whether or not we need a skate park in town

ways to recycle

how to make money this summer

_____

_____

_____

# III-9B. Ways to Become More Open-Minded

**Review**

Open-minded means _____
_____.

The opposite of open-minded is _____.

**Directions:** Use your responses to worksheet III-9A (How I Feel About…) to complete this exercise in becoming more open-minded. (Use another sheet of paper if you need more space for your answers.)

## Part 1: I have made up my mind about…

1. Choose one of your ideas. Write it here: _____
_____

2. Give reasons why you believe this so strongly. _____
_____

3. Is there any information about this idea that would ever make you change your mind? If so, what?

_____
_____

## Part 2: I am open-minded about…

4. Choose one of your ideas. Write it here: _____
_____

5. What thoughts do you have about this idea that need more exploring? For example, what aren't you sure about? What information would help you find out more?

_____
_____
_____

6. What sources could you go to that would help you make up your mind or form a definite opinion about this idea?

_____
_____
_____

## Part 3: I have given little or no thought to...

7. Choose one of your ideas. Write it here: _____

_____

8. Do you think this idea is important enough to find out more about it?

_____

9. How does it affect you and your life? _____

_____

10. What are some good sources who/that could help you learn more about this idea?

_____

## Part 4. Partner Activity

After you have completed Parts 1–3, pair up with a partner and discuss the following questions:

11. Have your partner choose one of the ideas you listed in Part 1. Explain to your partner why you feel very strongly about this idea. What happened in your life or thoughts to make you feel so strongly? Trade roles and question your partner about one of his or her ideas.

12. Have your partner choose one of the ideas you listed in Part 2. Together, come up with at least five sources of information that might help you form a more definite opinion about your idea. Then trade roles again.

_____

_____

_____

13. Have your partner choose one of the ideas you listed in Part 3 that you think is important. Together, come up with at least five sources of information that might help you form a more definite opinion about this idea.

_____

_____

_____

Do you think this topic will become more important to either of you now? Why or why not?

_____

_____

_____

# Quiz on Part 15: Open-Minded

1. What is meant by being open-minded? _____

_____

2. Which of the following people are showing open-mindedness?

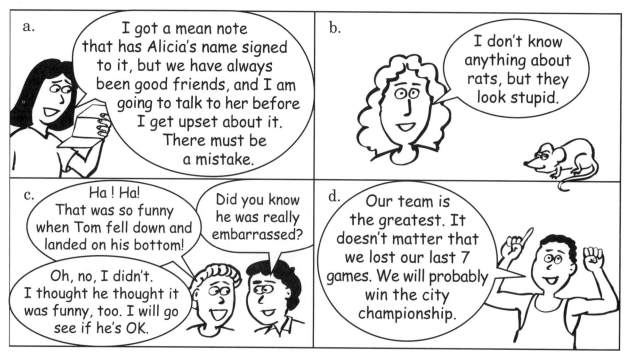

3. How could you show open-mindedness in each situation? Write your answers on the back of this sheet.

   a. Your neighbor wants everyone on the block to plant red tulips so that in the spring, all of the yards will look the same. She is going around having all of the neighbors sign a paper that says they want to do this. You have never given any thought to whether or not you care if there are flowers in everybody's yard or not. How will you make up your mind?

   b. Later, your mother comes home and says that she hates red tulips because they remind her of how much yard work she had to do when she was a child. In fact, she doesn't like flowers at all. She would rather just have bushes. What are your thoughts now?

   c. Later, your other neighbor comes over and says that someone has a truckload of red tulips and will donate them to the neighborhood. They are free! In fact, they will even have people come and plant them in people's yards so there is no yard work involved at all. What do you think you might do now?

   d. Finally, your mother says that she doesn't want to cause problems in the neighborhood, so if everyone else wants red tulips, there can be red tulips. But now she wants to start a letter going around the neighborhood for everyone to have blue mailboxes so they will all look alike. What are you going to do?

# Game for Open-Minded: Consider the Source

**Materials:**

- gameboard for each set of players
- spinner with 6 choices: good information, false information, reliable source, bad information, true information, not a trustworthy source
- 24 situation cards (see samples)
- game markers in two colors (one for each player)

**Objective:** To play 3 cards in a row on a 3 by 3 grid

**Players:** 2

**How to Play:**

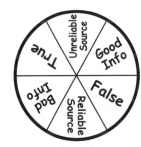

1. Shuffle the situation cards.
2. Each player takes his or her game marker pieces.
3. One player goes first by taking the top situation card and reading it out loud.
4. That player then spins the spinner to see whether or not his or her information is reliable. If it is, that player can put a marker on any square on the gameboard.
5. Play goes to the other player. He/she reads the next situation card and spins the spinner to see if the information is reliable. If it is, he or she can put a marker on any available square. If it is not, he or she loses that turn.
6. Play continues in this manner until one player has three in a row. (Game is similar to Tic-Tac-Toe.)

| | | |
|---|---|---|
| Your mother tells you to sweep out the garage, but your sister says you can do it later. | You think your bike is in good shape, but your brother says it is missing a wheel. | You want to stay overnight at your friend's house, but someone tells you your friend is mad at you. |
| You don't want to go to camp in the summer until you read a paper about it that describes how much fun it is. | You think your apple pie turned out awful until your neighbors tell you that it tastes really good. | You think the new boy in school is really nice until you hear that he smokes and drinks. |
| You think a friend is ignoring you, but someone tells you that your friend lost his glasses and didn't notice you. | You are laughing at a friend until he tells you that he is really upset that you are laughing at him. | You think a friend is bragging too much, but he tells you that he's just kidding, he's not really bragging. |

| | | |
|---|---|---|
| A friend didn't invite you to her skating party, and you heard it was because she didn't have enough money to invite everyone. | You think your new neighbors are OK, but your other neighbors tell you the new neighbors are crazy. | You always walk your dog on your neighbor's lawn until you get a note that says they don't want you on their property anymore. |
| You wonder why your neighbors always leave their new car outside. Your friend tells you they have a really expensive sports car that they keep in the garage. | Your neighbors are a different race and religion than you, but you heard that they are really interesting people who like to talk about their lives. | Your neighbors ask you if you could turn down your loud music, and they tell you that it's only because they have company over who is bothered by it. |
| Your teacher next year is Mrs. Jones, and you are worried because someone who had her this year said she is really tough on everybody. | You are really hungry, but you hear that the cafeteria is serving really bad hamburgers for lunch. | You think the bus driver is really crabby today, but you overhear someone say he is sick and doesn't feel very well today. |
| You want to read a mystery book for your next book report, but the librarian says they are all checked out so you should find something else. | You hate art class because you don't think you draw very well, but your art teacher tells you that you are fantastic! | You really want to be a starting player on the soccer team, but you hear that the coach said you don't try hard enough. |
| Your team practices once a week, but you hear someone say that your team is going to start practicing every day if they don't improve. | Your team is getting a lot of fouls called against it, and a parent says it is because the referee has a son on the other team. | The new kid on your team seems like he doesn't understand how to play, but you hear that he went to a special camp all summer for good athletes so he must be pretty good. |
| You think your team is never going to be able to beat your rivals from across town, but you hear that half of their players are sick and the other half skipped practice, so maybe you have a chance. | | |

# Consider the Source

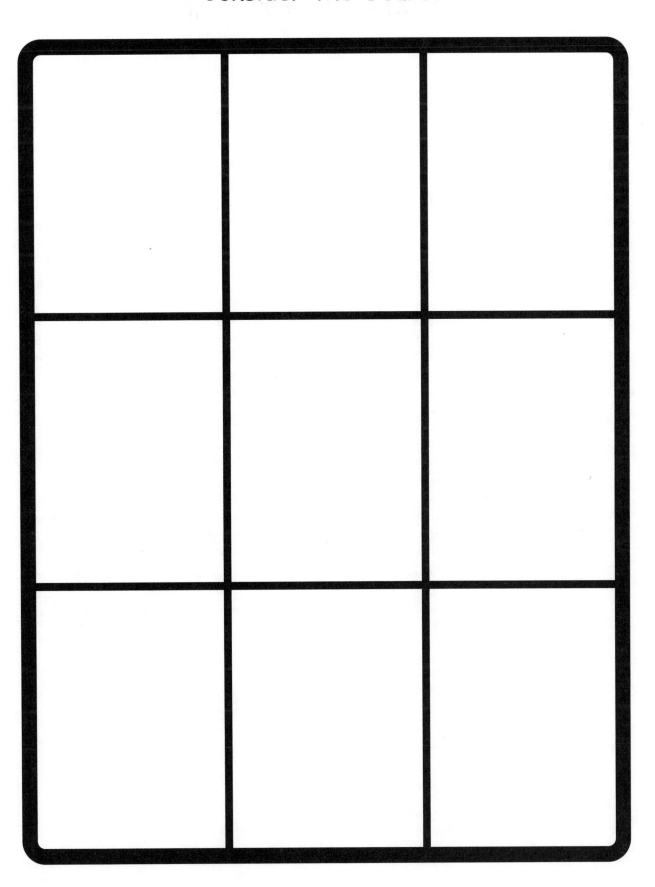

# Lesson III-10: Defining Initiative

**The contents of Lesson III-10 include:**

- Journal ideas
- Pre-/Posttest on initiative
- Worksheet III-10A, Knowing What Needs to Be Done…
- Worksheet III-10B, …and Doing It
- Worksheet III-10C, Taking Out the Trash

## Journal Ideas

Students can select these or other topics to write about in their personal journals.

## Pre-/Posttest

Pass out the pre-/posttest to students and have them identify opportunities to demonstrate initiative that are apparent in the picture.

### Answers

mow the lawn (grass is very high); bring in the bike (looks like rain); wash the dishes in the sink; take out the garbage; pick up the broom and put it away; take care of the crying baby; let the dog out; clean off the breakfast table; put the milk in the refrigerator; call the dentist (note tacked to refrigerator); put bottle of poison out of reach of the child; little boy has a cut on his leg (needs bandage)

## Worksheet III-10A, Knowing What Needs to Be Done…

1. Write the definition of *initiative* on the board or other place where students can easily see it. *"Initiative means knowing what needs to be done and doing it."*

2. Discuss these categories of knowing what needs to be done: (a) putting things in order—this is important to be organized and do things efficiently; (b) considering how a person feels—this is important to make sure relationships are smooth between people and to offer assistance if needed; and (c) safety issues—this is important to make sure that unsafe situations are prevented before accidents occur.

3. Pass out the worksheet to students and have them complete the review section at the top.

4. Directions for the rest of the worksheet ask students to categorize the items according to one of the three categories discussed above.

### Answers

1. c (safety); 2. b (person's feelings); 3. a (handling situation efficiently); 4. c (safety); 5. b (considering the baby's feelings); 6. c (safety); 7. a (taking care of the situation; or possibly b—considering how they feel); 8. a (efficiency); 9. b (person's feelings); 10. a (keep the mower running efficiently); 11. c (safety, so someone doesn't fall); 12. b (considering Dad's feelings)

**Discuss**

1. For the "a" responses, how would these actions help things run efficiently? Are these the kind of jobs that usually you have to wait for someone else to tell you to do them?

2. For the "b" responses, how are a person's feelings important in each situation? Why is it helpful to think ahead and try to determine how a person might feel in each situation?

3. For the "c" responses, how is safety an issue? What could possibly happen if the situation was not taken care of?

# Worksheet III-10B, ... and Doing It

1. Review the definition of initiative.

2. Pass out the worksheet to students and have them complete the review section at the top.

3. On the rest of the worksheet, explain that students are to read the situations and select the person in each example who is actually doing what needs to be done.

**Answers**

1. first person; 2. second person; 3. first person; 4. first person; 5. second person

**Discuss**

1. In situation 1, why isn't it enough for the little brother to check in with the big brother every half hour? *(safety issue—a half hour is a long enough time for him to get into trouble)*

2. In situation 2, what's wrong with the first person's response? *(if there's room, it would be efficient to squeeze more in; probably, however, the person is avoiding the task of taking it out)*

3. In situation 3, the message is that the library books are due tomorrow. What's wrong with the second person's response? *(he wants his mother to do his job for him)*

4. In situation 4, what's wrong with the second person's response? *(copying the answers is not the right solution; the first person took initiative to think ahead and make a list for the girl who was absent)*

5. In situation 5, the first girl is being polite. Why isn't this showing initiative? *(she's a nice girl, but is not taking initiative to think about what might be helpful to the neighbors while they are gone)*

# Worksheet III-10C, Taking Out the Trash

1. Review the definition of initiative.

2. Pass out the cartoon section of the worksheet.

3. Explain that you are going to read a story about some people who did not take initiative in a situation and what happened. Students should follow along with the pictures as you read and answer the questions.

**Answers**

See the teacher's script.

# Journal Ideas: Initiative

1. How good are you at taking initiative—seeing what needs to be done and then doing it? *Rate yourself* 0–5.

   0 = I never take initiative to do things.

   1 = I very seldom take initiative to do things.

   2 = I take initiative once in awhile to do things.

   3 = I sometimes take initiative to do things.

   4 = I usually take initiative to do things.

   5 = I always take initiative to do things.

2. What would you do if you saw an expensive camera left on the playground? How far would you go to try to find the owner?

3. Pretend you are planning a surprise birthday party for your mother or father. What things would you need to think about and organize to do it?

4. Your mother informs you that you are having company—your very old, very rich, very picky great-aunt—who is coming to visit for a month and she'll be staying in YOUR room. And guess what ! She'll be at your house in about 10 minutes. What are you going to do?

5. Make a list of 5 things that would make your school or classroom a better place. Now: What could you do about making them happen?

6. The dog's water bowl is empty and Fluffy is scratching at it, picking it up in her teeth and looking up at you. You have a lot of homework to do and it's not your job to take care of the dog. What will you do? Why?

7. The weather report is calling for a big storm to come, and you and your brother or sister left your bikes outside. The sky is sunny and it doesn't look like anything is going to happen. Would you go out to get them in the rain? Would your brother or sister?

8. Place an empty crushed soda can next to a trash container and position yourself where you can watch people pass by. Count how many of the first 10 people who pass by actually stop to throw it into the trash. Summarize your findings.

9. What jobs or careers would require someone with a lot of initiative to get things done? Why?

10. Who is someone you know who is a real "go-getter"? What does this person do that makes you think of him or her in this way?

© 2002 by The Center for Applied Research in Education

# Initiative Pretest/Posttest

Look at the picture below. If you were a person who takes initiative to do things, what are some opportunities that you can find in this picture? List your answers.

# III-10A. Knowing What Needs to Be Done...

**Review**

Initiative means k_____ what n_____ to be

d_____, and d_____ it.

**Directions:** Read the items below and decide which of these categories they fit into:

> **a. putting things in order**
> **b. considering how a person feels**
> **c. safety issues**

_____ 1. You see a board with a big nail sticking out of it.

_____ 2. It is your sister's birthday today and you know it is important to her.

_____ 3. The phone is ringing and no one is getting up to answer it.

_____ 4. Your brother is standing on a ladder to change a light bulb but no one is holding the base of the ladder and it's wiggling.

_____ 5. Your baby sister is crying in her crib.

_____ 6. There is broken glass on the kitchen floor.

_____ 7. Everyone is hungry and tired so you order a pizza for dinner.

_____ 8. You arrange for someone to take back a late library book.

_____ 9. You see a frightened child in the grocery store who is lost.

_____10. The lawn mower is low on gas, so you put some in.

_____11. There is a loose rug in front of the slippery doorway of your house.

_____12. Your dad is tired when he gets home late from work.

Name _____ Date _____

# III-10B ...and Doing It

**Review**

Initiative means k_____ what n_____ to be

d_____, and d_____ it.

**Directions:** Read each situation and circle the person who knows what needs to be done, and then is doing it.

1. "Don't let your brother play in the parking lot. It's too dangerous." "Stay here where I can watch you." "Check in with me every half hour, OK?"

2. "Time for the garbage to go out." "I can squeeze more in there." "I'll take it out."

3. LIBRARY BOOKS ARE DUE TOMORROW "I'll get them tonight and put them in my book bag." "Mom, would you take my book to the library?"

4. "Will you let me know the assignments I missed?" "I made a list for you." "You can just copy answers."

5. "We're going to Florida for a week." "Have a good time!" "Would you like me to get your mail for you?"

# For the Teacher
## (Script for Worksheet III-10C, Taking Out the Trash)

Follow along with the pictures as I read a short story about garbage. I will stop to ask questions after each picture.

**(Picture 1)** Early in the morning, the school custodian puts an empty trash can in the hallway. He puts a black trash bag in the can and takes the lid off. He puts it right by the door of the cafeteria.

**STOP.** What's the purpose of a trash can? *(to throw trash in)* Can you think of any other uses for a trash can? Do you think most people know what it's used for? Since it is close to the school cafeteria, what do you think might end up in the trash can? *(food, plastic bottles, school papers, etc.)*

**(Picture 2)** School starts, and the kids get off the bus and come into the building. Johnny throws a broken pencil into the trash can. Marie finds some old papers in the back of her folder and tosses them into the trash can.

**STOP.** How are these students showing initiative? *(they are using the trash can properly, to throw their unwanted things away)*

**(Picture 3)** At lunch, Rick crumples up his soda can and tries to shoot it into the trash can, as if he were playing basketball. He doesn't make it! The can hits the side of the trash can and lands on the ground. Rick laughs and walks on by. His friend, George, tries to do the same thing with his crumpled-up can, but his friend isn't very accurate either, and the can lands on the ground next to the trash can. Nick tries too, but without luck. Now there is a small pile of cans next to the big trash can.

**STOP.** What's happening now with the trash? *(kids are goofing around and not putting trash into the can)*

**(Picture 4)** Alison walks by the trash can as she leaves the cafeteria and sees the small pile of cans on the ground. "I wonder why there are so many?" she thinks to herself. "Maybe someone is collecting them to recycle them." She puts her soda can on the ground next to the others.

**STOP.** Why does Alison put her can on the ground instead of in the trash can? *(she saw so many of the cans she figured there was a reason)*

**(Picture 5)** As the day goes on, more and more kids put their soda cans on the ground next to the others. The pile grows and grows. Even the teachers and the principal see the stack and think someone is collecting them.

**STOP.** Why do you think it seems OK for there to be so much trash on the ground? *(there was a big pile and it was growing; no one was stopping the wrong thinking)*

**(Picture 6)** At the end of the day, people can hardly see the trash can because of all the soda cans surrounding it. The night custodian comes in after school and sees the message that is left for him: "Don't forget to empty the trash can by the cafeteria." He goes to the trash can, peeks in, and sees that it is practically empty. "Well, this will be easy," he says. He empties the trash can of a broken pencil and a few pieces of paper. He steps carefully around the piles of soda cans, thinking they are someone's project.

**STOP.** Why doesn't the night custodian pick up the soda cans? *(he thought they were there for a reason)* Did he properly do his job? *(he followed the written directions, but didn't take initiative to get rid of the cans)*

**(Picture 7)** The same thing continues for the next few days. No one uses the trash can, and everyone puts their cans next to it. Finally, the principal comes on the P.A. system and asks whoever is collecting the soda cans for recycling to come and get them, as the pile is taking over the school. The teachers all look at each other and ask who is collecting the cans. No one knows anything about them.

**STOP.** How do you think this problem will be resolved? *(Answers will vary.)*

**(Picture 8)** Rick, George, and Nick talk to their teacher about the soda cans. "We have an idea," Rick says. "Why don't we take the cans to the recycle center and use the money we get to put towards a new basketball hoop for the playground?" No one has a better idea, so the teacher says they may go ahead with the recycling idea. It takes a few months, but many cans are recycled and the boys raise enough money to buy a basketball hoop. The principal comes up to the boys and says, "You boys really took some initiative to make this happen. Fine job!" The boys smile and toss the basketball towards the hoop. Maybe you can guess… it didn't go in!

**STOP.** How did the boys use initiative in this situation? *(they recognized what needed to be done—get rid of the soda cans—and did something about it)*

# III-10C. Taking out the Trash

1.

2.

3.

4.

5.

6.

7.

8.

# Lesson III-11: Recognizing Initiative

**The contents of Lesson III-11 include:**
- Worksheet III-11A, Does This Show Initiative?
- Worksheet III-11B, What Could You Do?
- Worksheet III-11C, Initiative with Common Sense

## Worksheet III-11A, Does This Show Initiative?

1. Pass out the worksheet to students and have them complete the review section at the top.
2. Directions for the rest of the worksheet ask students to read the examples and write YES or NO to indicate whether or not it shows initiative.

### Answers

1. no (should do it sooner than next week); 2. yes (put them in safe-keeping before they become broken); 3. yes (thinking ahead to line it up before the night of the party); 4. yes (so the dog won't get lost or stolen or do damage); 5. no (you should open the door yourself!); 6. no (this shows knowing what needs to be done, but not doing it); 7. yes (you realized that milk needs to be put back in the refrigerator); 8. no (hamsters need more care than that)

### Discuss

1. Why isn't it showing initiative if you ask someone else to do a job that needs doing? *(this is delegating a job, which is OK in some circumstances, but if you are able to do the job, it would show following-through by finishing what needs to be done)*
2. In situation 4, what considerations might you have to think about if the dog was mean or if you didn't know the dog? *(safety issues—not getting hurt by the dog)*
3. In situation 6, the person is showing that he or she has a good idea about the track meet, but how could the person do what needs to be done? *(take care of providing ribbons for the track meet)*

## Worksheet III-11B, What Could You Do?

1. Pass out the worksheet to students and have them complete the review section at the top.
2. Students should write or draw a picture to show someone taking initiative for each example on the worksheet.

### Answers (examples)

1. cleaning up the room; 2. checking with the teacher to get assignments; 3. calling the bowling alley ahead of time to make reservations; 4. catching the dog, replanting flowers; 5. throw the ball back; 6. take sunscreen on your trip, wear shorts; 7. have a meal prepared for her; 8. make sure half of the pizza is without mushrooms

### Discuss

1. In each example, what needs to be done and what is actually being done to accomplish it?
2. Why is it important to take care of these things without waiting to be told by someone?

## Worksheet III-11C, Initiative with Common Sense

    1. Pass out the worksheet to students and have them complete the review section at the top.

    2. Have students read and respond to the situations on the worksheet, discussing how each depicts a situation in which common sense is not being used.

**Answers** (examples)

    1. it is obvious that the dog wants to go out, but the girl is not paying attention; 2. the boy knows what needs to be done, but he is not taking responsibility to complete the task; 3. it is good that she warned the boy not to play with matches, but she needs to do something about it; 4. it would take a long time to cover everything that is in the yard and it is probably unnecessary if it isn't going to rain; 5. two months are probably much more time than is needed to reserve the unpopular video; 6. the boy is being silly by not stopping the baby, which was not Mother's intention when she said to mind his own business

**Discuss**

    1. In each example, what task needs to be done?

    2. In each example, what could or should the person do to complete the task?

Name _____ Date _____

# III-11A. Does This Show Initiative?

**Review**

Initiative means _____ what

_____ to be done, and

_____ it.

**Directions:** Read each example below. Write YES if it shows initiative; write NO if it does not.

1. The grass is really high in your front yard, but you will wait until next week to mow it when you might have more time.  _____

2. Someone left a pair of glasses on the playground, so you take them to the lost and found.  _____

3. You are having a few friends over to spend the night on Friday, so you ask your friend on Wednesday if you can borrow her CD player.  _____

4. Your neighbor's gate was left open and their dog is running around the neighborhood, so you try to catch him and put him back in their yard.  _____

5. At the store, a man is carrying a very heavy bag so you tell your friend that he should open the door for him.  _____

6. Your class is having a track meet against another school and you think it would be fun to have ribbons.  _____

7. You poured some milk on your cereal at breakfast, and then you put the carton back in the refrigerator.  _____

8. Your family is going to be gone for two weeks, but you think the hamster will be OK if you leave him some food and water in a bowl.  _____

# III-11B. What Could You Do?

**Review**

Initiative means _____ what _____ to be _____,

and _____ it.

**Directions:** Write or draw a picture to show what you could do in each situation to demonstrate taking initiative. Use another sheet of paper for your answers.

1. Your room is a mess and company is coming very soon.

2. You have been sick for 3 days and missed a lot of homework assignments.

3. You want to have a surprise birthday party for your friend at a bowling alley.

4. Your neighbor's dog dug up all the flowers in your yard and is going through the trash.

5. You and your friends are playing catch in the park and someone's ball rolls over near you.

6. You listen to the weather report and hear that it is going to be sunny and over 100 degrees on the day of your outdoor field trip.

7. Your mother has been in the hospital for a week having surgery and is coming home today.

8. You are ordering pizza for a group of your friends and you realize that one of the people really does not like mushrooms, but everyone else does.

© 2002 by The Center for Applied Research in Education

Name _____ Date _____

# III-11C. Initiative with Common Sense

**Review**

Initiative means _____ what _____ to be _____,

and _____ it.

**Directions:** What's wrong with each situation? Why isn't the person using common sense to show initiative?

1.

Ellen! Let the dog out!

Why?

2.

Here, I made a list of everything everyone should do. Call me if you need me. I'll be playing games on the computer.

3.

You really shouldn't be playing with matches. See ya later.

4.

I'm going to cover everything in case it rains. It will just take me an hour or so.

The weather report says "sunny" for the next three days...

5.

We want to get that video for the party, so I'm going to plan ahead and take it now.

But the party is two months away and it's not a very popular video.

6.

Mom told me to mind my own business, so I'm not going to stop the baby from touching the wet paint.

# Lesson III-12: Applying Initiative

**The contents of Lesson III-12 include:**
- Worksheet III-12A, How Can I Show Initiative?
- Worksheet III-12B, My Personal Contract
- Quiz on Part 16: Initiative
- Activity: Create a Superhero!

## Worksheet III-12A, How Can I Show Initiative?

1. Pass out the worksheet to students and have them complete the review section at the top. Discuss how the opposite of initiative is being "lazy" or not hard-working.
2. Directions for the rest of the worksheet ask students to list specific ways that they can show initiative in a variety of situations in their lives.

**Discuss**

1. What are some ways you chose to show initiative at home? School? With your friends? In your community? Other areas?
2. Which of these will be the hardest for you? Which will be the easiest? Why?

## Worksheet III-12B, My Personal Contract

1. Pass out the worksheet to students and have them complete the review section at the top.
2. Students should complete a personal contract by following the steps on the rest of the worksheet. Guide students step by step through the process of selecting a behavior that they feel could be personally improved, identifying steps to show initiative, and enlisting the help of someone who will share the responsibility for working on this behavior. Over the next two weeks (or whatever length of time is feasible), each student should log his or her behavior and progress on this task. Signing and dating the contract (with a witness) is helpful to make the contract seem serious and official.

**Discuss**

1. Did you choose a behavior that seems easy to do or did you choose one that you think will be difficult?
2. How did you select someone to be your "helper"? Did you pick a friend or an adult? How will this person help you?
3. After you have worked on this task, evaluate your progress. What went well? What was difficult? Do you think you are better at taking initiative in this area now?

## Quiz on Part 16: Initiative

This quiz can be used as a follow-up activity for this lesson.

**Answers:**

1. *(definition)* Initiative means knowing what needs to be done, and doing it.

2. *(examples)* a. yes (the boy recognizes a safety issue and is getting help); b. yes (the girl is anticipating Grandma's dinner needs); c. no (the boy is very careless and thinks getting a new bike is the answer); d. no (the ice will melt; there needs to be a better solution)

3. *(applying)* Answers will vary.

## Activity: Create a Superhero!

Directions for this activity are at the end of this lesson.

# III-12A. How Can I Show Initiative?

**Review**

Initiative means _____
_____.

The opposite of showing initiative is being _____.

**Directions:** What are some ways you can show initiative in these situations?

## At home...

_____

_____

_____

## At school...

_____

_____

_____

## With my friends...

_____

_____

_____

## In my community or neighborhood...

_____

_____

_____

## In my sports, hobbies, other activities...

_____

_____

_____

# III-12B. My Personal Contract

**Review**

Initiative means _____
_____.

The opposite of showing initiative is being _____.

**Directions:** Complete the personal contract below to take steps to show initiative.

Select something you think you could improve on to show initiative. Some ideas are:

- cleaning up your room
- keeping your desk at school organized
- picking up litter on the playground
- setting the table at home without being asked
- making a new friend
- organizing a project or party

I would like to be better at: _____
_____.

How will you take steps to do this?

1. _____

2. _____

3. _____

Who is someone who can help you stay on track? (helper) _____

Report your progress every day for at least two weeks. (Use another sheet of paper.)

I will try to take initiative to be better at this task. Date starting: _____

Signed: _____

Helper: _____

Witness: _____

Name _____  Date _____

# Quiz on Part 16: Initiative

1. What is meant by initiative? _____

_____

2. Which of the following examples show someone taking initiative?

a. You have a cut on your leg! Stay here and don't move. I'll go get the teacher.

b. Grandma's coming for dinner. I know she doesn't like fish, so let's pick up some chicken. She will like that much better.

c. I guess I lost the key to my bike lock. Oh, well, I'll just get a new bike.

d. Hmmm. I can't put the ice away because the freezer is full. I'll leave it out until there's room.

3. How could you show initiative in one of these situations? Choose one and write about it.
   - taking care of a younger child
   - making sure you are ready for a week at camp
   - organizing a special event

_____

_____

_____

_____

_____

_____

# Activity for Initiative: Create a Superhero!

**Materials:** a task card for each student or group that is creating a superhero

**Objective:** To create a superhero with special powers related to student's ability to initiate and accomplish tasks

---

## Task Card

1. Superpower—What is your superhero's special ability? (organize, clean up, make something, fix something, etc.)

2. Name your superhero.

3. Design a cape for your superhero.

4. Create a poster showing your superhero in action!

5. Write a short story about your superhero "on the job"!

---

# Lesson III-13: Defining Optimistic

**The contents of Lesson III-13 include:**

- Journal ideas
- Pre-/Posttest on optimism
- Worksheet III-13A, Good Things about a Situation
- Worksheet III-13B, Being Hopeful about a Situation
- Worksheet III-13C, Hope for Buddy!

## Journal Ideas

Students can select these or other topics to write about in their personal journals. Perhaps each has a special time when they were particularly hopeful or optimistic about something that they can share with others.

## Pre-/Posttest

Pass out the pre-/posttest to students and have them circle the response that best shows someone being optimistic.

### Answers

1. c (hopeful that she will get better); 2. a (he is using the task to motivate himself to work faster); 3. b (she intends to keep looking); 4. d (she is hopeful that there will be a party); 5. c (still hoping that they can win—why give up?)

## Worksheet III-13A, Good Things about a Situation

1. Write the definition of *optimistic* on the board or other place where students can easily see it. *"Optimistic means finding good or hopeful things about something."*

2. Briefly discuss what it means to be optimistic, or an optimist. Use the terms interchangeably so students become familiar with hearing both terms. Explain that an optimist is a person who looks for good in things, but is also hopeful that these good things will happen. As they work through the tasks on the worksheet, students should begin to develop a clearer understanding of what optimism looks like, feels like, and how it can be a positive force.

3. Pass out the worksheet to students and have them complete the review section at the top. For the rest of the worksheet, they are to circle the response (a or b) that fits the definition of optimism by showing something good about the situation.

### Answers

1. a; 2. b; 3. b; 4. b; 5. a; 6. a; 7. b; 8. a

### Discuss

1. Does every bad situation have a good side to it? Is there always something good about a death, illness, or tragedy? *(something might be truly tragic, but the way a person reacts to it can affect their entire outlook. This is difficult for children to understand, but discuss the idea of finding something positive in every trial or hardship, even if that positive thing is a good attitude and personal strength.)*

2. Have you ever had to deal with a bad situation like any of the examples on the worksheet? How did it feel? Could you find anything good about it?

## Worksheet III-13B, Being Hopeful about a Situation

1. Review the definition of optimistic.
2. Pass out the worksheet to students and have them complete the review section at the top.
3. Remind students that optimism in a person can be expressed as an attitude, not necessarily just as someone who goes around trying to be happy all of the time. In the examples, words are used, but this is to help students understand what the characters are thinking and feeling. The idea of being "hopeful" should convey the feeling of expecting something positive to happen.
4. On the rest of the worksheet, students should circle the person who is showing a hopeful response to each situation.

**Answers**

1. first; 2. second; 3. second; 4. first; 5. second

**Discuss**

1. What is each person "hoping" for in the examples? *(a strike, a healed arm, a good test score, a friend, a good art project)*
2. How does "hoping" for something to happen make it more likely that it will happen? *(if the people are hoping, they might try harder to make it happen, look for opportunities to make it happen, be friendlier, etc.)*

## Worksheet III-13C, Hope for Buddy!

1. Review the definition of optimistic.
2. Pass out the cartoon section of the worksheet.
3. Explain that you are going to read a story about an injured dog and a girl who takes care of him. They should think about the definition of being optimistic—looking for positive things and being hopeful—while they listen to the story and react to the questions.

**Answers**

See the teacher's script.

# Journal Ideas: Optimistic

1. How optimistic are you? *Rate yourself* 0–5.

   0 = I am never optimistic, always seeing the gloomy side of things.

   1 = I am very seldom optimistic.

   2 = Once in awhile I am optimistic.

   3 = I sometimes am optimistic.

   4 = I usually am optimistic.

   5 = I am always optimistic, always seeing the good and hopeful side of things.

2. List 5 positive or good things that could happen as a result of a broken TV set. List 5 positive things that could result from a broken arm or leg. List 5 positive things that could result from moving to a new neighborhood.

3. Who is someone you know who is very optimistic? What does he or she do that makes you think he or she is an optimist? Do you like this trait about the person?

4. Can you think of any people who have gone through a terrible tragedy, such as a fire, death, sickness, etc., and have maintained a positive attitude? What did they say about the situation?

5. Some people find inner strength that gives them hope to cope with hard times through religion, reading, talking to other people, and so on. How do you find inner strength to help you?

6. What could possibly be positive or hopeful about going through a hard time, such as the tragedies mentioned in #4?

7. What is something that happened that really disappointed you or made you feel discouraged? How did you get over it? (or did you?)

8. What characters on TV or the movies have been optimistic? Describe a situation in which the character showed optimism.

9. What jobs or careers would best be filled by an optimistic person? Why? What might happen if a very negative person had the job?

10. What happens if people give up hope in something? Do you think that having strong hope might really make a difference in a situation? Can you think of any examples in which it did?

# Optimistic: Pretest/Posttest

Read each situation. Choose the response that best shows someone being optimistic.

1. Janelle catches a cold the day before she is supposed to perform the lead in the class play. She is home in bed taking medicine. What could she say?

   a. "This is so awful that it happened to me today."

   b. "Now Abby will get to play the lead instead of me."

   c. "If I rest well tonight, maybe I will be OK tomorrow."

   d. "I don't care if I do the play or not."

2. David wants to go out with his friends, but his father says he has to stay home and finish weeding the yard first. What could he say?

   a. "This will make me work faster!"

   b. "My dad is so unfair!"

   c. "I hate all these weeds."

   d. "All of this work makes me really tired."

3. Rachel can't find her little black kitten that wandered away in the morning. What could she say?

   a. "I guess the kitten found a better home."

   b. "I'll keep looking for her all over the neighborhood."

   c. "I bet someone stole her."

   d. "I wish my friends would help me search for her."

4. It's Danielle's birthday and so far no one has said anything about it to her. She wonders if anyone remembers. What could she say?

   a. "I guess I don't have any friends."

   b. "Hey, everybody, it's my birthday today!"

   c. "See if I get *you* any presents."

   d. "Maybe they are planning a surprise party for me."

5. Richard's team is behind in softball, 5–0, with one inning left. What could he say?

   a. "I hope it's all over soon!"

   b. "That team is just too tough for us."

   c. "The inning isn't over yet—there's still a chance!"

   d. "I think I should switch to basketball."

# III-13A. Good Things about a Situation

**Review**

Optimistic means f_____ g_____ or h_____

things about s_____.

**Directions:** Read each situation, then circle the response that shows something good about that situation.

1. Andy's bike is getting old and rusty.
   a. He might be able to get a brand new one.
   b. He can walk to school.

2. The field trip to the lake was cancelled.
   a. The class can stay at school.
   b. They can plan a new trip.

3. Jenna has to work on Saturdays.
   a. She can do homework later.
   b. She can make some money.

4. The grocery store is out of Ralph's favorite potato chips.
   a. He can talk to the manager about it.
   b. He might try another brand.

5. Jeff's basketball team is going to play a really tough team on Friday.
   a. They will try harder than usual to play well.
   b. They will be good losers.

6. The movie that Sara and her friends want to see is sold out.
   a. They can do something else together.
   b. They can complain to each other.

7. Kyle's teacher wants him to stay after school for extra help on a report that he did not do correctly.
   a. He will have to find a ride home.
   b. He can learn to correct his mistakes.

8. Chad's dog has cancer and has to be put to sleep.
   a. Chad will not have to see his dog suffer.
   b. Chad can ask his parents for a horse.

Name _____ Date _____

# III-13B. Being Hopeful about a Situation

**Review**

Optimistic means f_____ g_____ or h_____

things about s_____.

**Directions:** Which person in each example below is showing a hopeful response?

1. I need to get a strike to win.

I think I can do this!

I'll probably get a gutter ball!

2. The doctor says it will take six weeks for your arm to heal.

It will be a long six weeks!

I'll do everything he says and maybe it will heal faster.

3. Oh no! This test is really long and it looks hard!

I wonder if I'll finish.

I studied well, so I'll just relax and try to remember everything.

4. It's hard to be the new kid in school.

That person looks friendly. I'll sit by him.

Everyone is ignoring me.

5. I wonder if my art project is good enough to enter in the contest.

I'll just give up.

I think I can make some improvements to make it look a little better.

# For the Teacher
## (Script for Worksheet III-13C, Hope for Buddy!)

Follow along with the pictures as I read a story about a sick dog and a girl who doesn't give up hope. I will stop to ask questions after each picture.

**(Picture 1)** Kara is always bringing home stray dogs and cats. Her family live out in the country, so they have some room to keep a lot of animals, but Kara always wants her dogs and cats inside as much as possible. Sometimes Kara will work at the local animal shelter, walking the dogs and cleaning out their cages. She always hopes that people will come and adopt the stray animals and give them a good home.

**STOP.** What do you know about Kara at this point? *(loves animals, works with animals)* What is she hopeful about? *(finding homes for the animals)*

**(Picture 2)** One afternoon, when Kara stops by after school, she finds the other workers gathered around a dog that has just arrived. When she gets closer, she can see that he has been in some kind of an accident and his leg is broken and hurting. "He'll never make it," one of the workers says. "We should just call the vet to put him to sleep." Kara works her way to the front of the crowd and looks into the big brown eyes of a pretty black and white border collie. Even though he is in pain, he thumps his tail as he looks at her.

**STOP.** What is the situation now? *(the dog is hurt quite badly)* What do you think is going through Kara's mind? *(how to help the dog)*

**(Picture 3)** "No!" Kara cries. "I want him! I want that dog!" The other workers look at her and smile. Kara wants ALL of the dogs. "Honey, he's hurt quite badly," one of them says. "It would be better if he was just put to sleep." She looks at the dog. He is extremely thin and very weak. His eyes are not shiny. He can hardly hold his head up. But Kara is determined. After a few phone calls are made, the dog is taken to the vet to see how badly he is hurt. Kara knows one thing: She wants that dog.

**STOP.** What do you think Kara is hopeful about right now? *(that the dog will be OK, that she will be able to get the dog)*

**(Picture 4)** The vet has good news and bad news about the dog: His leg is so badly damaged that it will have to be taken off, but that is his only life-threatening problem, and he will probably be OK with some food, water, and love. The dog stays at the vet to have the surgery, and Kara informs her mother that there is going to be an addition to the family: Buddy!

**STOP.** What problems are still awaiting Kara and Buddy? *(Will he live? Will Mother let Kara have the dog?)*

**(Picture 5)** The next few weeks are very difficult for Kara. Buddy has to learn to walk on three legs—but first he has to be strong enough to stand up. Kara has to help him stand, carry him outside to go to the bathroom, and feed him by hand. He is so very weak that it seems as though he is getting worse. Still, his tail thumps on the ground when Kara pets him. "I'll do whatever it takes to help him," Kara says. She wags a finger at her mother. "You know I can help this dog!" Mother isn't so sure.

**STOP.** Do you think Kara will give up hope on the dog? *(probably not)* Does Mother feel hopeful? *(it seems as though Mother isn't sure the dog will be OK)*

**(Picture 6)** One day, Buddy can't even pick his head off the floor. Kara sits next to him and tries and tries to get him to eat, but he just doesn't seem interested. Kara thinks, "Maybe he's just going to die. Maybe I can't save him." Later that afternoon, a friend of Kara's comes over. "I have something for Buddy," says Rosie. "It's an omelet." Kara stares at her. "An omelet?" "Yes," says Rosie. "My dogs love omelets. Let's see if Buddy wants one." Rosie puts the omelet on a plate in front of Buddy's nose. His eyes open. He sits up. He sniffs the egg. Then he licks the omelet. Then he eats it! Rosie and Kara cheer. Thump, thump, thump, goes Buddy's tail.

**STOP.** Was Kara losing her optimism about saving the dog? *(yes)* Why? *(he wasn't responding)* Do you think she has hope now? *(yes)*

**(Picture 7)** Once Buddy begins to eat, he begins to get stronger. Each day he can stand a little better and hobble a little faster. One morning before school, Buddy follows Kara into her bedroom. She goes into the bathroom to brush her teeth, and when she comes out—there is Buddy on her bed! Somehow he had JUMPED up on the bed. He looks at her as if to say, "What's the big deal? I love beds!"

**STOP.** Do you think Kara is hopeful now? *(yes)*

**(Picture 8)** Today Buddy is healthy and fit. He chases the boys next door when they speed by on their four-wheelers. He takes walks with Kara and the other dogs, and, yes, he still sleeps on her bed. Whenever Kara pets Buddy's furry head, she is reminded about how important it is to never give up hope… and yes, this is based on a true story!

**STOP.** How will Buddy always help Kara remember to be hopeful? *(it was an experience that they went through that worked out well for her)* Do you think if Kara had given up hope when Buddy quit eating, he wouldn't have recovered? *(probably)* How did Rosie show hopefulness? *(she brought omelets for the dog)* Do you think every hurt dog can be saved, so we should be hopeful about all of them? *(no, but in this case the physical signs were good to begin with and the attention helped Buddy recover)*

Name _____ Date _____

# III-13C. Hope for Buddy!

1.

2.

3.

4.

5.

6.

7.

8.

# Lesson III-14: Recognizing Optimistic

**The contents of Lesson III-14 include:**
- Worksheet III-14A, Which Is the Optimist?
- Worksheet III-14B, Optimism with Common Sense
- Worksheet III-14C, Optimistic—Yes or No?

## Worksheet III-14A, Which Is the Optimist?

1. Pass out the worksheet to students and have them complete the review section at the top.
2. Directions for the rest of the worksheet ask students to choose which person in each example is showing an optimistic outlook.

### Answers

1. second (still hopeful that the dog can be found); 2. first (hopeful that she might feel better); 3. second (making plans to study); 4. second (still hopeful that they might do OK); 5. first (making plans to help the plants)

### Discuss

1. How is each person that you circled on the worksheet doing something that might help their situation? *(running ad, taking medicine, studying, playing harder, feeding the plants)*
2. Do you think an optimist can just feel good about something or would it help to actually DO something, like in the examples?
3. Is it possible that in each situation, the very worse might happen—the dog might be gone, the girl might continue to be sick, the plants might die, etc.? How would an optimist handle those situations?

## Worksheet III-14B, Optimism with Common Sense

1. Pass out the worksheet to students and have them complete the review section at the top.
2. Directions for the rest of the worksheet ask students to consider the situations and determine how the characters are not using common sense in their efforts to be optimistic. Remind them that being optimistic means finding good or hopeful things in situations, but they still have to be realistic and use common sense. These examples can be used as discussion starters.

### Answers

1. this girl is hopeful that she will do well, but she is not realistic—it is probably too late for her to pull up her grade that high; 2. this boy is annoying—this is a situation in which the other boy is truly sad and worried; he should be allowed to be sad! The boy should not expect his friend to show no grief.; 3. this boy is excusing the other person's behavior of stealing; 4. this girl is unrealistic—there are storm clouds and lightning; it probably is not going to stop raining no matter how hard she hopes; 5. this girl can hope all she wants, but she needs to read the book; 6. the boy is pretty sure that he won't get caught smoking and doesn't seem to care, but he is obviously too young to smoke anyhow and he probably will get caught (notice the adult in the background)

**Discuss**

1. In which examples are the characters being unrealistic about their optimism? *(first, fourth, fifth)*

2. In which examples are the characters being inappropriate about being optimistic? *(second, third)*

3. If you or a friend are doing something that might be harmful to you (drugs, smoking, unsafe situations), do you think it is appropriate to be optimistic that you won't get hurt? When should you be realistic about a situation, rather than just hoping for the best? *(when involved in a serious or dangerous situation)*

## Worksheet III-14C, Optimistic—Yes or No?

1. Pass out the worksheet to students and have them complete the review section at the top.

2. Directions for the rest of the worksheet require students to write YES or NO to show if the people are showing optimism. They should base their opinions on what the person is doing in each situation.

**Answers**

1. yes (he is being resourceful); 2. no (giving up); 3. yes (hopeful that she'll still be able to play); 4. yes (didn't let the accident stop him); 5. no (gave up on the whole day); 6. yes (he will meet his friends later; not upset by this); 7. yes (she apparently trusts her friend); 8. no (hoping is not going to be enough to stop the rain; unrealistic)

**Discuss**

1. Go through the examples that show YES responses. How would a person who was not optimistic handle each situation?

2. Go through the examples that show NO responses. How could these people handle their situations in an optimistic way?

Name _____  Date _____

# III-14A. Which Is the Optimist?

**Review**

Optimistic means _____ good or _____ things

_____ something.

**Directions:** Read each situation. Which person in each example is showing an optimistic outlook?

1.

2.

3.

4.

5.

# Worksheet III-14B. Optimism with Common Sense

**Review**

Optimistic means feeling _____ or _____ things about

_____.

**Directions:** These people are trying to be optimistic, but they are not using common sense. What is wrong in each situation? Write your answers on the back of this sheet.

1. I know I have five F's on my last few spelling tests, but that's OK! I'll pull up my grade. I can do it! I know I can! We have one more test, and I can still get an A on my report card! I hope!

2. My grandpa is really sick. I'm worried about him.

Don't be sad! Nobody wants to be around a sour puss. Smile! Put on a happy face!

3. I know you stole Jane's lunch money, but I'm sure you didn't mean to. You are a good person and that money just jumped right out at you! Don't even worry about it!

4. I am sure this rain will stop! It just has to!

5. I'm not going to read the book for my book report, but I know I can still fake enough to get a good grade. I am sure I can fool my teacher again!

6. If you smoke, you'll get in trouble!

Nobody will catch me, I'm sure about that! Smoking won't hurt me!

# III-14C. Optimistic—Yes or No?

**Review**

Optimistic means _____ good

or _____ things

_____ something.

**Directions:** Are these people showing optimism? Write YES or NO on the lines.

1. Barry's TV is broken and he can't watch his favorite TV show. He decides to go next door and watch the show with a friend. _____

2. Yvonne overslept and missed her first class, which was having a test. She told the teacher that she would just take an F on the test. _____

3. The coach promised Danielle that she could be a starter in the game. The coach was sick for the game, so he had a substitute coach. Danielle told the substitute that she hoped he would still let her start in the game. _____

4. Jamal spilled orange juice on his new shirt at breakfast. He quickly put some water on it and went to school. _____

5. Renee wanted to have her friend Janice come over on Saturday, but it turned out that Janice had to visit her relatives. Renee said that her plans were ruined and the whole day was wasted now. _____

6. Pete's mother asked him to babysit for his little brothers after school instead of going out with friends to the music store. Pete told his friends that he would catch up with them a little later. _____

7. Teresa lent her bike to a friend who was supposed to bring it back in an hour. After two hours, her mother said maybe her friend wasn't reliable. Teresa said she knew the girl very well and that something must have happened, because she knew that the friend would bring the bike back soon. _____

8. Jackie was excited about going on a boat ride with the neighbors when they invited her. At the last minute, it began to thunderstorm, so they cancelled the boat ride and asked her if she would like to come over for pizza instead. She said she was just going to wait outside for the rain to stop. _____

# Lesson III-15: Applying Optimistic

**The contents of Lesson III-15 include:**
- Worksheet III-15A, Being Optimistic
- Worksheet III-15B, Practice Being Optimistic
- Quiz on Part 17: Optimistic
- Game: Four in a Row

## Worksheet III-15A, Being Optimistic

1. Pass out the worksheet to students and have them complete the review section at the top. Remind them that the opposite of being an optimist is being a "pessimist" or someone who looks at the bad side of things. Decide which terminology you would like your students to use.

2. Directions for the rest of the worksheet ask students to demonstrate how they could apply being optimistic to the situations given. They can draw a picture or write down their ideas.

**Answers** (will vary)

1. plan for a lot of people; 2. include the new kid in activities with your friend; 3. go swimming every afternoon after summer school; 4. go out for ice cream; 5. open a lemonade stand; 6. camp out in the backyard with a tent; 7. help your brother clean up his room; 8. go see a different movie; 9. get lots of attention for your arm; 10. cheer for the team anyhow

**Discuss**

1. Which of the situations would be the hardest for you to be optimistic about?

2. Have you experienced any similar situations? How did you handle them? What happened?

## Worksheet III-15B, Practice Being Optimistic

1. Pass out the worksheet and have students complete the review section at the top.

2. Directions for the rest of the worksheet involve having students observe themselves during a period of time (perhaps a week) and take note of particular things that happen to them that trigger strong feelings or reactions. Certain events, for example, might make them feel sad, discouraged, happy, or experience other strong emotion. Each student should try to recall those situations and then record his or her response. Obviously, the intent is for students to try to be optimistic as much as possible in these situations. By recording and sharing their experiences, they may become more aware of how they tend to react.

**Discuss**

1. What types of experiences did you have this week?

2. Did you find that you reacted as an optimist to many of them?

3. What conclusions did you come to after this experiment?

## Quiz on Part 17: Optimistic

This quiz can be used as a follow-up activity for the lesson.

**Answers**

1. *(definition)* Optimistic means finding good or hopeful things about something.

2. *(examples)* b (there is time to improve the grade), c (he is hopeful that there are children who will play with him) [In **a**, the boy is not using common sense—it is extremely unlikely that he can possibly win the race. In **d**, the boy is complaining about the weather.]

3. *(applying)* Answers will vary.

## Game: Four in a Row

Directions and cards are at the end of this lesson.

# III-15A. Being Optimistic

**Review**

Optimistic means _____

_____ .

The opposite of being an optimist is being _____ .

**Directions:** How could you show an optimistic outlook for each situation below? Draw a picture or write about your ideas. Use another sheet of paper for your answers.

1. You are having a party and aren't sure how many people are going to come.

2. You notice that a good friend of yours seems to be spending a lot of time with a new kid who moved to your school instead of with you.

3. You find out you have to go to summer school.

4. Your swimming lessons were cancelled on a very hot day.

5. You need to save $100 to go to camp.

6. You have to give up your bedroom for three days while your relatives visit.

7. Your brother borrowed your favorite CD and can't find it in his room.

8. The movie you really wanted to see just left town.

9. You broke your arm falling off your bike.

10. You had to miss baseball practice because you were sick, and find out that someone else is now playing your position.

Name _____ Date _____

# III-15B. Practice Being Optimistic

**Review**

Optimistic means _____

_____.

The opposite of being an optimist is being _____.

**Directions:** Practice being optimistic! Record things that happen to you during your week and your reaction to them. Do you show a positive, hopeful attitude? If not, what could you do instead the next time?

Week of: _____

| **What happened:** (describe the event) | **How did I feel?** (sad, depressed, angry, discouraged, happy, proud, silly, excited, etc.) | **Was I an optimist?** | **Next time, I could...** |
|---|---|---|---|
| | | | |

**Conclusions:**

1. I learned this about myself: _____

2. How much of an optimist am I? _____

3. Are there things I could improve on to have a more positive attitude?

_____

_____

_____

Name _____ Date _____

# Quiz on Part 17: Optimistic

1. What is meant by being optimistic?

_____

_____

2. Which people below are showing an optimistic outlook?

 a. I know I can still win this race!

b. I got a C on the test, but I can study harder for the next one.

 c. I think there is a family with children moving in next door. I'll go over and see if anyone wants to play baseball.

d. Why does it always have to rain when we have outdoor recess? There's nothing fun to do indoors.

3. How could you show an optimistic attitude for one of the following situations:
   - entering a contest and finding out that you did not win
   - noticing that your best friend doesn't seem to be very friendly to you
   - finding out that your family is going to move
   - starting a new grade in school with a new teacher

_____

_____

_____

_____

# Game: Four in a Row

**Materials:**

- playing board
- set of 45 Situation Cards
- 5 WILD CARDS
- 2 sets of markers—one with smiles for the optimistic player and one with frowns for the pessimistic player (20 of each, in different colors)

**Objective:** To be the first player to get four of his/her markers in a row (horizontally, vertically, or diagonally) on the playing board

**Players:** 2

**How to Play:**

1. Situation cards are shuffled and placed near the gameboard.

2. Players choose or are assigned their roles: one is the pessimist (blue frowning face cards), the other is the optimist (yellow smile face cards)

3. Players take turns taking a Situation Card and reading it out loud. The player must respond to the situation as if he or she were an optimist or pessimist, depending on his or her role. For example, if the card says: "It is sunny out," the optimist might say: "It's a good day to walk in the park." The pessimist might say, "It's too hot and I'm sweating."

4. After responding, the player places his or her card on the bottom square of any of the 6 rows on the board.

5. Play continues to alternate between the two players, choosing cards and responding to them.

6. As play continues, players use strategies to attempt to put their cards in rows and columns that will help them achieve four cards in a row.

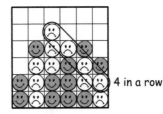

4 in a row

7. If a player draws a WILD CARD, he or she can pull out any marker already on the board which will cause all markers on top of that row to slide down. This might help the player get four markers in a row.

Pull this card; 🙂 now has 4 in a row

8. The first player to get four markers in a row is the winner.

| | | |
|---|---|---|
| It is a rainy day. | You are having broccoli for lunch. | You can't find a dollar that was in your wallet. |
| It is a sunny day. | You came in second place in a race. | You find a dollar on the street. |
| You have math homework to do. | You did not get the starring role in the play. | There is a letter for you in the mail. |
| You have no homework tonight. | You can't find your dog. | Your grandmother is coming to visit. |
| You have to redo an assignment for reading. | Your mom said you may get a kitten. | You have a dentist appointment. |
| You received an award for your drawing. | You have to read a mystery for a book report. | Someone accidentally knocked into you and you dropped your books. |
| You are having pizza for lunch. | You overslept for school. | You won $5.00 in a contest. |

| | | |
|---|---|---|
| Your best friend is moving. | You get to line up first for lunch. | You got new shoes that are too big. |
| The ice cream store is out of your favorite flavor. | The P.E. teacher is absent today, so there is no gym class. | You lost a tooth. |
| You have to read two books while on vacation. | You have to wear glasses. | You burned the chocolate chip cookies in the oven. |
| Your uncle gave you pajamas for Christmas. | You won the spelling bee for your class. | There is a long line for the slide at the water park. |
| Your friend borrowed your watch and broke it. | You got a pink sweatshirt with an angel on it for your birthday. | You got a C on a test. |
| Your class job this week is to pick up trash in the room. | You got a softball mitt for your birthday. | The computer in your room is broken. |
| Your cut your finger using scissors. | You are going to spend the night at a friend's house. | You have to rewrite your paper with better handwriting. |

| | | |
|---|---|---|
| There is only white milk in the lunch line today. | **WILD CARD** | **WILD CARD** |
| You only have a black marker that works. | **WILD CARD** | **WILD CARD** |
| You have to get your hair cut. | **WILD CARD** | |

# Lesson III-16: Defining Risk-Taking

**The contents of Lesson III-16 include:**

- Journal ideas
- Pre-/posttest on risk-taking
- Worksheet III-16A, Something New
- Worksheet III-16B, Something Difficult
- Worksheet III-16C, On the Team

## Journal Ideas

Students can select from these or other ideas to write about in their personal journals. Be sure to allow time for sharing ideas and comments.

## Pre-/Posttest

Pass out the pre-/posttest to students and have them select the response that shows someone taking an appropriate risk. As a pretest, students may not have thought about the difference between an "appropriate" risk and risk-taking in general.

**Answers**

1. b (she is using humor to help her with her insecurity about the darkness, but still being a part of the group); 2. c (it is probably a safe risk to approach the neighbors, even though they may not be interested in the seeds); 3. a (this is a risk that might end up being fun for him); 4. b (she is still going to take a risk, but practicing beforehand might help her feel more comfortable); 5. a (he can venture out a little towards the deeper end, but make sure he will be safe by having some type of flotation)

## Worksheet III-16A, Something New

1. Write the definition of *risk-taking* on the board or other place where students can easily see it. *"Risk-taking means trying something new or difficult."*

2. Discuss that a risk involves trying something new. This does not mean that a person should do anything for the sake of trying something new, but it does mean he or she should not hesitate to learn something or try to make something happen that is new.

3. Pass out the worksheet to students and have them complete the review section at the top.

4. Directions for the rest of the worksheet ask students to identify which characters on the page are trying something new by putting an X in the box in front of each item.

**Answers**

2, 4, 5

**Discuss**

1. In situation 1, what new thing is the person avoiding? *(learning a new language)*

2. In situation 2, how is the boy taking a risk to try something new? *(he's going to approach the town leaders and try to initiate something that doesn't exist in the town; he might be turned down)*

3. In situation 3, how could the girl take a risk? *(sign up for the class and learn something about art)*

4. In situation 4, how is the boy taking a risk? *(he's approaching someone he doesn't know)*

5. In situation 5, what is new for the girl? *(she wants a new, innovative haircut)*

6. In situation 6, what could the girl do if she wanted to take a "reading risk"? *(try to read about something that she is not already familiar with)*

# Worksheet III-16B, Something Difficult

1. Review the definition of risk-taking.

2. Pass out the worksheet and have students complete the review section at the top.

3. Directions for the rest of the worksheet ask students to identify those characters who are taking a risk by trying something that is difficult for them. They should put an X in the box to show their choices.

**Answers**

2, 4, 5

**Discuss**

1. In situation 1, how could the boy take a risk that is difficult for him, but might be a better option? *(he could talk to the neighbor, admit what he did, pay for the window)*

2. In situation 2, what risk is the girl taking? *(learning to swim)*

3. In situation 3, what risk might the boy take if he invites his grandfather to the school party? *(he might be embarrassed)* Should he take that risk? *(it would be nice if he did, especially if his grandfather would have a good time)*

4. In situation 4, what risk is the girl taking? *(hoping that her father will be understanding of the bad grade)*

5. In situation 5, how is the boy taking a risk by skipping the movie that his friends are going to? *(his friends might be upset with him, laugh at him, not include him the next time)*

6. In situation 6, what risk could the girl take? *(she could risk getting a lower grade by taking harder projects)*

# Worksheet III-16C, On the Team

1. Review the definition of risk-taking.

2. Pass out the cartoon section of the worksheet.

3. Explain that you are going to read a story about two friends who take a risk by joining a running team at school. They should follow along with the pictures as you read and stop to ask questions.

**Answers**

See the teacher's script.

# Journal Ideas: Risk-Taking

1. How much of a risk-taker are you? *Rate yourself* on this scale:

   0 = I always have to feel safe.

   1 = I almost never try something new.

   2 = I sometimes try new things.

   3 = I usually am up for trying something different.

   4 = I almost always take risks.

   5 = I love to try new things and take risks.

2. List five things that are really difficult for you. Which one is the hardest for you? Why?

3. When is the last time you were really frightened? What scared you? How did you react?

4. Have you ever been positive that you would not like something, then after you tried it you discovered that you did? Tell about it.

5. What is the bravest thing you have ever done? How did it make you feel after you did it?

6. If someone dared you to spend a night in a haunted house, alone, on Halloween night, would you do it? Why or why not?

7. Who are some community heroes in your town or school? What did they do? What reward or recognition (if any) did they get?

8. What do you think of the latest fashion fads? Are you usually one of the first to wear something really different or try something that people aren't ready to accept yet?

9. Who are some people or characters in books or movies that you think are courageous? Why do you feel that way about them?

10. If no one else was around, would you go into a burning building to get:

    a. a school book?

    b. a TV set?

    c. your money?

    d. a pet

    e. your clothes?

    f. your brother or sister?

    g. something from your bedroom?

    Would you go into the building if there was just a little smoke and the fire department was on the way? How would this change things for you?

# Risk-Taking Pretest/Posttest

Circle the response that shows someone taking an appropriate risk.

1. Kathryn is afraid of the dark. She goes to a slumber party where the other girls want to turn out the lights and tell ghost stories. She could…
   a. Say she has to go home now.
   b. Ask to hold a flashlight (to hit the ghosts!).
   c. Suggest they leave the lights on.
   d. Complain that it isn't very much fun.

2. John is selling flower seeds for a school fund-raiser. He sees his unfriendly neighbors outside on their front porch. He could…
   a. Walk past them.
   b. Run past them.
   c. Tell them about the seeds and ask if they are interested.
   d. Ask his mother to call them on the phone.

3. The boys in the class are invited to go to a roller skating birthday party. Evan has never skated before and he thinks he might fall down and look silly. He could…
   a. Give it a try.
   b. Say that his parents won't let him go.
   c. Sit and watch the others skate.
   d. Stay home.

4. Amelia wrote a beautiful story that her teacher wants her to enter in a reading contest, but she's afraid to get up in front of people. She could…
   a. Skip the contest.
   b. Practice with her teacher until she feels more comfortable.
   c. Tell her teacher that she'll do it next year when she's older.
   d. Ask the teacher to read it for her.

5. Nick is not a very strong swimmer. Some of his friends want to play tag and they are in the deep end of the pool. He could…
   a. Wear floaties and stay near the edge of the pool.
   b. Stay in the shallow end where he is comfortable.
   c. Go in the deep end but hang on to a friend.
   d. Tell his friends that he doesn't want to play.

Name _____  Date _____

# III-16A. Something New

**Review**

Risk-taking means t_____ s_____ n_____ or
d_____.

**Directions:** Which person below is trying something new? Put an X in front of each risk-taker.

1. ☐

Why do we have to learn to speak another language? I just want to speak my own.

2. ☐

I think we need a place to ride our skateboards in town. Let's talk to the mayor and see what we have to do to get one.

3. ☐

ART CLASSES
WEDNESDAY
SIGN UP NOW!

I have never taken an art class. I don't think I'd be very good at it, so I won't bother signing up.

4. ☐

Hey, there's a new kid in our neighborhood. Let's find out if he would like to play baseball with us.

5. ☐

I want to look like this!!

6. ☐

I always read horse stories during free reading time. I don't want to read anything else.

# III-16B. Something Difficult

**Review**

Risk-taking means t_____ something n_____ or

d_____.

**Directions:** Which person below is trying something difficult? Put an X in front of each risk-taker.

1. ☐

   "I broke the neighbor's window, but she'll never know it was me. Thank goodness!"

2. ☐

   "I don't want to get in the water, but it's important to learn how to swim."

3. ☐

   "I am so embarrassed when Grandpa starts talking so much when we're with my friends. I won't invite him to the school party."

4. ☐

   "Dad, I got a bad grade on the spelling test. May I explain what happened?"

5. ☐

   "Jerry, I really don't want to go to that R-rated movie. I think I'll just see you guys later."

6. ☐

   "I can get a better grade if I do the easy projects, so I'll do those."

# For the Teacher

## (Script for Worksheet III-16C, On the Team)

Follow along with the pictures about two girls who joined a cross country team while I read the story. I will stop to ask questions after each picture.

**(Picture 1)** Dana and Teresa are good friends and like to do a lot of things together. When their school starts a cross country team for girls, Dana really wants to join it. "It'll be lots of fun," she tells Teresa. "All you have to do is run. It's easy! Let's do it together!" Teresa isn't convinced, but she says she will give it a try.

**STOP.** How much of a risk does this seem to be for Dana? *(not too much)* How much of a risk does this seem to be for Teresa? *(a bit more—she is not convinced she'll do well or have fun)*

**(Picture 2)** Practice is held after school and on weekends. At first it is really fun. The girls get to run through the park next to the school and all through the neighborhoods. The coach is a lot of fun, too, and they enjoy being with the other girls.

**STOP.** Even though this is something new to the girls, are they enjoying it? *(yes)* Why? *(having fun running, enjoying the coach and other runners)*

**(Picture 3)** As time goes on, however, Dana realizes that she isn't a very strong runner. She gets tired of running after a mile and never seems to get any faster. It is sometimes hot in the afternoon after school, and Dana thinks she would rather be home reading fashion magazines than running in the woods.

**STOP.** How does Dana feel about the situation now? Why? *(she is losing interest because it's more work than she thought and sometimes not easy)*

**(Picture 4)** Teresa, however, discovers that she is a fast runner. It seems that once she gets started running, she can run for a long, long time and it doesn't bother her. She is surprised to find out that she can keep up with the older girls. In fact, she even leads the pack sometimes and the coach uses her to set the pace.

**STOP.** How are things turning out for Teresa? *(she's enjoying it)* What did she discover about herself? *(she has some talent for running)*

**(Picture 5)** Finally the team is ready for their first meet against the school across town— their best rivals! Teresa and Dana are both ready to run. They stretch, they warm up, and they are all set to run! Girls from both teams line up, ready to run! Ready… set… go!

**STOP.** How do you think each girl feels now? *(excited about the thrill of competition)*

**(Picture 6)** Teresa is surprised to find that she is able to pass a lot of the girls while they are running. Finally, there is one girl in front of her. Teresa grits her teeth and pumps her arms and runs harder… harder… harder…! She is even with the girl for a long time. Finally they make the last turn and the finish line is right in front of them. People everywhere are cheering! She can hear the coach's voice screaming: "Come on, Teresa!! You can do it!"

**STOP.** What is Teresa's challenge now? *(trying to beat the girl in front of her)*

**(Picture 7)** And she does! Teresa pulls ahead and wins the race! She bends over and stops to catch her breath and she watches the other girls cross the line. She has finished ahead of many girls who are older than she is! Finally she sees Dana coming up to the finish line. "Come on! Finish strong!" she yells. Dana smiles and waves as she crosses the line.

**STOP.** Do you think Dana is discouraged? *(looks as though she's a good sport, smiling and waving)* How do you think Teresa feels? *(very excited)*

**(Picture 8)** After the race, Dana comes over to Teresa. "You were great!" she cries. "You won the whole race!" Teresa laughs. "I never would have tried out for this if it wasn't for you, Dana," she said. "This is your victory, too!" Dana is happy for Teresa and happy to be part of the team. "But, next year," she tells Teresa, "I'm going out for soccer instead!"

**STOP.** Both girls took a risk, trying something they had never done before. How did it turn out for each of them? *(for Dana, it was an experience she may not do again; for Teresa, she has discovered a talent she didn't realize she had)*

# III-16C. On the Team

1.

2.

3.

4.

5.

6.

7.

8.

# Lesson III-17: Recognizing Risk-Taking

**The contents of Lesson III-17 include:**
- Worksheet III-17A, Is This Risk-Taking?
- Worksheet III-17B, What's New or Difficult?
- Worksheet III-17C, Risk-Taking with Common Sense

## Worksheet III-17A, Is This Risk-Taking?

1. Pass out the worksheet to students and have them complete the review section at the top.
2. On the rest of the worksheet, students should write YES or NO to indicate whether or not the character is showing risk-taking.

**Answers**

1. yes (risking changing her appearance); 2. no (he seems to be embarrassed about telling his friend where he's really going to camp); 3. yes (she's anxious to walk past the kids, but she's doing it anyhow); 4. no (he did the least amount of work that was required); 5. yes (he's trying something new!); 6. yes (she's admitting what happened to her friend)

**Discuss**

1. In situation 1, the girl is changing her appearance. What are some other ways that people can take risks in changing how they look? *(the clothes you wear, tattoos, make-up, etc.)*

2. In situation 2, the boy is concerned about appearance, too, but this time he is wondering how he will "appear" to his friend. What do you think his concern really is? *(he thinks it sounds more exciting to say he's going to a sports camp rather than a church camp; he's worried about what his friend will think of him)*

3. In situation 3, what is difficult for Jenny? *(walking past kids)* Why? *(she doesn't know them, doesn't know what they are saying about her)*

4. In situation 4, Tony is showing little effort to go beyond what is required of him. What risk could Tony take? *(he could set a goal for himself to do more than he thinks he is able to do)*

5. In situation 5, why is this a risk? *(Alex may think that he doesn't like the Hawaiian pizza, but he wants to fit in with his friends so he's going to try something new)*

6. In situation 6, what is difficult for Kathryn? *(telling her friend about losing the cards)* Why? *(perhaps her friend has a temper or is not understanding)*

## Worksheet III-17B, What's New or Difficult?

1. Pass out the worksheet to students and have them complete the review section at the top.
2. On the rest of the worksheet, students should read the examples and discuss what they think is new or difficult for the characters. Since this is a discussion page, no writing is required.

## Answers

1. the boy is giving his dad some possibly frightening information; 2. the girl is confronting the younger girl about swimming in the pool; 3. the boy is afraid of the ball, but he's still playing; 4. the boy is in a restaurant and is going to sample some food he isn't sure about; 5. the girl is on a horse for the first time and is probably a little nervous; 6. the girl has a tough decision to tell her mother, so maybe she isn't sure how her mother will react; 7. the boy is going to push himself to work for extra credit on an assignment; 8. the boy is turning down the peer pressure to smoke; 9. the kids are going to ride a tandem bike—somewhat unusual; 10. the kids are walking past a barking dog, but hope that he is securely tied up

## Discuss

1. What is difficult for one person might not be difficult for another. As you look at the characters and situations on the worksheet, how do you think you would react in a similar situation?

2. What advice would you give to kids who have to confront others, such as in situations 1, 2, 6, and 8?

3. In situations 3, 5, and 10, the kids are somewhat frightened or anxious, but still doing what they need to do. Do you think they will continue to be frightened or could they learn from the situations? *(situations 3 and 5 involve learning skills, so these people could probably get better; in situation 10 the kids are walking past a dog, but if they get to know the dog they may feel safe around him)*

# Worksheet III-17C, Risk-Taking with Common Sense

1. Pass out the worksheet to students and have them complete the review section at the top.

2. The characters on the rest of the worksheet are facing some risks, but they are not using common sense. Students should try to figure out what the problem is in each situation and write their answers on the line next to each item.

## Answers

1. going down a hill without a helmet; 2. thinking she can go up 8 stories to help a kitten; 3. risky to try to cross the tracks with the signal flashing and gates down; 4. the boy telling the fire chief what to do; 5. thinking he knows all there is to know about riding a motorcycle by reading a book (he can't even get on it by himself); 6. assuming that by admitting the problem to her dad there is no further obligation to make things right

## Discuss

1. Can you think of any people who like to take risks that are unsafe? *(thrill-seekers, daredevils)* What would make someone take risks like that? *(desire for excitement, perhaps money and attention)*

2. If you know that something is really going to be unsafe, why would you do it anyhow? *(peer pressure, poor judgment)* Can you think of any examples in your life or with your friends? *(pressure to smoke, unsafe driving, etc.)*

3. In situation 6, why does the girl think she should be rewarded? *(she confessed and that was difficult for her)* What do you think? *(she's doing what she should be doing, so no need to reward that!)*

Name _____  Date _____

# III-17A. Is This Risk-Taking?

**Review**

Risk-taking means _____ _____ new or

_____.

**Directions:** Read about each person below. Decide if that person is showing risk-taking. Write YES or NO on the line after each item.

1. Alicia has always had really long hair. She decides to get it cut very
short and styled in a different way.                          _____

2. Ricardo is going to church camp, but he tells his friends that he is going
to a sports camp because it sounds more exciting.            _____

3. Jenny notices some kids staring at her while she is walking down the
street and it looks as though they are whispering, but she keeps right
on going.                                                    _____

4. Tony needs to read five books to get all of his book report points, so he
stops after he reads the fifth one.                          _____

5. Alex is at a pizza restaurant with his friends and they want to try a
Hawaiian pizza with pineapples on it, so he says that sounds
interesting and to count him in.                             _____

6. Kathryn borrows her friend's game and loses a few playing cards. She
tells her friend what happened and says she will replace them.  _____

Name _____ Date _____

# III-17B. What's New or Difficult?

**Review**

Risk-taking means _____ something _____ or

_____.

**Directions:** What is new or difficult for each character in the situations below? Discuss your answers.

1. Dad, I think you should know that Sis is hanging around with some kids who are in a lot of trouble at school.

2. Rachel, you shouldn't be in the deep end of the pool.

Get out or I'll pull you out myself!

Oh, leave me alone!

3. Please don't come to me! Don't hit the ball over here! Please!!

4. Try this—you'll like it.

Well, OK. Just a small bite.

5. OK, what do I do first?

6. Mom, I've decided I want to live with Dad.

7. I'm going for extra credit!

8. No, thanks, I'm not smoking.

9. What a weird-looking bike! Let's ride where people can see us!

10. That dog is tied up... I think we will be safe.

Name _____ Date _____

# III-17C. Risk-Taking with Common Sense

**Review**

Risk-taking means _____ something _____ or

_____ .

**Directions:** These characters seem to be taking risks. What is a problem in each situation? Write your answers on the back of this sheet.

1. It's a big hill, but I'm a good skater. I don't need to wear a helmet.

2. I'll save you, little kitty! It's only eight stories high!

3. I can get across the tracks in time!

4. Stand aside, Chief, I will rescue those people from the burning building!

5. I read a book on how to ride a motorcycle, so I think I'm ready. Umm, could you give me a leg up, please?

6. Dad, I want to admit that I didn't study very hard for my test and I got an F. Now that I've been brave enough to confess, I expect you to completely forgive me, forget about this, and reward me for being so honest!

# Lesson III-18: Applying Risk-Taking

**The contents of Lesson III-18 include:**

- Worksheet III-18A, Self-Assessment
- Worksheet III-18B, Complete the Sentences
- Quiz on Part 18: Risk-Taking
- Game: Take a Risk

## Worksheet III-18A, Self-Assessment

1. Pass out the worksheet to students and have them complete the review section at the top. Remind them that the opposite of taking risks is playing it safe or staying the same. Discuss some examples of not taking appropriate risks.

2. Directions for the rest of the worksheet ask students to consider 15 items and score them according to how likely they would take that risk. They can draw a smiling/frowning face or use an X to indicate their response.

### Discuss

1. What type of physical risks are you likely to take? Do you think you are likely to try things that involve doing something? What?

2. Is it risky for you to do things involving people, such as speaking in front of people, confronting people, or involving yourself in activities with other people? What particularly is risky for you?

3. What are some "fun" risks that you like to take, such as eating new foods, wearing interesting clothes, changing your appearance?

4. Do you think you should take more risks in certain areas? What?

## Worksheet III-18B, Complete the Sentences

1. Pass out the worksheet to students and have them complete the review section at the top.

2. Students should complete the sentences on the rest of the worksheet by writing examples that apply to them.

### Discuss

1. Do you think your fears are very different from other people's or pretty much the same?

2. Do you think you have gotten "better" about risk-taking in some areas? What?

3. How would you evaluate yourself as far as a risk-taker now?

## Quiz on Part 18: Risk-Taking

This quiz can be used as a follow-up activity for this lesson.

### Answers

1. *(definition)* Risk-taking means trying something new or difficult.

2. *(examples)* a. no (it might be new to him, but it isn't appropriate); b. yes (she's fearful but is going to try it); c. yes (he isn't excited about going, but knows he should); d. no (this boy doesn't swim well enough to be diving)

3. *(applying)* Answers will vary.

## Game for Risk-Taking: Take a Risk

Directions and cards are at the end of this lesson.

# III-18A. Self-Assessment

**Review**

Risk-taking means _____

_____.

The opposite of taking risks is _____.

**Directions:** How likely are you to do the following things? Score each item:

☹ = would not do   X = might do this   ☺ = would definitely do this

○  1. Dive in the deep end of a pool to try to get a penny.

○  2. Ski down a really big hill.

○  3. Try hang gliding.

○  4. Sing a solo in front of people you don't know.

○  5. Try out for a big speaking part in a play.

○  6. Climb a tree to rescue a kitten.

○  7. Sell cookies door-to-door in a neighborhood close to yours.

○  8. Walk past a group of people who are staring at you.

○  9. Get a tattoo or have something pierced on your body.

○  10. Pick up a snake.

○  11. Raise your hand when someone asks for a volunteer.

○  12. Try eating food from another country.

○  13. Teach an adult how to do something you know how to do.

○  14. Go on a roller coaster.

○  15. Talk to your parents about a problem you have.

# III-18B. Complete the Sentences

**Review**

Risk-taking means _____

_____.

The opposite of taking risks is _____.

**Directions:** Complete each of the following sentences as the situations apply to you.

1. I am very brave when it comes to _____

_____

2. It scares me to _____

_____

3. I get very nervous when I have to _____

_____

4. It is hard for me to _____

_____

5. At school, I don't like it when _____

_____

6. I don't want people to laugh at me when I _____

_____

7. If I had to talk to someone I didn't know, I _____

_____

8. I feel like I'm in danger when _____

_____

9. I was very courageous when _____

_____

10. I didn't think I would like this, but I found out _____

_____

# Quiz on Part 18: Risk-Taking

1. What is meant by risk-taking?

_____

_____

2. Which of these people are taking appropriate risks?

a.  I'm going to try something new. I've never had a glass of beer before!

b. I think I'll try reading a poem in front of the class. Maybe they will laugh at me, but... here goes!

c.  I don't want to go into that nursing home. Old people scare me! But I know Grandma would like to see me. I'll take some flowers for everyone in her hall.

d. I want to dive! I'm going to dive off the high dive! I've never done it before, but I'm learning to swim and it looks like fun.

3. How could you show risk-taking in one of these situations?
- a friend asks you to do something that is not what your parents would want you to do
- your face is spotted with chicken pox and you don't want to go to school
- you accidentally damaged something belonging to your new neighbor

_____

_____

_____

_____

# Game: Take a Risk

**Materials:**

- 26 Risk Cards, each assigned to a point value of 2, 3, or 5; one worth 10
- 2 Lose It All Cards
- Score sheet for players to tally their points (one player can act as scorekeeper)

**Players:** 2–4 (may want to add additional cards for more players)

**Objective:** To be the first player to get to exactly 15 points

**How to Play:**

1. Shuffle the Risk Cards and place in a pile.
2. Each player takes a card off the top and reads the risk.
3. The player can "accept" or "reject" the card. Rejected cards go to the bottom of the pile.
4. Players tally the point value of the card on the score sheet.
5. The first player to reach exactly 15 points is the winner.
6. If a player gets a "Lose It All" card, all cards are returned to the pile and he or she starts over.

**Strategy:**

Players need to keep track of their points to make sure they don't go over 15; thus, they may need to reject some of the risks.

**Cards**

*10-point card:*

- Rescue the entire planet from an alien attack.

*5-point cards:*

- Save a child from a burning building.
- Pull a trapped person out of a car.
- Dive into a pool to rescue a drowning child.
- Start a community clean-up program.
- Walk past a rattlesnake.

*3-point cards:*

- Climb a tree to rescue a cat.
- Admit to breaking a window.
- Sign up for dance lessons.
- Join the track team.
- Swim in the deep end of the pool.
- Learn how to inline skate.
- Visit a sick person in the hospital.
- Do volunteer work at a nursing home.
- Invite someone you don't know well to your party.
- Try out for the lead in the school play.

*2-point cards:*

- Try riding a pony.
- Learn to speak a different language.
- Make conversation with someone you don't know very well.
- Work on the scenery in the school play.
- Walk past a big dog.
- Walk past a group of scary-looking kids.
- Get a new haircut.
- Wear really odd clothes that are in style.
- Eat one of Mom's new recipes.
- Play chess with your father.

****Lose it all!! *****

****Lose it all!! *****